American Trails Series
XXII

Washington Peck, circa 1850s, from a tintype.
Courtesy of John Wells Heap.

On the Western Trails

The Overland Diaries of Washington Peck

Edited and with Biographical Commentary by

Susan M. Erb

The Arthur H. Clark Company

An imprint of the University of Oklahoma Press

Norman, Oklahoma

2009

Library of Congress Cataloging-in-Publication Data
Peck, Washington, 1801–1889.
On the western trails : the overland diaries of Washington Peck / edited and with biographical commentary by Susan M. Erb. — 1st ed.
p. cm. — (American trails series ; v. 22)
Includes bibliographical references and index.
ISBN 978-0-87062-379-0 (hardcover : alk. paper) 1. Peck, Washington, 1801–1889—Diaries. 2. Pioneers—West (U.S.)—Diaries. 3. Frontier and pioneer life—West (U.S.) 4. Overland journeys to the Pacific. 5. Wagon trains—West (U.S.)—History—19th century. 6. Oregon National Historic Trail—Description and travel. 7. California National Historic Trail—Description and travel. 8. California—Gold discoveries. 9. Santa Fe National Historic Trail—Description and travel. 10. Salt Lake City (Utah)—History—19th century. I. Erb, Susan M., 1944– II. Title. III. Series.
F593.P434A3 2009
978'.02092—dc22
2009004672

On the Western Trails: The Overland Diaries of Washington Peck is Volume 22 in the American Trails Series.

The paper in this book meets the guidelines for permanence and durability of the Committee on Production Guidelines for Book Longevity of the Council on Library Resources, Inc. ∞

1 2 3 4 5 6 7 8 9 10

To my husband,
Derek,
whose endurance
on this long journey
equals that of Washington Peck

Contents

Illustrations

Maps

Preface

WASHINGTON PECK'S two wagon trail diaries make an important contribution to the saga of America's westward expansion. His multiple travel routes were unique.

In 1850–51, Washington, his wife Mercy, and two sons traveled the Platte River Road (the Oregon-California-Mormon Trail corridor), taking the Mormon-California Trail to Salt Lake City. Then they took the southern route toward California (picking up the Old Spanish Trail) and finally rode up the California coast to the gold fields. This entire trip took over a year. Among its entries, the 1850–51 diary contains a description of what Washington calls a "Mammoth Wagon," a huge beast with double-spoked wheels. He reports the excitement of seeing the great buffalo herds, recounts many cordial meetings with American Indians, including the great Ute chief Wakara, and explains how he cured a bloated ox by stabbing it in the stomach with a knife. He records the names of many people who died along the trail and whose names do not appear in lists published to date.

In 1858 the Pecks traveled west again, this time as a family group of women and children. They traveled along the Santa Fe Trail and then took the new Beale Wagon Road along the 35th parallel from Albuquerque to California. In his 1858 diary, Washington describes driving his family through a gathering of five thousand Indians and a shocking murder by a mountain man near the Raton Pass. He records how four young men traveling with him and his family stole some Indian ponies, thus endangering them in the heart of the Navajo War. And Washington compassionately describes meeting the starving survivors of the Rose Party Wagon Train Massacre. After sparing what flour they could, the Pecks turned back to retrace their steps across 350 miles of hot desert with drying water holes.

Differences between the trips are evidenced in the diaries by the amount of trail traffic and the speed that the Pecks traveled. On the trip to the gold rush, they were never out of sight of other wagons, and a sense of urgency kept them moving, stopping only on the Sabbath to rest. On the Santa Fe Trail in 1858 they met few emigrants, but the trail was busy with two-way freighting traffic. On the final leg along Beale's Wagon Road, the small family wagon train of women and children traveled alone, proceeded more slowly, and stopped more often to rest.

Throughout both diaries, Washington maintained an obvious and remarkable daily appreciation for God's creation in all its elements: from his care of his animals, to his constant comments on the beauty of the lands, to his extreme reverence for the dead (in graves) that he and his family came upon.

When my cousins and I, all Peck descendants, began researching annotations for the diaries, we discovered that Washington Peck had led a far more adventuresome life than we had realized, extending well beyond his travels on western trails. After we put together a paper trail, primarily of land deeds and letters, the book evolved from a publication of Washington Peck's diaries to a biography of his life. Our fascination as well as difficulty in researching and recording the Peck story was due to his extensive moves and travels, in which he often would leave a married child behind. Thus, the research trail got longer and wider. Our task grew from annotating two years of trail diaries to filling in the other eighty-six years of his life. More important than documenting when and where Washington moved or traveled was to figure out why he chose a particular place and then what happened politically, climatically, or economically that caused him to pick up and move yet again. As my Peck cousins and I followed their trail through decade after decade in state after state, we began to realize how many historical events the Pecks had witnessed. Researching Washington Peck's life (1801–1889) became a journey for me—and is now a journey for the reader—through the history of the nineteenth century.

A number of diarists who traveled at the same time help to fill in details that add depth to Washington Peck's diaries. John Udell's diaries

(1850, 1853, and 1858) are important because his travels paralleled the Pecks. He traveled the Mormon Trail in 1850 two to three weeks ahead of them. He returned via the Isthmus of Panama four months before the Pecks, and he traveled the Santa Fe Trail in 1858 where Washington and Udell finally met. Udell credits Washington Peck with saving his life. Henry Atkinson Stine (1850) arrived at Fort Laramie on the same day as the Pecks. He provided details of the activities taking place at the fort and on the trail from there to Salt Lake City. David W. Cheesman (1850) traveled with the Pecks from Salt Lake City to California and provides a second voice to the events that occurred. A number of women's diaries were used to speak for Mercy Peck because Washington never recorded her activities, and yet there is sense of their duality that comes from Washington's use of "we" and "our" in his daily entries. Other diarists who traveled in the same year or who experienced similar situations contributed details that I was able to use to add depth to the story.

Acknowledgments

The way this book came about is a story of its own. It was pieced together like a gigantic jigsaw puzzle by descendents of six of Washington's children: Elizabeth, David, Egerton, Mary Ann, Jane, and Emma (these children are identified below in parenthesis). These descendants, including myself, spent many years researching their branch of the family, which they then generously shared so that I could compile and write this story.

Dr. Thomas Martin Zanna (David). I owe Tom a huge thank-you because without him this book would not have come together. He revealed the existence of the 1850 Diary to me and shared the names of other Peck family descendants he had located. When Dorothy (Peck) Lynch visited a cousin in 1968 in Atchison, Missouri, she asked about the Peck diary. To Dorothy's dismay, the cousin began rooting around in the bottom drawer of a desk to locate it. Seeing its poor condition and realizing its historical value, Dorothy persuaded the family to send it to the Burton Historical Collection at the Detroit Public Library where it could be properly stored and preserved. Accompanying it was a typescript, which had been published in serial form in the *Tarkio Avalanche* in Tarkio, Missouri, in 1965.

Vernon Paul Fleming (deceased) (David) obtained a photocopy of the diary and a copy of the typescript from Dorothy. He soon discovered that the typescript had numerous errors and left out important historical information, although unfortunately subsequent researchers have used the flawed typescript. Vern painstakingly produced a more accurate transcription, so this is the first time Washington Peck's 1850–51 diary has been published as he wrote it.

Nicholas Peck (David) prevailed upon the Burton Historical Collection to produce a microfilm of the diary in 1991, which he has generously shared. This was many years after microfilming for Merrill Mattes (during his research for *The Great Platte River Road,* published 1969) had been ruled out due to the fragile condition of the diary. The paper is very brittle and the writing pale. After being told how faint the writing was, Mattes commented, "Perhaps someone in Michigan with a strong magnifying glass or connections with the FBI Laboratory will be willing to tackle this problem" [*Platte River Road Narratives,* 288–89].

Carolyn Dodds Schaeffer (Egerton) became interested in covered wagon history as a child. She and her sisters played "wagon train," pretending that they were traveling west. Because of her interest, she was given the family papers, which included three letters Washington had written in the 1870s to her great-grandmother, Anna Eliza Peck, which are included in this book along with numerous family photos. Carolyn has also contributed extensive genealogical research on the family.

John Wells Heap (Mary Ann) brought a significant piece to the puzzle—a family sampler listing the names of Washington Peck, his second wife, Mercy Mary, and his eight children. The sampler is unique because the middle names given for the children are not their legal names. Carolyn Dodds Schaeffer surmised that they were baptismal names or included a godparent's name, traditions not usually found in the early Methodist Wesleyan church to which the Pecks belonged. Our best guess is that Mercy, her daughter Mary Ann Banghart, or one of Mary Ann's daughters stitched the sampler.

Susan Rector Erb (Emma) inherited the 1858 Wagon Trail Diary from her grandfather, Fred Rector, as a result of her interest in family history. He revealed that her great-great-great grandfather Peck had written many diaries but that the others had been destroyed when the Rector family ranch house burned in 1939. The wagon trail diary survived because it was considered the most interesting and had been loaned to someone to read.

Calvin Uridge Whiffen, II, (Elizabeth) shared his research and some beautiful family photos, which fortunately a wise family member had inscribed with names.

Wesley "Junior" Labrier (Jane) lived on a ranch in Kenton, Oklahoma, where the Keys had settled in the 1880s when it was called No Man's Land. Junior grew up hearing family stories that went with the old homesteads on the ranch. He shared both his stories and family photos before he passed away on August 24, 2003.

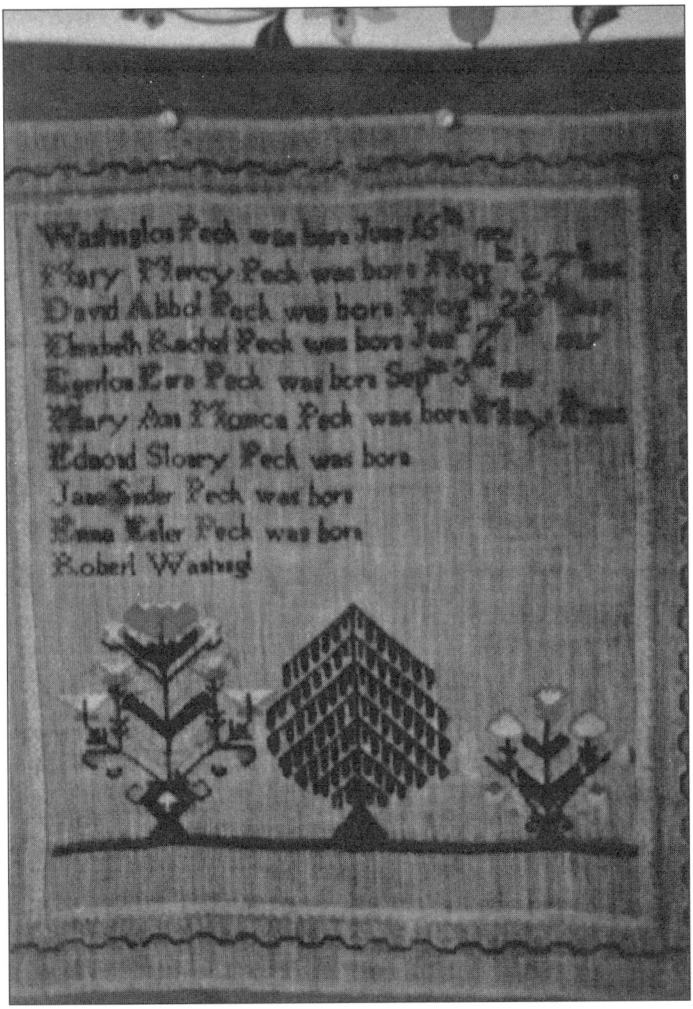

The Peck family sampler was handed down in the Banghart family. Stitcher unknown. *Courtesy of John Wells Heap.*

John "Jack" Taylor (Jane) had worked on the Keys family history for many years. He generously shared his photos and information, including the fascinating story of two Keys daughters who themselves became pioneers when they accompanied their newspaper husbands to the gold rush in Alaska and the Yukon in 1898.

I AM MOST GRATEFUL to my publisher, Bob Clark, for his editing expertise and guidance, to Bill Nelson, for his drawing of detailed maps, and to the many historical librarians and local area experts listed below who generously offered their help and expertise. Any errors are my own.

1850–51 WAGON TRAIL DIARY: Trevor J. Bond, librarian, Special Collection, Veterinary Medicine, Washington State University; Richard M. Davis, author, wagon wheel expert; Mark L. Gardner, author, wagon expert; Levida Hileman, author; Philip Holmes, author, information about Henry C. Smith at Mission San Jose; John H. Peck, Consulting Geologist, Las Vegas; David L. Poremba, former Manager, and Mark Patrick, Manager, Burton Historical Collection, Detroit Public Library; Martha Whittaker, Reference Librarian, Sutro Library; Lesley Wischmann, author, OCTA (Oregon-California Trails Association).

1858 WAGON TRAIL DIARY: Donald W. Aldrich, copy of Ed Akey's story; Bob Power (deceased), historian, copy of 1858 Udell Diary; Emmy E. Werner, author, Julia Brown story.

ARIZONA: Dove Menkes, author; Dr. Melanie Sturgeon, Division Director, History and Archives Div., Arizona State Library; Kathryn E. Vohs, Micrographic Supervisor, Yavapai County Microfilm Department; Michael Wurtz, Sharlot Hall Museum Research Library.

CALIFORNIA: Marilyn Peck, San Marino Historical Society; Shawn Lum, Vacaville Museum.

ILLINOIS: Elmer Dickson, Kendall County historian; Janny Johnson, slave child story; Stephanie Todd, Kendall County Historical Society; Glennette Tilley Turner, author.

MISSOURI: Elaine Davis, copy of *Early Times of Atchison County Missouri*; Susan McCormack, Reference Specialist, State Historical Society in Columbia, who located a microfilm of *The News*, Holt County, 1857–1858; Sharon L. Meyer, Circuit Clerk and Recorder, Atchison County;

Pat O'Dell, Coordinator of the Atchison County, Missouri, website for RootsWeb.com.

Oklahoma: Allan Griggs, Kenton Mercantile, for putting me in touch with Wesley (Junior) Labrier.

New Mexico: Bobbie Battler (deceased), Lucy Mima Wright's Diary; Karen Mills, Lincoln County Historical Society; John P. Ryan, author; John P. Wilson, author, map of Washington Peck's Rancho and additional assistance.

Upper Canada: Judith Argent, Cloverdale Branch, Surrey Public Library, genealogical expert on source materials; Ruth Burkholder, genealogist; George W. J. Duncan, Heritage Coordinator, Richmond Hill, information on Burr House; Janet E. Fayle, information on the land swap between W. Peck and R. Burr; Randall Reed, Information Officer of Montgomery's Inn; Mary Lloyd, Librarian, Richmond Hill Public Library.

Washington Territory: Angie Leventis, reporter, *Tacoma News Tribune*; Shannon Stevenson, Thurston County Historic Commission.

I especially thank family members who shared their stories: Robert (Bob) Butterworth (deceased), Viola Butterworth (deceased), Doris Colvin, Ruby Labrier, Bill Lynch, Eldon Morrill, Donald Rector, Fred Rector (deceased), Lester (Buster) Rector (deceased), Betty Steel, and Jo Anne Rousseau (deceased).

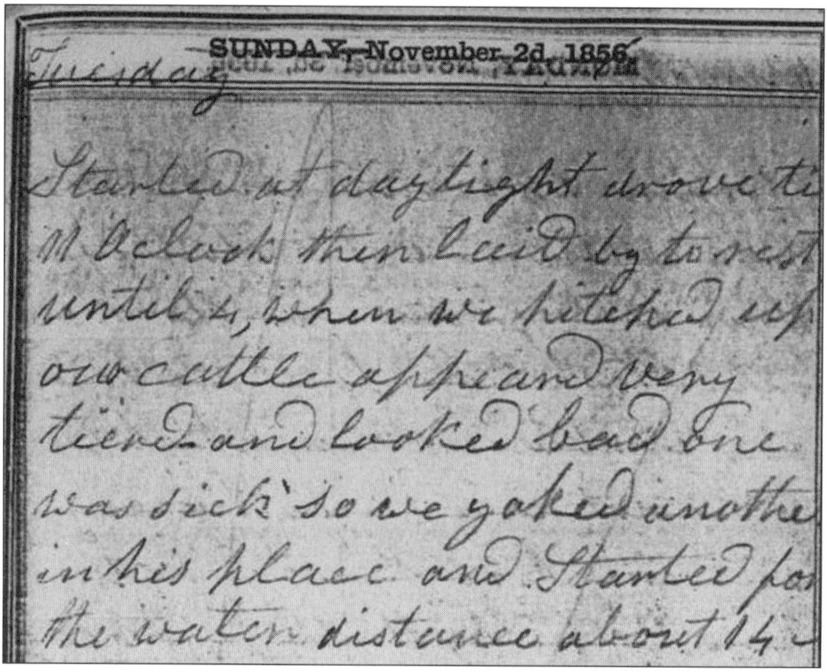

SUNDAY, November 2d, 1856.
Tuesday

Started at daylight drove ti
11 Oclock then laid by to rest
until 4, when we hitched up
our cattle appeared very
tired and looked bad one
was sick so we yoked another
in his place and Started for
the water distance about 14

Sample of Washington's handwriting from 1858 diary.
From author's collection.

Editorial Procedures

THE 1850–51 WAGON TRAIL DIARY is a foolscap journal, 7½ × 13 inches, with almost legal-size pages. The paper is brittle, with missing corners, holes, and foxing that obscures some of the faint writing. It is very difficult to read. Entries for many days are written on one page. Washington begins with the month, date, and day of the week: April 22, 1850, Monday. The subsequent entries include only the date and day of the week: 23 Tuesday. The month is identified only on the first day of the month. I have added the month in brackets [April] 23, Tuesday for clarity.

The 1858 Wagon Trail Diary is a small black leather diary, 4 × 6 inches with 1856 preprinted at the top each page, which Washington laboriously crossed out day after day. It is made of thin onionskin paper that is stronger than the foolscap paper of the 1850–51 diary, but again the writing is very faint and difficult to read. The last few pages and back cover are missing. The date from the preprinted heading has been placed at the beginning of each day's entry: Tuesday, July 13, 1858.

The diaries have been transcribed as accurately as possible. Lack of punctuation makes the diaries difficult to read, so a literary transcription style was used, which added punctuation and capitalization where obvious. Spelling and grammar were not altered. Parentheses are Washington's own. Holes or illegible words are indicated by [——]. Brackets enclose clarifications by the author.

Washington Peck Family Tree

Washington Peck (1801–1889)
m. (1825) Sophia Willcox* (1805–1832)
1. Elizabeth Rachel Peck (1827–1882)
m. (1845) Thomas Whiffen (1816–1891)
2. David Abbott Peck (1829–1897)
m. (1850) Eliza Jane Carey (1829–1885)
3. Egerton Ezra Peck (1831–1903)
m. (1855) Hannah Maria Woodhull (1837–1885)
m. (1832) Mercy Mary Wilcox* Card (1806–1899)
Widow of Thomas Perry Card (1806–1829)
4. Mary Ann Monica Peck (1833–1881)
m. (1850) George W. Banghart (1823–1895)
5. Edmond George Peck (1834–1910)
m. (1873) Ellen Serena Alexander (1855–1887)
6. Jane S. Peck (1836–1917)
m. (1858) Calvin S. Keys (1830–1911)
7. Emma Ester Peck (1840–1925)
m. (1858) George W. Rector (1837–?)
m. (1866) Ignatius Colvin (1829–1898)
8. Robert Washington Peck—b. after 1840

*Sophia Willcox and Mercy Wilcox were not related.

Introduction

Washington Peck lived a remarkable life as an eyewitness to many of the major historical events during the 1800s. He worked as a cooper and a farmer, and he witnessed the changes brought about by the California gold rush, the Mormon building of Salt Lake City, the 1837 Patriot Rebellion in Canada, the Underground Railroad in Illinois, the build-up to the Civil War in New Mexico, travel on the Butterfield Overland Mail Route during the outbreak of the Civil War, devastating floods and droughts in southern California, a stage coach robbery in the "wild west," and the creation of a territory (Utah) and a state (Washington). Washington's story explains how those events affected the lives of ordinary citizens and how his leadership skills, honed by experience, led to his election as a wagon train captain and a territorial legislator.

A unique story unfolds in Washington's own words as related through two wagon trail diaries (1850 and 1858) and several letters. He expresses a creative personality characterized by thoughtful morality and persistent hard work. He remained dedicated to his family and managed to keep himself and them safe from threatening epidemics and Indian attacks. He was, indeed, a survivor.

Washington and Mercy, his wife, were ardent Wesleyan Methodists who founded a church on their first property. But after sixty years, they became entranced with the Spiritualism movement that swept through the country in the 1860s, which led them to some intriguing activities and beliefs.

Mercy was at Washington's side throughout their travels, but Washington never once mentioned her by name. On rare occasions he referred to her as *wife* or *mother*. His diaries recorded unusual events, his sons' and son-in-law's activities, men's work, problems with animals, and the weather, but nothing about the Peck women on the trail.

After living in Ontario until age thirty-eight, Washington Peck made his first wagon trip west, to Illinois. Over the next twenty-five years, Washington continued to travel, spreading his growing family across the continent. Although his final twenty-five years were anchored in Washington Territory, he and Mercy moved several more times.

Wherever he went, Washington bought and sold property, so his moves are tracked and dated from land records. Mercy often signed the deeds, either with or without Washington, showing that she not only was capable but was, in a sense, treated as an equal. In some cases she appears to have gone ahead or stayed behind to take care of legal details while Washington dealt with other matters. She also contributed to the women's suffragette movement in Washington Territory in the 1870s. All of these experiences helped to make up Mercy's full and busy life, although it is not evident in Washington's diaries.

As the Pecks continued to migrate, their children grew to adulthood, married, and often stayed behind. The result of this was twofold: first, the Peck family became spread from Ontario to Washington Territory by 1864, and second, those who "stayed behind" dropped out of Washington's main story.

This book weaves together two significant wagon trail diaries with the biography of Washington and Mercy Peck, who traveled both the Oregon and Santa Fe trails as a couple, a unique occurrence. Their lives spanned the settlement of the West. Their travels and experiences bring that history to life.

1

The Early Years

York, Upper Canada, 1814

Washington Peck was born on July 26, 1801, but his place of birth is unknown. Various census records point to Massachusetts, Connecticut, and New York. By 1814 he had immigrated to Upper Canada with his father Caleb, a cooper, and likely with his mother.

Conditions were primitive. York (Toronto) was a small muddy village of a hundred households clinging to the shore of Lake Ontario. Cows and pigs wandered through the mud along the main street, eating from the garbage tossed there. Picket fences were built to keep animals out of yards, not in, and the mud was horrendous. Historian Margaret Atwood wrote, "The roads were only completely safe [in winter] when they were frozen solid."[1] The *Canadian Freeman* reported that garbage piled up throughout the year until spring when the dead horses, dogs, and manure were heaped together on the frozen lake to await the spring thaw, the same lake that supplied their drinking water.[2]

The Pecks settled in the village of Weston in York Township on the banks of the Humber River, which ran down into Lake Ontario. The Humber's waterpower had attracted millers, who built gristmills, sawmills, and distilleries along its banks from Upper Canada's earliest days. When the Pecks arrived, the gristmills were operating at full capacity producing flour for the troops involved in the ongoing War of 1812.[3] The need for barrels was enormous, so coopers were in great demand. Everything, it seemed, was packed into barrels—flour, molasses, whiskey, potash, salted fish, and meat—both for personal storage and for shipping. Caleb quickly found work, and over the next few years, as his son grew into a tall, lanky young man with a shock of unruly hair, he began teaching Washington coopering skills.

[1] Atwood, *Days of the Rebels*, 11.

[2] Raible, *Muddy York Mud*, 9.

[3] Mossman, "Weston," *Villages of Etobicoke*, 106.

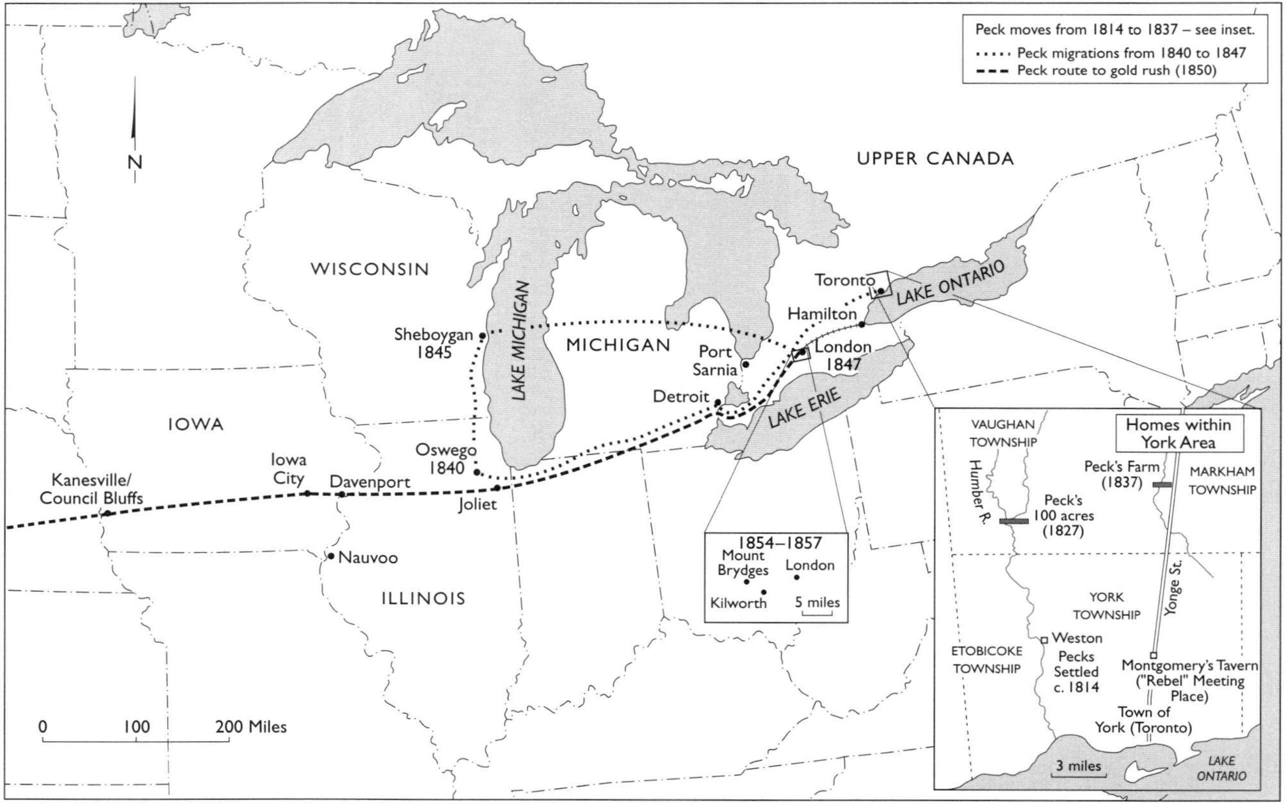

Peck travels from 1814 to 1857

Around 1814 Washington Peck immigrated to Canada and settled with his father in Weston, a few miles west of York (Toronto). In 1827 he acquired his first property in Woodbridge, and in 1837 he moved to Yonge Street in Toronto. In 1840 the Pecks migrated to Oswego, Illinois; in 1845 to Sheboygan, Wisconsin; then back to Canada in 1847. In 1850 the Pecks joined the masses heading west to the California gold rush. By 1854 the Pecks had returned to Ontario where they remained until 1857.

The Pecks likely were attracted to Upper Canada by the government's offer to settlers of two hundred acres of free land. Canada needed settlers. So many Americans had moved into Upper Canada to take advantage of the free land grants that by the beginning of the War of 1812, two-thirds of the population were American.[4]

The Pecks found that life in Upper Canada was markedly different from the United States. Since Upper Canada was a colony of Britain, the government-appointed officials controlled everything, and they were a little nervous about Americans who were used to self-government. During the next twenty years the Pecks lived through a battle for religious freedom, revisions to the land laws, and a rebellion that supported constitutional reform.

The land system was the underlying reason for all three problems. One in every seven lots was designated as a Crown Reserve, which would provide government revenue, and a second lot became a Clergy Reserve, to fund the Church of England. The Reserves were sprinkled throughout the township in a checkerboard pattern amongst the remaining five lots, which were held for settlers. Most lots were two hundred acres.

Getting free land was not easy. A settler had to apply for land in a groveling tone of humility, with a set wording that appears in page after page of applications. On April 22, 1819, Caleb Peck's application came before the committee, "Praying for a grant of land as a settler."[5]

One of the men making the land-granting decisions was Reverend John Strachan, head of the Anglican Church in Canada. Strachan controlled the Clergy Reserves and also sat on both the Legislative and Executive Councils for many years. His was the most influential voice in Upper Canada.[6] Unfortunately for the Pecks, Strachan loathed Americans, especially Methodists, and the Pecks were both.[7] Thirty-eight applications from settlers were reviewed on April 22, 1819, and all were granted one hundred or two hundred acres, except one. Caleb's application reads, "Not recommended."[8] It was a crushing blow, one that had a lifelong impact on Washington, who vowed from that day forward that he would own his own land.

The religious freedom the Pecks had known in the United States did not exist in Canada at that time. The 1793 Marriage Act decreed that only

[4] Bowler, *War of 1812*, 14.
[5] National Archives of Canada, Microfilm C103, Upper Canada Land Book K, 89.
[6] Scadding, *Toronto of Old*, 380.
[7] Fraser, *Eminent Canadians*, 19.
[8] National Archives of Canada, Microfilm C103, Upper Canada Land Book K, 89.

the Church of England could perform marriages.[9] Not only was it illegal for Methodist ministers to perform marriages or baptisms, they could not own land for churches, parsonages, or cemeteries.[10] Undeterred by the rejection of his land grant, Caleb Peck helped found a new Episcopal Methodist Church in Weston in 1821 on a donated acre of land.[11]

The battle between the churches began to heat up in the summer of 1825. During a funeral sermon Reverend Strachan delivered a blistering attack on Methodist preachers, stating that they were too ignorant and too American. In fact they were neither, but Strachan was trying to retain the clergy reserves for the exclusive use of the Anglican Church. He did not want to share the revenue from land sales with other Protestant churches, especially Methodists. His sermon, published in the spring of 1826, created an uproar.[12] After years of discrimination, the Methodists were outraged by Strachan's attack and decided that someone must write a rebuttal. The man chosen was Egerton Ryerson, a young Methodist preacher, who had just been assigned to the York circuit, which included the Weston church that the Pecks attended. Editor William Lyon Mackenzie, an ardent political reformer, published Ryerson's reply under a pseudonym in the *Colonial Advocate*. Strachan's power had finally been challenged, and historian Chris Raible concluded that his "influence would never again be quite the same."[13] The Methodists began their own newspaper, chose Egerton Ryerson as editor, and published the first issue of the *Christian Guardian* on November 22, 1829.[14] Within four years the laws were changed to allow Methodists and other denominations to perform marriages and christenings and to own land for churches.[15]

On July 17, 1825, Washington, almost twenty-four, married Sophia Willcox, then twenty.[16] After their first child, Elizabeth Rachel Peck, was born on March 7, 1827, Washington set out to find a home for his young family. He headed into the wilderness, traveling north on an ancient Huron Indian trail alongside the Humber River. Six miles upriver he came to the confluence of the Humber and East Humber Rivers, part of a long portage

[9] Somerville and Macfarlane, *History of Vaughan Township Churches*, 3.

[10] Damania, *Egerton Ryerson*, 15–16.

[11] Cruickshank and Nason, *History of Weston*, 104–105.

[12] Damania, *Egerton Ryerson*, 15.

[13] Raible, *Muddy York Mud*, 226.

[14] The paper evolved into McGraw-Hill Ryerson, which continues to publish today.

[15] Damania, *Egerton Ryerson*, 19, 21.

[16] Reaman, *History of Vaughan Township*, 286–87.

(now called the Toronto Carrying Place) that passed from Lake Ontario to Huronia.[17] It was an incredible piece of land described by historian Sydney Fisher as having "fine stands of pine and a forest of mixed hardwoods."[18] It was exactly the land Washington needed to begin a cooperage.

On June 30, 1827, Washington leased one hundred acres, the western half of a Crown Reserve lot, from the government.[19] In contrast to the U.S. Township and Range system of square grids oriented on true north-south, land in Upper Canada was laid out in concessions that were divided into rectangular two-hundred-acre lots, one and a quarter miles wide by a quarter mile deep. The long, narrow lots were laid out in whatever direction best accommodated the land.[20]

Washington built a log cabin that was described by Elizabeth Burr Tyrell, who lived in the house as a child, as a "hewn log house, which although small, was comfortable and free from dampness as in stone or brick."[21] Washington, Sophia, baby Elizabeth, and his father Caleb moved in.

They built a cooper's shop and began turning out barrels, buckets, and washtubs for the settlers who were sprinkled sparsely around the township. The cooperage was a busy place filled with smoke from the small fires needed to steam and bend staves and noise from hammering metal hoops into place. Customers stayed to visit while Washington worked, and they discussed their concerns, which included political reform.

The government needed increased capital and more settlers, so in 1824 they sold 2.5 million acres of unoccupied Crown Reserves to the newly formed Canada Company.[22] Five years later the Canada Company purchased the Crown Reserve in the Woodbridge area, including the lot where the Pecks lived. The company improved the road, eliminating the previously poor access that had saved the forest on Washington's property from the clear-cutting that had taken place downstream on the Humber.[23] Washington continued to lease the land from the Canada Company for the next few years.

---

[17] Sawdon, *Woodbridge Story*, 1–2; *Woodbridge Mackenzie Site (AkGv-2)*, report by Meryl Oliver. Three hundred years earlier an Iroquois longhouse village and palisade had been built near this confluence. The site has been dated to 1520 and is designated as a heritage site.

[18] Fisher, *Merchant-Millers of the Humber Valley*, 125.

[19] Coleman, *Canada Company*, 22, 217–18.

[20] Raible, *Muddy York Mud*, 220.

[21] Letter from Mrs. William (Elizabeth) Tyrell (daughter of Rowland Burr), May 20, 1891, 3. William Tyrrell Papers.

[22] Craig, *Upper Canada*, 134–36.

[23] Fisher, *Merchant-Millers of the Humber Valley*, 125.

Washington and Sophia had two more children. David Abbott Peck was born on November 22, 1829, and Egerton Ezra Peck arrived on September 3, 1831, named in honor of minister Egerton Ryerson. Eight months later, on April 5, 1832, Sophia died at age twenty-seven. Her obituary simply said that she "died after a short illness."[24]

Three months later, Washington married a young widow, Mercy Mary (Wilcox) Card, who despite the similar last name was not related to Washington's first wife. She was as short as he was tall. Born in Nova Scotia on November 27, 1806, Mercy had married Thomas Perry Card in 1824 and then moved to Upper Canada with a large Card family entourage.[25] Thomas died in 1829 and left her with two small children, who apparently died in one of the many epidemics that swept through the area. Whatever drew Mercy and Washington together—mutual grief, love, or practicality—they were married on July 17, 1832, with Caleb Peck and James Rose as witnesses.[26]

In May of 1834 Washington purchased his leased hundred acres for 75£ from the Canada Company.[27] From that day forward Washington was never again without land.

He donated one acre for a Wesleyan Methodist Church, the first church in the district, sometimes called Peck's Appointment. The small log church sat on the high point of Washington's property overlooking the Humber Valley.[28] Historian George Reaman described the Church members as a group of "ardent Christians" who followed the teachings of John Wesley.[29]

Three more children were born: Mary Ann (May 11, 1833), Edmond George (December 28, 1834), and Jane (October 1836). As the family grew, a small village developed on and around Washington's land. James Rose, a shoemaker, and Mercy's cousins from Nova Scotia, Stephen and Mary Burgess, lived on the property and were members of their small Methodist church.[30]

---

[24] *York (Ont.) Christian Guardian*, Apr. 18, 1832.

[25] Obituary of Mercy Peck, Nov. 3, 1899, *Chehalis (Wash.) Bee Nugget.*

[26] Records of the Registrar General, Marriages in the Home District 1823–1845, in Archives of Ontario, Microfilm MS248, Reel 1: Index 59.

[27] Canada Company to W. Peck, May 17, 1834, Old York Registry, Vaughan Township Deed 10930, Lot 8, Conc. 7.

[28] Old York Registry, Vaughan Township Deed 13814, Lot 8, Conc. 7, July 9, 1834; and Reaman, *History of Vaughan Township*, 159. The trustees were Francis Bunt, a fellow cooper, James Rose, a witness at his wedding, James Farr, Nathan Martin, and Robert Coates.

[29] Reaman, *History of Vaughan Township*, 159.

[30] Walton, *City of Toronto and the Home District*, 141.

The movement for political reform developed slowly. Unrest grew at a grass roots level against the small, privileged group who controlled the government. During the summer of 1831, Washington attended a meeting at Keffer's Schoolhouse to sign a petition thanking the King of England for his support of constitutional reform. It was a backhanded but safe way for settlers to support change. Hundreds signed throughout the township but little change occurred.[31]

In late February of 1837 Washington traded seventy-eight acres to Rowland Burr for a sixty-five-acre farm on Yonge Street. He sold one acre to his friend James Rose, turned the cooperage over to Francis Bunt, a fellow church member, and attended to the sad task of burying his father Caleb in the little churchyard.[32]

Rowland Burr was a builder who had been eyeing Washington's property for years.[33] Burr's daughter Elizabeth recalled that he immediately "employed men to remove the great forest trees and clear the chosen site for his improvements," which were a saw mill, a flour mill, and a woolen factory.[34] The developing community was named Burwick, and later Woodbridge.[35]

The Peck's new farm was just off Yonge, the main road that pushed north into the wilderness from Toronto. Burr retained the Yonge Street frontage, which had a sawmill and a gristmill, called Greenfield Mill.[36] The Pecks likely moved into the house Burr built in the 1820s.[37]

The Pecks then had a ringside seat to the Patriot Rebellion of 1837, which occurred a few months after they moved in. Grumbling against the government had grown into a reform movement led by the fiery

---

31 *York (Ont.) Colonial Advocate*, July 7, 1831, 3:2 and Oct. 6, 1831, 4:2.

32 Old York Registry, Vaughan Township Deeds 13812 and 14566, Lot 8, Conc. 7; Deed 13969, Lot 41, Conc. 1; Mulvany, *History of Toronto and County of York, Village of Woodbridge*, 196–97; Sawdon, *Woodbridge Story*, 42–43; "Sketch of the History of Vaughan Including Woodbridge," Nov. 9, 1899, *Woodbridge (Ont.) Leader and Recorder*; and Somerville and Macfarlane, *History of Vaughan Township Churches*, 235–36. Caleb Peck was the first burial in Peck's Burying Ground, later called the Old Methodist Church Cemetery. The gravestones (not Caleb's) were later moved and set into a stone wall creating a cairn.

33 Fisher, *Merchant-Millers of the Humber Valley*, 125.

34 Letter from Mrs. William (Elizabeth) Tyrrell (daughter of Rowland Burr), May 20, 1891, 3. William Tyrrell Papers.

35 Reaman, *History of Vaughan Township*, 125. Woodbridge is now part of the city of Vaughn, and Washington's original one hundred acres can be seen in the Humber River Valley along Meeting House Road, as part of the Woodbridge Country Club golf course.

36 Sawdon, *Woodbridge Story*, 35.

37 Mulvany, *History of Toronto and County of York*, 128; Sawdon, *Woodbridge Story*, 35; and Duncan, "Early Houses of Richmond Hill and Vicinity," *York Pioneer*, 1995, 90:18–19. Burr House is now designated as the oldest house in Richmond Hill and is home to the Richmond Hill Historical Society.

newspaper editor, William Lyon Mackenzie, who had been elected to Parliament. Historian F. R. Berchem noted that people were weary of the small privileged group, called the Family Compact, who continued "to run the colony much as they pleased and for their own benefit, ignoring the needs of the people they were supposed to be serving."[38] The complaints had a familiar ring: high taxes, excessive pay for government officials, and too little money spent on roads and education. When Mackenzie began to advocate taking over the government by force, more moderate men, including Egerton Ryerson, withdrew their support.[39]

Mackenzie proceeded to organize the patriot uprising for early December of 1837. Five hundred rebels gathered at Montgomery's Tavern on Yonge Street, south of Peck's farm. Armed with a few muskets, pitchforks, and sticks, they began the four-mile march down Yonge Street to take over the government in Toronto. There they had a brief skirmish with twenty men led by Sheriff Jarvis. When the front line of rebels fired, they dropped down so those behind could fire over their heads. The untrained young farmers, thinking their men had been shot, panicked and fled. Two days later the government assembled fifteen hundred soldiers and marched them up Yonge Street to Montgomery's Tavern where the rebels had regrouped. Historian Robert Stamp noted that they routed the rebels within half an hour, "burned the tavern, and leisurely marched back to Toronto." The Patriot Rebellion was over.[40]

The discontent that remained after the aborted rebellion fueled an emigration to the United States made attractive by cheap land in Illinois, Michigan, and Iowa. By August of 1838 the *Toronto Mirror* reported that if matters continued at the present rate, "one half of Canada [would] be in Illinois and the Far West before long." Reverend John Ryerson wrote to his brother, Egerton, "I find some of the best farmers in those parts have sold, and others are trying to sell . . . and have left for the States."[41] Washington was one of them.

On May 1, 1840, Washington sold his farm for 500£, which was substantially more than the 75£ he had originally paid to the Canada Com-

[38] Landon, *Exile from Canada to Van Dieman's Land*, 38; and Carter, *Newmarket, The Heart of York Region*, 25.

[39] Berchem, *Yonge Street Story 1793–1860*, 131.

[40] Stamp, *Early Days in Richmond Hill*, 96–97.

[41] Landon, *Western Ontario and the American Frontier*, 197–201.

pany.[42] At thirty-eight years old, Washington was setting out as a pioneer for the second time. He packed up Mercy, who was pregnant, and their six young children (ages three to thirteen), piled everything into a wagon or two, and started west.

Kane/Kendall Counties, Illinois, 1840

The Pecks drove forty miles west of Chicago through fields of wildflowers and grasses that stretched across the level prairie as far as they could see. The horizon was broken by an occasional grove of trees that served as landmarks.[43] Historian Robert Howard wrote, "The blue-stem prairie grass, often as high as a mounted horseman . . . rippled a golden yellow in the late summer breeze."[44] The Pecks arrived at Oswego, a small village on the Fox River, just before Emma Ester was born in September of 1840.

Two miles south of town, Washington staked a claim to open prairie with a beautiful stream flowing through it—Morgan Creek. The family became squatters, the name used for settlers who staked a claim to government-owned land, and they set to work. After the land was surveyed into sections and townships, it would be put up for sale. Washington could establish preemptive (presale) rights by obtaining proofs from those who could verify his claim.

In November Washington bought a seven-acre wood lot in one of the groves to provide firewood, building logs, fence rails, and the hardwood for coopering.[45] The trees growing along Morgan Creek on his farm were left standing to provide a break against the constant prairie wind.

Life on the prairies was dangerous. Wolves roamed the area, children got lost in the tall grass, and the prevailing westerly fall winds swept fire across the grasslands until it reached water, making a stream on the property doubly important. Settlers plowed extra furrows around their fields and homesteads for protection. One pioneer remembered seeing as many as fifty fires burning at one time, turning the night sky into day.[46]

[42] W. Peck to John Atkinson, 65 acres, May 1, 1840, Old York Registry, Vaughan Township Deed 17273.

[43] Hicks, *History of Kendall County*, 203.

[44] Howard, *Illinois: A History of the Prairie State*, 2.

[45] J. Sullivan to W. Peck, Nov. 17, 1840, Kendall County Deed Book A:203.

[46] Farren, *Bicentennial History of Kendall County*, 74, 76.

At the beginning of 1841, Kendall County was created from neighboring counties and became part of the Ninth District Circuit Court.[47] Young circuit lawyers would arrive with the district judge to resolve any legal matters or disputes before the court. In the adjoining Eighth District Circuit out of Springfield, one of the young lawyers riding the circuit was Abraham Lincoln.

By 1842 the surveyors had completed work on the first section of Washington's farm, at which time he purchased it.[48] Land sales were fraught with problems. The going rate of $1.25 per acre had to be paid for in cash—in gold or silver.[49] The government did not accept bank notes for two reasons: banks frequently failed after issuing more paper than they could back and counterfeiting was rampant because bank notes were easily copied.[50]

When a sale was announced, all those living on the land got together to plat out the division, making sure each one's claim was agreed upon in advance. One man was chosen to bid on the whole parcel at the land office in Chicago. A group of neighbors went along to guard the moneybox and help make sure the sale went as planned. Speculators often tried to buy improved properties, either to keep or to sell back to the original settler at a hefty profit. To keep speculators from bidding, guards stood at the door to prevent strangers and speculators from entering. A speculator who did manage to buy a settler's land would be prevented from entering the building until the payment deadline had elapsed, thus freeing the land to be resold to the settler with preemptive rights.[51]

Property taxes also had to be paid in cash, so most settlers earned money by doing something other than farming; those who could not pay their taxes often lost their land.[52] A month after Washington's first land purchase, he bought four town lots in Oswego, including a prime location at the main intersection of the village, where the road coming south across the Fox River met the road coming from the east.[53] The river crossing was a natural ford where shallow water flowed over a solid sheet of limestone. Historian Roger Matile pointed out that a ford "slowed the

---

[47] Hicks, *History of Kendall County*, 221–23.

[48] Bateman, *Historical Encyclopedia of Illinois*, 700. Preemptive Certificates 9482 and 11702, July 10, 1844.

[49] Ibid., 712.

[50] Hicks, *History of Kendall County*, 213.

[51] Ibid., 208–209; and Bateman, *Historical Encyclopedia of Illinois*, 712–13.

[52] Farren, *Bicentennial History of Kendall County*, 76.

[53] Kendall County Deed Book A:204, May 12, 1842.

traffic and afforded business opportunities."[54] It was an ideal location for Washington to start a cooperage, especially with Nathaniel Rising's gristmill across the Fox River generating a need for barrels.[55]

At the next land sale, in July of 1844, Washington bought a second quarter section, and Stephen Burgess, Mercy's cousin from Woodbridge, bought an adjoining farm.[56]

The abolitionist movement, which reached an early flash point when white abolitionist newspaper publisher Elijah P. Lovejoy was murdered in 1837, was strengthening and gaining momentum throughout Illinois. The Underground Railroad ran from Quincy, on the Mississippi River, through Kendall County, along the Fox River and on to Chicago, primarily helping slaves fleeing from Missouri. Almost every village in the county had stations to hide runaways. From Chicago the slaves boarded ships that delivered them to freedom in Canada, where slavery was prohibited.[57]

Written records by those who were involved in the Underground Railroad are rare. The need for secrecy was great because aiding runaway slaves could result in fines of $500 and jail sentences.[58] That a farm could be lost for unpaid taxes of as little as $2.94 emphasizes how large that fine was.[59] Years later, when Washington's eldest son, David Abbott Peck was interviewed for his own biography, he revealed that Washington had been a conductor on the Underground Railroad.[60] Author Raymond Bial explained what conductors did in his book *The Underground Railroad*: "'Conductors' undertook the most dangerous work. . . . They either led 'passengers' on foot or hid runaways in wagonloads of straw or vegetables" to deliver to the next station.[61] To protect the identities of all, a conductor would know only the next stop on the route.

A cooperage provided good cover for such activities, with farmers coming and going. A false bottom fitted partway down a barrel, with the top

---

[54] Matile, *150 Years Along the Fox*, 7.

[55] Farren, *Bicentennial History of Kendall County*, 99; and Bateman, *Historical Encyclopedia of Illinois*, 886.

[56] Bateman, *Historical Encyclopedia of Illinois*, 700. Certificates 11701 and 11702, July 10, 1844.

[57] Bateman, *Historical Encyclopedia of Illinois*, 766; Siebert, *Underground Railroad*, 147; and Hicks, *History of Kendall County*, 215.

[58] Farren, *Bicentennial History of Kendall County*, 129; and Bateman, *Historical Encyclopedia of Illinois*, 765.

[59] *Nauvoo (Ill.) Neighbor*, Apr. 2, 1845.

[60] *Biographical History of Page County*, 642–43.

[61] Bial, *Underground Railroad*, 10.

filled with grain or flour, provided a good hiding place. More commonly, a farm wagon had a false bottom with a hidden compartment.

Secret passwords and lamps lit in certain windows or hung on a hitching post were only part of an elaborate system used to signal whether the station (a house or barn or hollow haystack with a blind entrance) was safe or whether the runaways should continue on to the next place.[62]

To maintain secrecy and prevent accidental disclosure, children were usually kept unaware of runaways, which the following story illustrates. One little girl, sensing something was going on, joined her mother in the kitchen where she heard a noise in the stove. She opened the door and was startled to see two eyes peering back at her from the darkness. She looked at her mother, who simply nodded but said nothing, so she closed the door. Nearby slave hunters were searching for runaways. Her father later moved the child to their barn, but nothing was said to the young girl about it—ever.[63] It is not surprising that the younger Peck children did not mention Washington's involvement in written or oral biographical stories because secrecy by those directly involved was maintained for decades.

Was Washington a conductor? There is only David's testimony, but by 1845 when the family left Illinois, David was almost sixteen and working with Washington, so he likely witnessed it firsthand. David's biographical material is particularly accurate in all other events that he reported, which lends credence to his assertion. In addition, the Pecks were devoted followers of the Wesleyan Methodist Church that had long supported abolitionism.

Adherents to the Mormon Church had emigrated from Missouri, where they had met persecution, engaged in armed conflict, and eventually been expelled by state forces. They had arrived in Illinois at the same time as the Pecks. They lived peaceably for a few years, building up the community in Nauvoo, until new problems began to arise. With the help of Secretary of State, Stephen A. Douglas, they had obtained a special city charter, allowing their founder and prophet, Joseph Smith, to be head of the law within the community, rather like president of a city-state.[64] City council meetings were often conducted like court proceedings.

In a record of a meeting in Nauvoo on June 8, 1844, a Washington Peck testified that Joseph H. Jackson had come across the river to Peck's store

[62] Bateman, *Historical Encyclopedia of Illinois*, 765.

[63] This story was handed down in Janny Johnson's family. The young girl told her story years later after she became a grandmother.

[64] Howard, *Illinois: A History of the Prairie State*, 215.

and offered him some jewelry in return for cash.[65] While there, Jackson, a Mormon, admitted to being involved in producing counterfeit money, "making bogus" he called it. When asked if Joseph Smith knew of it, Jackson replied that he did not. Further, anyone who dared tell Smith would be murdered. After Jackson left, Washington discovered that the jewelry traded to him was stolen property.[66]

The minor controversy over counterfeiting occurred at the same time that dissension within the Mormon Church had prompted the creation of a rival newspaper, the *Nauvoo Expositor,* whose first issue was printed on June 7, 1844. Smith was so incensed at the accusations it contained that he ordered the press destroyed.[67] In the resulting uproar Joseph and Hyrum Smith were ordered to stand trial. They were arrested and jailed in nearby Carthage where on June 27, 1844, an angry mob murdered them both, just three weeks after Washington Peck testified in Nauvoo.

During the chaos of the next few months, Jackson was one of the men accused of plotting the Smiths' murders. He fled to Missouri. When the sheriff went to arrest him, Jackson refused to surrender and thereby avoided being sent to Carthage for the murder trial that began in May of 1845. Historians Oaks and Hill described the men who stood trial as being "among the most prominent men in western Illinois." They included a state senator, a newspaper editor, and four officers from the local militia who had been assigned to guard the jailed Smiths. All were acquitted. Jackson, who admitted helping in the planning, enlisted to fight in the Mexican War of 1846–47 where he died of yellow fever.[68]

The bitterness that had been unleashed against the Mormons soon led Brigham Young, who had assumed leadership of the Church, to conclude that they would have to leave the United States to find peace. By 1847 the first Mormon pioneers would arrive at their new "Zion" in the Great Basin beside the Great Salt Lake.

In the Peck household, eighteen-year-old Elizabeth married Thomas Whiffen on March 16, 1845.[69] The Whiffen family had arrived in the spring of 1844 and settled on a nearby farm. Thomas had come from England with

---

[65] In spite of extensive research, the definitive identity of the Washington Peck who testified at Nauvoo has not been proven.

[66] *Nauvoo (Ill.) Neighbor,* June 19, 1844, 2.

[67] Ibid., 3.

[68] Roberts, *Comprehensive History of the Church of Jesus Christ of Latter-day Saints,* Century I, 2:313–14, n. 15; and Oaks, *Carthage Conspiracy,* 4–5, 38, 227. See the *Carthage Conspiracy* for complete details of the trial.

[69] Kendall County Marriage Book A1:12.

his father, Uridge, and four siblings in 1842. After stopping in Oneida County, New York, most of the family had continued on to Kendall County.[70]

Newton and Mary Goodell, also from Upper Canada, bought land adjoining the Whiffen farm.[71] At the beginning of September 1845, the Goodell, Whiffen, and Burgess families sold their farms, Washington sold his business lot in town, and they all migrated to Wisconsin.[72] Thomas and Elizabeth Whiffen stayed behind until their son, Uridge Peck Whiffen, was born and then they caught up with their families.[73]

Washington had abandoned a 320-acre farm (not selling it until two years later). This implies some unknown urgency to their move. Was Washington being threatened for testifying in Nauvoo? If he wasn't the Peck who testified, had he been mistakenly identified? Or had he been exposed as a conductor on the Underground Railway? Their reason for migrating north remains a mystery.

Sheboygan, Wisconsin, 1845

The trip to Wisconsin was hard going. The only first-hand account is that of ten-year-old Nathan Goodell, Newton's eldest son, who told his story to the *Sheboygan Press* many years later. "They stopped wherever night overtook them . . . always in the forests, for roads were . . . scarce." From Port Washington, they had to cut through the forest along an Indian trail. It took them four days to travel twenty-five miles.[74] In one of the wagons jolting along the rough trail was a pregnant Mary Ann Burgess, who gave birth to a son, David, on October 15, 1845, just as they arrived in Sheboygan.[75]

Sheboygan had about three hundred settlers, attracted by the sawmills and gristmills. Realtors were trying to bring more immigrants to Sheboygan County by distributing promotional pamphlets, mostly in Germany.[76] Washington and Mercy bought three scattered parcels from the

---

[70] *Portrait and Biographical Record of Sheboygan County*, 667.

[71] Bateman, *Historical Encyclopedia of Illinois*, 701; Preemption Certificate 19664A, Feb. 18, 1846.

[72] W. Peck to Daniel B. Jewell, Sept. 27, 1845, Kendall County Deed Book D:64.

[73] T. Whiffen to A. B. Smith, May 28, 1846, Kendall County Deed Book D:50.

[74] Federal Census, 1850, Wisconsin, Sheboygan County, District 14, Roll 1006, 132; and "Pioneer of the Many Pioneers," *Sheboygan Press*, Jan. 16, 1915.

[75] Wesleyan Methodist Baptismal Registers, Reel 1, 453.

[76] "My First Visit to Sheboygan," *Sheboygan Times*, Aug. 24, 1895; and "Sheboygan of 78 Years Ago Described by Dr. Brown in the Old Sheboygan Mercury," *Sheboygan Press-Telegram*, Oct. 1923, 1895.

government land office, and along with the Goodells and Whiffens, the Pecks set to work clearing the land for farms.[77] Within eighteen months they sold the cleared acreages at a profit, implying that they may have been engaged in a real estate venture rather than resettlement. The wave of immigrants brought in by the promoters increased the population in Sheboygan County from 1,600 to 8,300 between 1845 and 1850.[78]

Little is known about life in Sheboygan during the years that the Pecks lived there. There was no newspaper until 1847, and a courthouse fire in 1860 destroyed all but the deed records, but even they were left incomplete. It is known that a widespread smallpox epidemic swept through the area in the winter of 1846–47 killing many, perhaps including the Pecks' last child, Robert Washington Peck, who is presumed to have died very young. About thirty people, perhaps including the Pecks, organized the Methodist church in 1846.[79]

In July of 1847 Washington had the good fortune to meet Christopher Williams, who owned a farm that he wanted to sell in the London District of Ontario. Washington traded his 320-acre Illinois farm for the 95-acre farm in Canada, which had equal value.[80] By the end of the month, the Pecks were on their way back to Canada. Their stay in Sheboygan had lasted twenty-one months.

Washington's daughter and her husband, Elizabeth and Thomas Whiffen, took their baby son to Canada too, but they settled in Port Sarnia (now Sarnia), where Thomas purchased a couple of town lots and went into the potash business. The Whiffens remained in Sarnia for the rest of their lives where they helped build the early community. Of their nine children, three died in childhood. Thomas served on the local school board for almost thirty years and was elected to Town Council concurrently for five years.[81]

The rest of the Whiffens remained in Sheboygan, and the Burgess family returned to Woodbridge.

---

[77] Green Bay (Wis.) Bureau of Land Management-General Land Office Records Certificates 4422, 6754, and 4493; Sheboygan County Deed Book C:456, 459 and Deed Book F:461–62; and Zillier, *History of Sheboygan County*, 1:315.

[78] Writers' Program (U.S.) Wisconsin, *Wisconsin, A Guide to the Badger State*, 285.

[79] Buchen, *Historic Sheboygan County*, 15, 97; and Zillier, *History of Sheboygan County*, 320.

[80] Middlesex County Deeds, Lobo Township, Instrument 14, Lot 6, Conc. 2, July 31, 1847; and Kendall County Deed Book E:73, July 30, 1847.

[81] G. Durand to Thomas Whiffen, Aug. 21, 1847, Lambton County Deeds, Town of Sarnia, Deed 8566. Potash was a by-product produced when trees were burned during land clearing. It was a cash crop that was shipped, mostly to England, to make diverse products, ranging from soap to gunpowder.

London District, Canada West, 1847

Upper Canada was then called Canada West. Washington and Mercy mortgaged the farm they had purchased from Williams within three months and in January of 1848 bought a small lot in Kilworth, a couple of miles away.[82] A road ran from Woodhull's Bridge over the Thames River, through the middle of their lot and into the village. The deed described the land in roods and rods, perches and poles, and chains and links, with site line directions given in degrees and minutes of north, and it included a marker designated as a certain maple tree. All these complicated measurements added up to a little over half an acre.

It was an ideal location for Washington's cooperage, especially with Woodhull's gristmill just over the bridge on Springer's Creek. The village of about two hundred had a general store, a tavern, a wagon maker, a saddler, shoemakers, blacksmiths, a doctor, and a teacher—everything necessary to make a village thrive. The saw, grist, and fulling (cloth) mills owned by Benjamin Woodhull and Sutton & Comfort provided employment for many.[83]

In April, Mercy bought a hundred acres in Caradoc Township, a few miles west of Kilworth.[84] Although it is unusual to find a married woman making a land purchase, she had purchased land as a young widow and she had considerable experience in the process with her husband.

Within a few months the newspapers were filled with stories of gold discoveries in California, many greatly exaggerated. On January 30, 1849, the *Canadian Free Press* reported: "Lumps are found daily of from one to two pounds. Several have been found weighing as high as sixteen, and over twenty-five pounds. Many men who came here poor have realized from $40,000 to $50,000." Although the story went on to warn that "there was a great deal of distress for want of the common necessities of life, and attended with very extensive sickness and mortality," the warnings had little effect. In late April a story reported how easy it was to find gold in the dry creeks and gullies with just a shovel, pick, or pocketknife. By August contradictory articles were running side by side, with one exhort-

---

[82] W. Peck to Thomas Mee, Nov. 8, 1847, Middlesex County Deeds, Lobo Township, Lot 6, Conc. 2, Instruments 14 and 15; Middlesex County Deeds, Delaware Township, Broken Lot B of Gore (triangular-shaped) North of Conc. 3, Instrument 42, Jan. 14, 1848.

[83] Taylor, *Ontario Directory of 1851*, 74.

[84] Middlesex County Deeds, Caradoc Township, Lot 19, Conc. 4, SE half, Instrument 43.

Elizabeth Rachel Peck Whiffen and Thomas Whiffen surrounded by their children, circa 1870: (back) Mary Ann, Albert Uriah, Washington, Uridge Peck; (front) Alice Adaline, Charles John, and Susan Jane. Uridge Peck Whiffen, named for his two grandfathers, was Washington Peck's first grandchild. *Courtesy of Calvin U. Whiffen III.*

ing men to bring their wives and families, while the second warned of lawlessness, depredations, and lynchings taking place in the diggings.[85]

By late March of 1850, Washington and Mercy had caught the fever and began making arrangements to go to California. A flurry of activities took place during the following month: sixteen-year-old Mary Ann Peck married George Banghart on March 26 and moved onto the large Banghart family farm in neighboring Westminster Township; three

[85] *London (Ont.) Canadian Free Press*, Jan. 30, 1849, 2:4, April 24, 1849, 3:6, and Aug. 22, 1849, 1:3–4.

weeks later David Peck married Eliza Jane Carey and took over the cooperage;[86] and Washington collected the remaining mortgage payment for his farm, which he used to buy necessities for their trip, leaving the remaining money to take care of the family staying behind.[87]

Egerton and Edmond, at eighteen and fifteen, were going to California with their parents. Jane and Emma, thirteen and nine, wanted to go too, but they were sent to live with their older sister, Mary Ann, at the Banghart's. Jane also lived for a time at the Scrimshaw's neighboring farm.[88] Many young children who were farmed out to other families are found sprinkled throughout 1851–52 Census, which listed many husbands and sons as being "absent" or "gone to California."

[86] Marriage Certificates 642 and 633. Archives of Ontario MS248, Reel 3.

[87] Middlesex County Deeds, Lobo Township, Lot 6, Conc. 2, Instrument 196, Apr. 15, 1850.

[88] Census 1851, Roll C11738, Westminster Township, Division 2, 107; and Delaware Township, Division 1, 23.

(*opposite, left*) Mary Ann Peck Banghart and George Washington Banghart, circa 1850. *Courtesy of John Wells Heap.*
(*opposite, right*) David Abbott Peck and Eliza Jane Carey Peck, circa 1850. *Courtesy of Carolyn Dodds Schaeffer.*
(*right*) Mercy Mary Wilcox Card Peck, circa 1850s, from a tintype. *Courtesy of John Wells Heap.*

Washington and Mercy began assembling what they needed for the trip. With their previous travel experience, they knew better than most what to take. Each needed two or three changes of clothes sturdy enough to survive six months of strenuous work, and they had to make wagon covers and tents.[89] They assembled the usual provisions—flour, rice, bacon, salt, coffee, and sugar—as well as some preserves and dried fruit, such as apples, that could be used to make pies. Mercy also took along enough butter to last until July. Butter and eggs were usually packed in barrels of flour or meal to protect them.[90] Everything had to fit into the two wagons they were taking.

Washington's trip was unusual in two ways. At forty-eight he was far older than the mostly younger men who rushed off to the gold fields, and second, he took his wife. By April 21, 1850, the Peck's two horse-drawn wagons were ready to depart, along with some extra ponies and a dog.

[89] Faragher, *Women and Men on the Overland Trail*, 68–69.
[90] Ibid., 47.

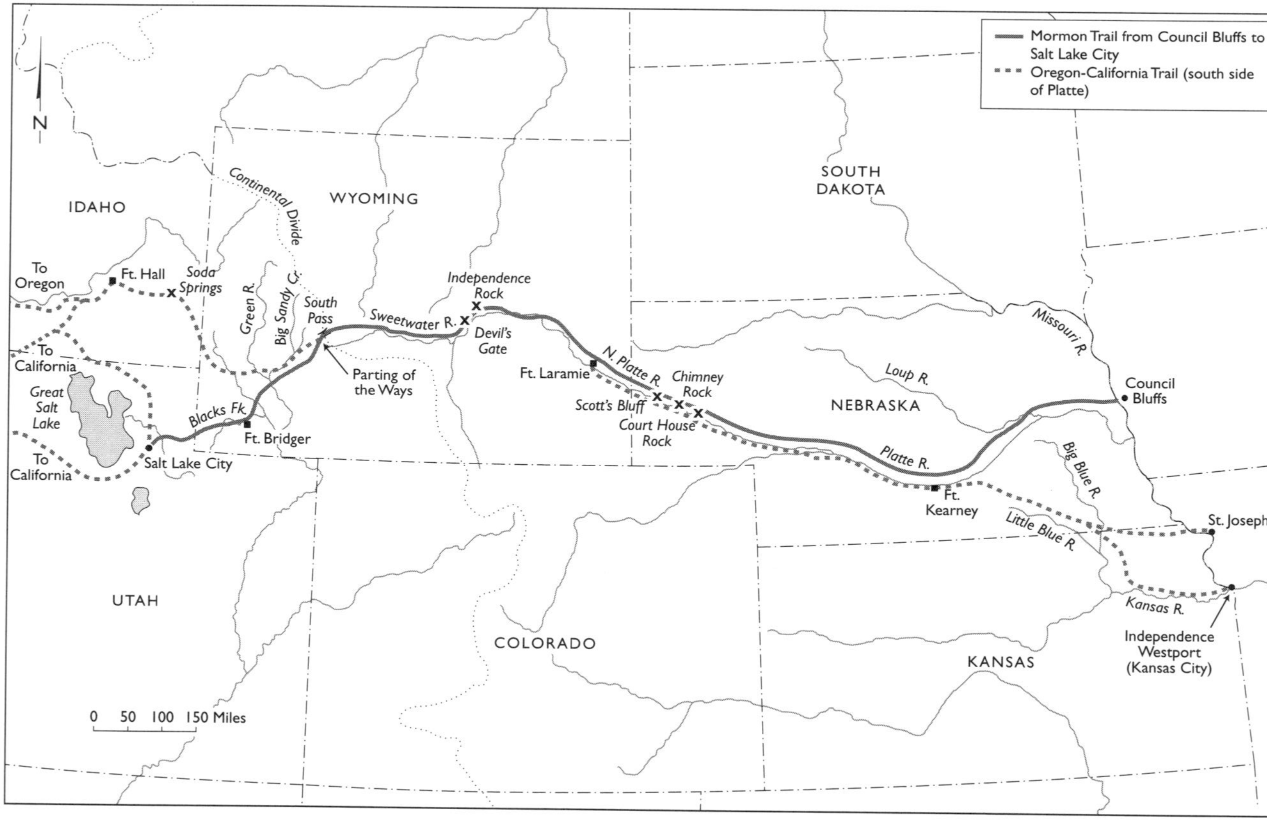

In 1850 the Pecks followed the Mormon Trail from Council Bluffs to Salt Lake City.
Adapted from Kenneth Holmes, *Routes of the Covered Wagon Women*, Vol. 1. Courtesy Arthur H. Clark Co.

2

1850–1851 Wagon Trail Diary: Ontario to Salt Lake City

April 22, 1850, Monday. 9 oclock we bid farewell to friends and acquaintances and started for California. Road muddy. In afternoon very bad and squalley. Made 25 miles.

The Pecks left Kilworth, Ontario (near London), crossed into the United States at Detroit, and made their way southwest into Indiana, through Illinois, and into Iowa, passing through many small villages, which Washington described in detail. (See map on p. 28.) He remarked on the development that had taken place since their 1840 trip to Illinois. He noted many improvements to the transportation network as they passed trains on the Michigan Central Railroad, steamboats on the rivers, and canal boats on the Michigan and Illinois Canal. From Indiana, their route roughly followed Interstate 80.

They continued through Iowa to pick up the trail to the West at Kanesville/Council Bluffs. From there they would follow the Mormon Trail on the north side of the Platte until it merged with the Oregon-California Trail at the Upper Platte Ferry (now Caspar, Wyoming). West of South Pass at the Parting of the Ways they left the Oregon Trail and veered southwest past Fort Bridger and on to Salt Lake City.

Washington, Mercy, Egerton, and Edmond traveled in two wagons pulled by ponies, not horses. The ponies may have been what Margaret Frink described in her 1850 diary as "hardy Canadian ponies, small but tough, and capable of enduring greater hardships than ordinary horses."[1]

The first four weeks of travel through settled areas were uneventful, so the daily entries have been omitted. The following entry is typical.

[1] Holmes, *Covered Wagon Women, 1850*, Vol. 2 (Journal of Margaret A. Frink), 81.

[May] 8 Wednesday. Morning foggy, wind west. Swaped dogs and paid 50 cents [to] boot. Got one half bull, watchful. Passed Valperaso, a smart village, and drove over some hilly land and dined by the road side. After we'd passed Valperaso, found the road bad. Reached Grand Prairie. Stoped for the night at a point of brush near a tamarack swamp.

Washington revealed no emotional attachment to the dog they sold, and the new dog was never mentioned again.

One problem Washington mentioned in early diary entries was the late spring weather, which was significant because the wagons could not leave until forage was available, which in an average year was about April 15. Merrill J. Mattes, in his definitive *The Great Platte River Road,* noted that it was important to leave as soon as grass was available in order to arrive at the end of the trail by the first of October, before winter weather set in.[2] In late April of 1850 Fort Kearney's commanding officer dispatched an urgent message to all the major "jumping off" places "that due to a late spring the prairie grasses were not yet able to support forage."[3] Fort Kearney was two hundred miles west along on the trail from the jumping off points, the small towns along the Missouri River where emigrants massed to make final preparations before leaving the United States to begin their trek on one of the western trails.

Finally by mid-May the Pecks crossed the Mississippi River into Iowa. Here the settlements thinned out, the number of travelers increased, and the Pecks began to experience the problems and events specific to the western trail experience.

[May] 18 Saturday. Morning cool. Wind from the west. Drove over dry beautiful Roleing Prairie, well watered, with only three or four houses on the road with a few at a distance. The scarsity of timber will prevent this country, for a long time at least, from becoming densely populated. Grain very scarse. We fear that we cannot get it at any price as we cannot hear of any. The number of teams that has gone on this one road this spring, bound for California, must have consumed, at a moderate calculation, ten thousand bushels of corn and oats while passing through this state (Iowa) which accounts for its scarsity. Camped at Mariners Grove by the side of Sugar Creek 25 miles from Davenport.

[2] Mattes, *Great Platte River Road,* 53.

[3] Unruh, *Plains Across,* 227, 468 n.107.

The enormous grain consumption Washington noted was a sign of the immense number of people on the road ahead of them. People were traveling from all directions toward the staging areas, where the small trickles came together to form a large swarming mass of people and wagons and animals, all anxious to cross the Missouri River and get started along the trail.

[May] 19 Sunday. Spent the day by our wagons. Our companions in travil drove on for to gain time to sell some goods they had without detaining us, when we expect to meet after a day or two. Day pleasant with a brisk west wind. Very dry. No rain for a long time. Vegitation very backward. Apple trees just in bloom and the woods presents a yellowish green appearance, the leaves just coming out. Evening pleasant. Wind blew hard in the night from the east.

The emigrants traveling with the Pecks were typical of some who brought goods to sell enroute so they could finish outfitting themselves at the jumping off places.

[May] 20 Monday. Morning rained at daylight. Cold wind. Rain over at six oclock. Started. Passed a small village called Tipton, the county seat of Cedar County. Drove over a beautiful country, well settled with plenty of timber, to Cedar River, a fine clear stream of about 30 rods [500 feet] wide. Water low. The ferry boat stuck on a bar. We had to lighten her by making the ponies wade to shore. Then the boat floted and we got safe on Tera Firmia. Drove about a mile and stoped to dinner. After noon passed some fine rooling prairie with small patches of timber and an abundance of spring creeks, then drove through a large grove of oak openings, a few settlers, to a creek with a saw mill at the road and put up for the night, 3 miles from Iowa City. Grass scarse.

[May] 21 Tuesday. Morning pleasant but cool. Drove over a hilly country to Iowa City, the Capital of the state. Population 3000. Quite a number of good Brick and stone buildings. The Capital is a splendid Building of cut stone. The city is situate[d] on the Iowa River about a hundred miles from its junction with the Mississippi. Navigable for steam boats in high water up to the city. It is a place of considerable business. Contains 7 Meeting houses [churches]. Crossed the River in a ferry boat. Drove on about 9 or 10 miles. Swaped wagons and got one lighter. In the afternoon crossed a hilly country neither prairie nor timber, but

betwixt and between. Not settled. Wind East all day. Afternoon very warm. Camped on a beautiful rolling prairie with a few scattering trees. Plenty of grass for the ponies.

[May] 22 Wednesday. Morning fine, neither cold nor hot. Started early. Drove about 8 miles. Came to the Iowa River again. Here we found three companyes of soldiers incamped with all their aquipage. They have been sent on to remove the Indians that have returned from beyond the Missouria River in small companies for several years and now the government is going to remove them again. It is said that they are very loath to go and some thinks that their will be a collition [collision] between them and the soldiers. Five miles farther up we passed Marengo, a town just springing into existence, the county seat of Iowa County. Drove about a mile farther and dined by the road side. Afternoon continued our course up the river for about 6 miles. Bought one bushel of corn for which we paid one dollar, three shillings more than we have paid before, and expect that we cannot obtain any more at that price. Left the river. Crossed a Hilly country and stoped for the night on a large prairie in a hollow where we could see no timber except in one point. All the rest looks as if the clouds and the grass were imbracing each other. Appearance of rain. Day warm and pleasant. Wind south.

Washington's conversation with the soldiers revealed that in spite of the government efforts to relocate the Indians across the Missouri, some had returned to live and hunt in the areas where they previously resided. Paula Mitchell Marks, author of *In A Barren Land*, explained that resettlement of the Indians had begun in 1830 with the passage of President Andrew Jackson's Indian Removal Act, which gave him the authority to "transfer any eastern tribe" west across the Mississippi River. The Illinois and Wisconsin tribes were soon moved into what would become Iowa. When the land between the Mississippi and the Missouri Rivers became Iowa Territory in 1838, the Indians were required to move west yet again. By 1850, in present-day Kansas, thousands of Indians had been resettled from numerous tribes, including according to Marks: "Missouri Sacs, Iowas, Kickapoos, Shawnees, Delawares, Chippewas, Munsees, Ottawas, Peorias, Kaskaskias, Weas, and Piankashaws."[4]

[May] 23 Thursday. Morning showery. Passed Bear Creek in Poweshiek

[4] Marks, *In a Barren Land*, 63, 119–20.

County and a grove. Then we entered a large prairie. Stoped at a point of timber to wood, then started across the prairie 18 miles. Continued showery til noon, then cleared up with a heavy squall of wind from the south East. Took off our wagon covers to save them from being torn. Afternoon pleasant. Reached a grove and put up. Beautiful country of land. Game scarse.

Although Washington described the land, the day's travel experiences, and the weather, he never mentioned Mercy's day-to-day chores. They would have begun before the wagons rolled out in the morning and lasted long after they stopped for the night. In his exhaustive research, John Mack Faragher, author of *Women and Men on the Overland Trail,* found a pattern in the women's general routine, which was to get up about 4 A.M., before the men, start the fire, and cook breakfast. After breakfast, while the men hitched up the animals, the women washed the dishes and packed everything into a grub box on the wagon. At the nooning, lunch consisted of a cold meal that the women had prepared the night before, and at the evening halt women unpacked the wagons, Faragher continued, and began "four or five hours of sustained work." After they built a fire, hauled water, and cooked dinner, they began baking for the following day.[5]

In 1849 emigrant John A. Johnson discovered just how difficult women's work was when he traveled west in an all-male company. Johnson was found to be one of the best cooks in his outfit, so he was offered the cook's job on a permanent basis, with the added incentive of being excused from all other duties, including guard duty. He could walk or ride in the wagon all day, and after dinner he could go to bed and sleep all night. Only one week later, he had given it up. "It is more slavish work than I had anticipated and by far the hardest post to occupy. I found I was working all the time during our halts while others were . . . resting." As for guard duty, that only came around every second or third night.[6]

[May] 24 Friday. Morning high wind from South East. Drove over a hilly country 12 miles to a house. Crossed four or five creeks. Scenery delightful, the hills high but not steep or abrupt and beautifully rounded off at the peaks, the surface smoth as if rolled, and all covered with a beautiful carpet of the richest green spread out by the hand of the Creator. Timber scarse. Stoped to dinner by a creek, north fork of Skunk River, in sight of

[5] Faragher, *Women and Men on the Overland Trail,* 76–77.
[6] Ibid., 81–82.

a saw mill. Dined on greens and ham. Afternoon passed a beautiful dry levil prairie to Newton, the county seat of Jasper County. We can say but little about the town as it has not fairly passed its egg state. Then drove over hills, dales and creeks and through groves to a large flat on a creek with good grass and put up. The wind has gone down. Some appearance rain. Warm and pleasant. From the Iowa River the settlements is very thin. Plenty of land and timber to be had at government price, the land of the best quality. Wind rose in the night and blew hard til day light.

[May] 25 Saturday. Morning crossed a branch of Skunk River, about 30 ft wide, clean, and about 2 ft deep. Drove two or three miles and came to the main stream which we had to ford, a fine stream about fifty ft wide and 2½ deep. Bottom hard. Drove over some exelent prairie and stoped to dinner near a grove. Saw some fine groves of timber. Overtook our Company that had gone ahead. Afternoon drove over some beautiful hilly prairie to a settlement on the banks and flats of the Desmoines. It is only four years since the settlement of this country commenced. Plenty of timber in this vicinity. Put up for the night 4 miles from Fort Desmoines. Evening wind high. Thundering and lightning. Every appearance of a stormy night, then blew off to the north. No rain. Wind blew hard all night, the fourth night that the wind has blown hard from the South East.

[May] 26 Sunday. Morning sprinkling of rain. Concluded to drive on to find a better location (grass scarse here). Passed Desmoines. Crossed the river in a ferry boat and Raccoon Fork, the ferrys close together. The Desmoines, a fine clean stream of about 30 rods [500 feet] wide. The Raccoon about 15 do [ditto]. Drove about 2 or three miles in the prairie and spent the remainder of the day. Fort Desmoines is on the point between the Desmoines and Raccoon fork. It is the county seat of Polk County, contains about 2000 inhabitants, some good Brick buildings. It was once a fort before the Indians surrendered the country. The Barracks are now occupied as dweling houses. Did not go into the town as the small pox is their. Afternoon cleared up. Evening fine and warm. 51 deg after sun set.

Fort Des Moines began as Fort Raccoon, a military garrison, but in 1843 the name was changed to Fort Des Moines. By 1846, when Iowa became a state, it was no longer a military post; it was a town, so the word *fort* was dropped from its name.

Smallpox! This was the first mention of disease by the Pecks. Their reaction—to avoid it—will be seen again.

[May] 27 Monday. Morning early came on a storm of hail, rain, and wind. The thunder and lightning was terrific. The horses broke from their fastenings and trembled like an aspen leaf through fear. Hitched up as soon as the storm was over and drove about a mile and a half and came to a small creek, which was so swollen that the water came into our waggon boxes while on the bridge. Bank very steep and slippery. Hard work to get up, (The banks is generally in this country ten or twelve feet high at the edge of the streames and narrow, and the bridges is commonly placed about half way down, and in high water, it runs over the bridge). Kept on our way. Roads slippery. Country hilly. Timber scarse. Afternoon came to Badger Creek. Found it high but fordable. Came up to the waggon boxes. A bad hill after we got over to raise. About two miles farther came to another fine stream called North River. It empties itself into the Desmoines, about 40 feet wide, rapid, but not much swollen. Very steep in and out. Flat stones in the bottom. Drove about a mile and half farther and stoped for the night in a beautiful place of high gently sloping hills dot[t]ed with small patches of timber. Country not much settled. Passed only two houses near the road today. Saw two or three more at a distance. All kinds of provisions very scarse here about. We could not obtain any thing eatable today and still worse, when wind changed to the north west in the night and blew hard and cold.

At their first crossing of the day, the water came up to the wagon boxes, which meant that the water was about three feet above the bridge deck. A sketch by Joseph Goldsborough Bruff shows how precarious a crossing could be. Along with the steep bank and sloping bridge, add three feet of water rushing over the deck.[7]

Often the animals were so frightened at the rushing water that they refused to cross. Teamsters had their own methods of dealing with these obstacles. One family was stalled at a water crossing until "a burly fellow came down on the other side and said, 'throw me that whip' and presto! that whip began to pop like a volly [*sic*] of musketry and the woods fairly roared with the oaths he rolled out, and those oxen lined up on the bank as if they meant to cross the plains that day. The man handed back the whip with the remark, 'You don't know how to drive cattle. You must swear at them.' "[8]

[7] Bruff, Joseph Goldsborough, *Diaries, Journals, and Notebooks, 1849–1850*.

[8] Faragher, *Women and Men on the Overland Trail*, 93.

Washington did not note that this day was Mercy's forty-fourth birthday, making her not only one of the few women on the trail, but one of the oldest. Between the miserable weather, difficult fords, and lack of food, perhaps it was a birthday to be forgotten.

[May] *28 Tuesday. Morning cold, overcoat and mittens again useful. Drove over a fine country with plenty of timber. Got a bushel of corn for $1.25 and 21 cents worth of corn meal and went on our way rejoicing. Stoped near a house and dined. We are told that it is sixty miles to the next house on the road. Afternoon saw some small patches of small timber at a distance on the right and left. Land exelent and well watered, but no timber. The Elk must have been numerous in these parts at some time. Since we have left Iowa River, we have seen a number of horns or parts of horns every day. Today we saw a scull with a large part of the horns fast to it and quite a number of others. We measured one across the end where it separated from the head, and it measured 4⅛ by 3½ inches in diameter. A large part of the length was gone. The remainder measured two ft, 7 inches. Put up for the night about a mile from any timber. Had some bark in our wagons. Went to the grove and brought a few sticks to cook our supper. Evening calm and pleasant, but cool.*

Biologists suspect that the elk antlers were probably from a large bull elk (not abnormally large) of the Eastern Elk, a subspecies that is now extinct.[9]

[May] *29 Wednesday. Morning clear, calm, and pleasant. Crossed Middle River, a small stream with a few small patches of timber on its margin, not sufficient to fence or build with. In the afternoon we overtook a mammoth wagon with six wheels from Milwakie, bound for California. We had seen the track of the critter for two hundred miles, but never got sight of it til today. When we discovered it, we put on a little more steam and came up to it. The fellows* [felloes] *is eight inches wide with two tiers of spokes set about four inches apart in the hub. It is 22 inches wider than a common waggon. There is an apperatus attached to one wheel that measures the distance every revelution of the large wheel, which is a rod fixed like the face of a clock so that they*

[9] Erick Cole, biologist at the National Elk Refuge in Wyoming, telephone conversation of May 8, 2002; Jeff Bates of the Skyriver Ranch, e-mail message to author, May 8, 2002; and Dick Solum of the Rocky Mountain Elk Foundation, e-mail message to author, May 13, 2002.

Joseph Goldsborough Bruff's sketch with notation "Ugly descent & crossing of Salt — (stinking) Creek." *Courtesy Yale Collection of Western Americana, Beinecke Rare Book and Manuscript Library, WA MSS 50.*

can tell every mile and its fractional parts. There is seven persons with it and four large horses. Their load is 35 cwt. It looks like a clumsy logy concern. If they get through with that, I think that we shall have no difficulty. The country is hilly, as usual destitute of timber. Saw no house today. Evening pleasant.

The Pecks had encountered one of the most interesting sights on this trip, what Washington called the Mammoth Wagon. This was one of the few times that Washington revealed excitement in his matter-of-fact writing style. The wagon's dimensions were substantially larger than a common farm wagon. The felloes, the outer curved part of the wagon wheel, determined the wheel width. Eight inches was huge. Wagon expert Richard M. Davies explained that wheels were usually 1½ to 2" wide and 60" apart. Thirty-five hundred pounds was double the load carried by most emigrants, and it was a very large load for four horses to pull over an extended distance.[10] The double-spoke wheels were very unusual, and the odometer, although not widespread, had been in use for a few years. Wagon experts have not identified this unusual wagon. Along with a few other one-of-a-kind wagons that were built, such as James Reed's Palace Car and the Wind Wagon with its giant sail, this one seems to be unique.[11]

[*May*] *30 Thursday. Morning a slight sprinkling of rain. Drove through a small grove of timber chiefly polls* [*poles*]. *Crossed a creek, very steep in and out. The Mammoth waggon had considerable trouble in getting through the grove and creek. Near night came to River Nishnabotna, some four rods* [*50 feet*] *wide, flag stones at bottom. Good ford, but very steep in and out. Two pitches in coming in to the water, ten or twelve feet each, with a space of about ten or twelve feet between them and crooked. The mammoth waggon was behind on the top of the first pitch. It started as they were going to fix the lock to the wheel and they could not stop it and all cried who*[*a*] *which caused the leaders to stop, so that the driver could not guide them nor stop on the space between the two pitches. The leaders swung round to the left as they entered the second pitch with a tremendious rush, which brought the leaders round along side the wheels, which threw the rear wheel horse. The tong*[*ue*] *of the wagon struck the bank at the side of the road, broke the neck yoke and run into the bank some three or four feet and stoped just as the wagon was on the point of upsetting, which would have thrown it into the river where the water was 2 feet deep. Smashed one wheel and sprung another. Very little injury done to the horses. They took out their load and commenced repairing. We camped in sight. Night cool and pleasant.*

The Mammoth Wagon encountered two difficulties because of its size. First, a wagon two feet wider than the track cut through the woods required extra chopping and clearing. Second, the immense weight on the steep pitch caused the drivers to lose control of the wagon. As the endless stream of wagons crossed the creeks, they broke down the banks and cut deep ruts, which created dirt sidewalls that enclosed the wagons as they went down the steep pitch, almost like an open tunnel. Running into the sidewall had saved the big wagon. The Peck men would have

[10] Richard M. Davis, wagon expert, provided details on common farm wagons in personal correspondence, June 27, 2000. For further information, see Mr. Davis's article, "Where Have All the Wagons Gone?" *Overland Journal* (Autumn 1997 and Summer 1998).

[11] Stewart, *Ordeal by Hunger*, 11–12; and Gardner, *Wagons for the Santa Fe Trade*, 134–35.

helped sort out the wagon and horses because, as Edward Allen noted in 1852, "in fording the rivers and creeks no sooner was one team over than all went to the aid of the remainder. Unacquainted emigrants worked together for as long as it took to complete a task."[12]

[May] 31 *Friday. Morning they were not likely to get the mammoth waggon repaired to start before near noon, so we left and went on. Drove a mile or two and came to a Mormon settlement of about ten families. Their fields lay open, they keeping their cattle on the other side of a creek. They told us that they intend going to Salt Lake Vally next spring. Passed nine ox teams of Mormons, five of them on their way to Salt Lake. The other four are going to stop near Council Bluff til next Spring, Drove over prairie fifteen miles to a few more families by a small grove, then five more to the west branch of Nishnabotna River. Very steep in and out, the bottom hard. Here is another settlement. Went about a mile farther and camped. The day has been delightful and the roads first rate, better than we have found them since we came into this state. Passed one ox team, two men and two boys bound for the gold diggings.*

Council Bluffs, also called Kanesville, continued to be the major stop-over place for the Mormons migrating west. It was the place they called their Winter Quarters. Brigham Young established the settlement in 1846 during the Mormon exodus from Nauvoo, Illinois. The Mormons continued to use this as a stopping place while they prepared for the overland trek to Salt Lake.

The Pecks' horse-drawn wagons easily passed the slow moving ox teams because men guided the oxen by walking beside them. There were no reins.

June 1 Saturday. Morning started early intending to reach the Bluff. Passed sixteen wagons, 14 of these bound for Salt Lake Vally. The other two are going to the mines, all ox teams. Came to a small settlement of Mormons at Silver Creek, ten or twelve families. They intend moving to the vally next spring. The land in these parts has not come into market. Many of the Mormons, after they were dispersed at Nauveau [Nauvoo], have squatted til they could acquire the means to go on to the Mormon settlement. Stoped to dinner by a small creek far from timber. Three men came looking for some stray oxen. The three men from Ohio

[12] Faragher, *Women and Men on the Overland Trail*, 29.

that has been in company with us consisted of a man and his son and one of no relation to them. It appeared from the statement of the young man and some admissions of the old man that they had put in about an equal amount of property in fitting out, but the old man held the purse strings, and it appeared as if he wanted to get in a quarrel with them for a pretext to keep the property and threatened in my hearing of leaving them at the Bluff and said that the property all belonged to him. Now we were drawing near the Bluff, the young men felt very uneasy for they had put in their all, and one of them had a small family, and now to fail would be ruin, so they concluded to try to bring the old man to terms. So when from our large dining hall (the three men being in company looking for the oxen) one of them took the lines to drive up a hill that lay just before us, (The old man had drove and ordered them about with all the authority of a southern niger driver) and the other mounted the odd horse. We had started on a little before them, and the three men before mentioned a little before us, and as we were raising the hill, the one on the horse broached the subject to the old man, and he giving no satisfaction, they cracked the whip and passed us like a shot and left the old man on the road. He ran and hollered after them and wanted us to persue or let him have a horse, but we were not inclined to do either. Then he tried the three men, and we explained the matter to them as we understood it, and they said, let them go. After they got some ways ahead, they stoped and put out the old man's chest of cloaths and a box containing a quantity of books and a set of double harness. We took them up and the old man to take them to town, but we stoped about three miles from town on account of grass being scarse nearer. The old man went on, full of wrath, for a warrant to arrest them for robery, but we think he will fail. The young men appear to be honest, respectable young men, but the old man, we think, is a hard case.

This would be the last place that the old man could obtain a warrant because after they crossed the Missouri River, they had left the United States and entered Indian Country, which historian Alan Wexler pointed out was administered directly by Washington D.C. through army officers stationed at a few widespread forts.[13] There was no civil law from this point on; people had to solve their own differences. Mattes noted that effective law came from within and from social expectations.

[13] Wexler, *Atlas of Westward Expansion*, 89 (map), 123–25.

"Under trail circumstances . . . informal justice was sometimes brutal, sometimes fickle, but its unseen presence doubtless served as a powerful deterrent."[14] Surprisingly few crimes were committed along the trail, considering the many thousands who were on the road. John Phillip Reid's study of law in the "vast legal no-man's land" revealed that the emigrants were remarkably well informed on law and conducted their affairs accordingly. They had a "working knowledge" of law that they drew upon "to guide disputants to a mutually agreeable settlement," particularly involving division of mutually held assets when companies broke down and emigrants went their separate ways.[15]

[June] 2 Sunday. Morning a slight sprinkling of rain. Cleared up when sun rose. Removed to the river bottom on account of feed being more plenty. The scenery is grand. The bottoms is 4 or 5 miles broad, as levil as a floor, surrounded on the north East side with Bluffs, 2 or 3 hundred feet high and very broken, presenting the apearance of hills on hills in the wildest confusion piled. The whole bottom, as far as we can see, is dotted with groups of covered waggons, several hundred being in sight. It is said that 500 waggons of Mormons will leave this place for the vally this summer. Day warm. Sprinkels of rain in the evening.

This scene of hundreds of wagons covering the river bottom was in startling contrast to the vast empty prairie the Pecks had crossed four days earlier where they did not see one house. This massing of emigrants was typical of the jumping off places, and because this was the northernmost site, the starting time was somewhat later than in the towns further south. Detailed Mormon records reported that a Mormon train of 206 people left on June 3 and another group of a hundred wagons (with three to nine people in each) crossed the Missouri the day after the Pecks, so the Pecks were sandwiched in between the two trains, with more behind them.[16] From this time onward, they were never out of the sight of other wagons, not only those ahead and behind, but also those on the other side of the Platte River.

[June] 3 Monday. Laid in our stock of provisions. The old man that went for a warrant failed, but got possession of the horses and wagon by lynch law, but was afterwards frightened to the degree that he gave up

---

[14] Mattes, *Great Platte River Road*, 77.

[15] Reid, *Law for the Elephant*, 8, 11, 183–84.

[16] *Kanesville Frontier Guardian*, June 12, 1850.

the horses and waggon and fitted them out well, and they are going on and the old man is going back. In the Evening rained heavy. Thunder and lightning beat through our wagon covers.

[June] 4 Tuesday. Started for the Ferry. Rain. Stoped at Kanesville. This is the town at the Bluff. It is called Council Bluffs for fifty miles. The town is in a deep ravine and buildings is mostly made of hewed logs and covered with a kind of long split oak shingles, if they can be called shingles, and some is shingled with straw. Others has a layer of straw or something els[e] and is covered with old mother Earth. We saw one man hoeing on his house. What kind of grain or vegitables is produced on them, we did not inquire. There is a great amount of goods sold here during the time of starting to California and Salt Lake. Nearly all the inhabitants of town and vicinity are Mormons. Rain continued. Drove about 3 miles and stoped. The upper ferry is twelve miles above Kanesvill, which we cross in takeing the northern rout. Heavy rain in the evening.

Washington's surprise at the sight of a man hoeing on his roof indicates that it was unusual.

The Pecks had decided to travel along the north side of the Platte, which was called the Council Bluffs Road but is now referred to as the Mormon Trail.[17] Washington may have decided that there would be fewer wagons and thus more forage for his animals, a major concern considering the large numbers headed west.

[June] 5 Wednesday. Morning drove on to the ferry, raining nearly all the way. There was 19 wagons to cross. Got 3 over. A sudden squall of wind continued to blow two hard to cross for 3 or 4 hours. Crossed some more in the evening. We remained all night on the Iowa side. The [Missouri] river is forty or fifty rods [650–800 feet] wide, strong current, the water so thick and muddy that an object cannot be seen a quarter of an inch beneath its surface. Continues the same except during the hard frost of winter. Rained a smart shower in the evening. Iowa is a country of exelent land, very few marshes or sloughs, and must be healthy as soon as brought into a state of cultivation. Exelent water and plenty of it with abundance of water power, but a great deficiency of timber, but it is hilly clear through the state where we passed.

[17] Mattes, *Great Platte River Road*, 129.

The reason it took so long to get the wagons across the Missouri at the Upper Ferry was because the ferry was so small. When Catherine Haun crossed in 1849, she described the ferry as a flat boat big enough for two or three wagons, which had to have the wheels removed. Her party of seventy wagons took a week to cross.[18] The delay caused by the storm prevented the Pecks from crossing until the next day. This was common at all the busy jumping off places.

[June] 6 Thursday. Morning crossed the turbid waters of the Missouria. Road slippery, very steep getting up the bank. Drove across the bottom and ascended a long steep hill, and when on the top, stoped and looked back to take a last fare well of sivilization, and all the trace that we could discover of it with all the advantages that cluster around. It was a distant view of an insignificant leg, but Sivilization has been fading away for three hundred [miles] until when we passed the line, the change was hardly perceptible. Drove over a hilly country road, cracked but good, until we came to a creek 18 miles from the ferry and camped. There we found a team with three men who had run off the bridge and upset their wagon into the water, 5 feet deep, and wet all their provisions. Spoiled their hard bread. Evening pleasant.

The Pecks were then in Indian Country where there were no towns to provide orientation, and thus Washington's reference points became rivers and landmarks based on mileage. Apparently he bought a copy of William Clayton's *Latter-Day Saints' Emigrants' Guide* in Council Bluffs, which was published in 1848. Clayton had traveled to Salt Lake with Brigham Young in the first Mormon emigration in 1847. During that trip Clayton became convinced that they should attach some kind of device to the wheel to measure distance. He lacked the know-how to build it himself and was having difficulty convincing anyone else of its importance, so he measured a wagon wheel and found that 360 revolutions would equal one mile. He then walked behind the wagon and tediously counted the revolutions, maybe by tying a rag on the wheel. He continued this for four more days, all the while nagging the leaders until they finally agreed to build a roadometer. After arriving in Salt Lake, the device was improved, so in the fall when he returned to Council Bluffs, he re-measured the distances and then published a guide for use by those

[18] Schlissel, *Women's Diaries* (Diary of Catherine Haun), 173.

who followed. He included detailed information about water supply, road conditions, and alternate routes.[19]

[June] 7 Friday. Morning drove to the Elkhorn River, a stream of about six rods [100 feet] wide, three feet deep at low water. We had it to ferry, for which we paid $2 per team. Afternoon organised a Company and drove twelve miles to the Platte and camped. Was visited by a number of Indians, one a Chief, most of them naked except a small strip of cloath about the loins. Large flats or bottom land in this place vary from ten to fifteen miles wide, but no timber for farming purposes. Another company came up. Our Captain behaved very imprudent both to the company and to the Indians, which gave general dissatisfaction. Two Chiefs and a boy camped with us for the night. Manifested great friendship. (Lost our sausepan.)

The Pecks had no sooner entered Indian Country than they met their first Indians. For many this was frightening because emigrants had been warned of the dangers of attack and were newly armed. It was only after a few personal encounters that they began to realize that they were not necessarily in danger. Washington appeared to be at ease with the Indians in camp, but he was annoyed at the Captain's behavior, which could have offended the Indians. They were travelers through the Indians' land, so good manners were common sense. Many Indians expected the emigrants to pay some kind of toll in the way of food or goods, perhaps a saucepan.

The Pecks had now become part of an organized company, which most emigrants did, both as protection against the Indians and to help each other with anticipated difficulties. After reviewing numerous diaries, Mattes wrote, "They might organize at their home town, at a jumping-off place, or somewhere along the trail, but sooner or later they organized. And sooner or later (with few exceptions), the organizations disintegrated." Some companies had so many rules that they barely survived to the jumping off points. The more overorganized they were, the quicker disintegration began. Mattes concluded that the "American tradition of self-reliance and rugged individualism was never displayed more dramatically than westward along the Great Platte River Road." When men disagreed with the rules, they just moved on.[20]

[19] Kimball, *Latter-Day Saints' Emigrants' Guide*, 4–5.

[20] Mattes, *Great Platte River Road*, 32, 34–37.

[June] 8 Saturday. Morning warm and pleasant. Drove 12 miles and dined by the river. Very hot. Thermometer up to 85 in the shade. No wind. Afternoon drove to Shell Creek. Here it rained heavy yesterday. Every hollow full of water. Creek high. Met with number of Indians. One of them speaks English. He told us that their had been a battle fought near this spring between the Pawnees and Souis, about 200 killed. They were all friendly, but beggars. Saw no fire[arms] around here. All used bows and arrows pointed with iron. We gave them some small bits of hoop iron for that purpose, which they received with marked thankfulness. In the evening the wind changed to the north west and blew cool. Some Indians camped with us and 18 wagons, mostly ox teams. Here we and one other wagon left the company that we belonged to and joined Capt Duncan's Company from Michigan.

Washington misunderstood the Pawnees' story, perhaps a language problem. The annual routine of the Pawnees was to plant crops in the spring, go buffalo hunting during the summer, and return in the fall to harvest their crops. Clayton explained that in 1846 while the Pawnee were away hunting, the Sioux burned their village of two hundred earth lodges, but none were killed. The Pawnees rebuilt most of their village, but the Sioux burned it again, except for one lodge, so the Pawnees had moved from the Cedar River to this location near Shell Creek, where they "routinely extracted tolls," according to editor Stanley Kimball.[21]

[June] 9 Sunday. Laid by and washed. In the evening drove on to find better feed. Every slough flooded with water. Some difficulty in crossing. Came to another worse and had to camp without fire. Grass first rate. Saw an Elk and a deer.

[June] 10 Monday. Morning commenced crossing the slough. We with one other team attempted to drive round or find a crossing place higher up. Drove all day two or 3 miles from the road without finding the desired spot. At night a number of men from the company came and helped us over a much worse place that [than] that crossed in the morning, so we gained a loss. Saw a company on the South side of the River. Camped by a small creek. A party of packers passed us. They go 30 miles per day. Saw a number of deers. Weather fine.

---

[21] Clayton, *William Clayton's Journal*, Apr. 24, 1847; and Kimball, *Latter-Day Saints' Emigrants' Guide*, 43.

Washington's concern for his horses prompted his search for a better crossing because sloughs were terribly hard on the teams. Eighteen-year-old Ester Hanna (1852) experienced just how treacherous they could be when her wagon became mired: "I am now sitting in our carriage in the middle of the slough. Our mules all fell down attempting to get through. I have never witnessed anything like it! We have put 14 yokes of oxen to the wagons to get them out."[22]

The packers, who were unencumbered by wagons, covered many more miles in a day than the wagon trains, which made fifteen to twenty miles on a good day.

[June] 11 Tuesday. Morning cool and pleasant. Crossed a creek. Steep getting out. Afternoon came to Beaver River, a stream of about fifty feet wide. Water high. Had to carry our stuff across on a foot bridge made with a large cotton wood tree that had fallen across and swim the horses and towed the wagons over with a long rope. All got over safe, except two or three wagons, which upset in the stream, but no loss. Got all loaded up at night ready for a start in the morning. At night the mammoth wagon overtook us. Some fears was entertained of the Indians as a few was seen skulking about at a distance. Doubled the guard, but no Indians made their appearance.

[June] 12 Wednesday. Found the road good. A few ravines, but not difficult to pass. Crossed the Ceder River, about six rods [100 feet] wide. Good fording at low water. Some packed their stuff on the top of the wagon, but others raised their box and all got safe over. Passed a grave with a board at the head ingraved with a knife. Joseph Percevil, Died June 18th 1849 Aged 67. Camped at night by a small creek. No timber in sight but small willows and some other small brush. Here we passed the grave of Lucretia Cox, Died June 15th 1848, Aged 6 years and 7 months. Saw some deer. On the East of Ceder River is the remains of an Indian village belonging to the Pawnee tribe. The houses were raised, about twenty five feet in diameter, dug out in the bottom like a dish, and the earth placed round the edge so as to form a wall in which were placed poles to support the roof. At each side of the door was an earth wall 12 or 15 feet long and roofed over. At each house was one or more holes dug large enough to admit a persons body, then dug out in the form of a wine bottle, six or eight feet in diameter, we suppose, for a store house. The

[22] Allen, *Canvas Caravans*, 26.

whole vilage was inclosed with a wall of sods and a ditch out side. Some is now standing 5 feet or more high. It was burned by the Souis in 1846.

These two graves are the first of many that Washington recorded in his diary, perhaps the only record that exists for many of them. Lucretia Cox was in Mormon Heber Kimball's wagon train to Salt Lake when she fell out of the wagon and was killed, either by falling under the feet of the oxen or by being run over by a wagon wheel. Although not all died, Mattes noted that many children were bounced out as wagons jolted over rutted uneven ground or large boulders.[23]

[*June*] 13 *Thursday. Morning drove six miles to the ford of Loop Fork, fifty or sixty miles from its junction with the Platte. Their has been a ferry kept til within a few days. The ferry man left and the boat cannot be found. So we had no choice of how we should cross. We found a company of ox teams that had been waiting since noon the day before, studdieng how they would get over, and some were making a raft. The bed of the River is about sixty rods* [*800 feet*] *wide, the stream from 30 to 40 rods, the water from 2 to 3½ feet deep with a current of about six miles per hour and the bottom quick sand. We came to a decision at once. Some of the men led the horses over while others went to work kalking a wagon box that was built skow fashion. When done, we unloaded a wagon at a time into the skow, and 8 or 10 men waded and towed it across. Then another company hitched a long rope to the wagon, waded, and hauled it over, and in this way we got all over before night, 15 wagons, after which about ten teams of the oxen borrowed the skow and got across in the same way. Here we found four graves. One was drowned last year in fording, another was shot for his money, and the other two died of cholery. Here we saw the irons of a wagon that had been left and burned for fire wood.*

The Loop Fork ford was noted as a dangerous crossing in the *Emigrants' Guide* because the river channels were constantly changing. The reason they could not find the ferryman or the boat was that the ferry had sunk. A few weeks earlier, in May of 1850, Thomas Christy wrote that it "required three or four men bailing constantly to keep the leaking raft afloat." John D. Unruh, author of *The Plains Across*, reported that it sank, not once, but twice in 1850.[24]

---

[23] Kimball, *Mormon Trail*, 19; Harwell, *Manuscript History of Brigham Young 1847–1850*, 123; and Mattes, *Great Platte River Road*, 91–92.

[24] Unruh, *Plains Across*, 268, 482, n. 8.

Washington's company had decided to make a raft from one of the wagons to avoid wheeling the wagons across the quicksand bottom, a danger that could not be underestimated. Once a wagon started across, it dare not stop. Diarist Luzena Stanley Wilson described a hair-raising crossing by their party in 1849. When she looked back, she saw "the team behind us stop in mid-stream. The frantic driver shouted, whipped, belabored the stubborn animals in vain, and the treacherous sand gave way under their feet. They sank slowly, gradually, but surely. They went out of sight inch by inch, and the water rose over the moaning beasts. Without a struggle they disappeared beneath the surface. In a little while the broad South Platte swept on its way, sunny, sparkling, placid, without a ripple to mark where a lonely man parted with all his fortune."[25]

[June] 14 Friday. Drove over a hilly sandy road for several miles, then crossed a low flat wet prairie to Prairie Creek, 24 miles. Camped without wood. Passed no timber today. Wind high. Blew all night. Here is two graves. One of A. Kellogg, Died June 18 1849, aged 23 years. The other an infant, died July 1847, aged 7 months, named J. O. Egbert.

The number of graves is increasing as they approach the Platte River. These two, a young man and a baby, seem particularly isolated and poignant. At the beginning of the trip, funerals were emotional affairs carried out with decorum. It was wrenching to leave a friend or family member behind in a grave that would never be seen again. Even eight-year-old Florence Weeks was able to put the emotion into words. In 1859 she wrote, "One had the oddest feeling seeing those graves in such lonely places, but it made no difference to the ones who was gone. It was the thought of going on without them."[26] Later on, after weeks on the trail, when they were worn down with exhaustion and had buried one after another of their party, many became numb. In 1857 Helen Carpenter gave evidence of just that. When they noticed that they had built their campfire on a grave, they left it there. "I have mentioned our growing indifference and can but think that what we are obliged to endure each day is robbing us of all sentiment. It is to be hoped that we will not be *permanently changed.*"[27]

[25] Henry, *My Checkered Life (Luzena Stanley Wilson '49er)*, 13.

[26] Werner, *Pioneer Children on the Journey West*, 124.

[27] Myers, *Ho for California* (Diary of Helen Carpenter, 1857), 127.

The baby was likely Joseph Orson Egbert, the son of Mormons Joseph and Mary Egbert, who traveled to the Salt Lake Valley in 1847.

[June] 15 *Saturday. Morning reached the Platte. Crossed Wood Creek. Saw where several Buffaloes had been killed. Afternoon saw 8 buffaloes and 2 calves. Fired 2 shots at them. Wounded one, but failed in getting it. We are just on the border of Buffalo country. The sight of them produces quite an excitement, which in some measure accounts for our failure in getting one. Passed 2 graves. The first had the following inscription: In memory of Mrs Carter, Died June 5th 1849, aged 25 years, the other Moses Wade, Died July 1 1849 of Cholery, aged 48. Camped near the river. Plenty of wood. Wind south. Blew hard.*

The Pecks have reached the beginning of the buffalo grasslands, which ranged from Canada to Texas and west to Wyoming. Nothing generated more excitement than the first sight of buffalo. It echoes throughout trail diaries. Wizlineus (1839) wrote that men anticipating their first glimpse of a buffalo "kept scanning the horizon expectantly, like shipwrecked sailors searching for an island."[28] Despite advice to the contrary, Faragher wrote that "men who otherwise stressed the importance of continual movement above all else would stop their wagons, saddle all available mounts, and head out for the kill at the slightest sign of a distant buffalo herd."[29] Little meat was salvaged from most of the buffalo killed, but one may as well try to stop a flood as to prevent the men from chasing off on the hunt.

[June] 16 *Sunday. Rested by baking and washing. Some of the company was after buffaloes. Saw a great many. Wounded one, but got none. Had preaching at one oclock by a Methodist local preacher (but now a traveling preacher). Day very warm, 87 in the shade. We are now 185 miles from Missori River.*

Mercy's day of rest meant doing laundry, probably all day, under the hot summer sun. After reviewing numerous diaries, Faragher concluded that women did laundry whenever the wagon train stopped long enough. "In most parties women spent a full day washing about every two weeks." Due to the scarcity of fuel, clothes were usually scrubbed in cold water with harsh soap. Rebecca Ketcham (1853) found that "a day of sun, wind,

---

[28] Mattes, *Great Platte River Road*, 253.

[29] Faragher, *Women and Men on the Overland Trail*, 85.

soap and water could be a painful combination," that resulted in sunburn and chapped hands.[30] A few women even ironed their laundry, at least at the beginning of the trail, as they attempted to maintain their housekeeping standards from home.[31] While the clothes dried in the sun, Mercy could begin baking.

[June] 17 Monday. Found the road first rate except a few narrow sloughs. In the morning soon after we started, a herd of buffalo was seen about a mile to the right of from fifty to a hundred. The horses that could be spared from the teams was manned and five or six foot men [men on foot] started to atact the buffaloes which was soon done. The herd sho[w]ed fight, but as the hunters did not charge but chose to keep at a distance and try their rifles on them, they did not come in close contact enough to have a regular battle. The result of the whole was that one fine buffalo bit the ground, which was soon dressed and divided among the company and was pronounced to be the best meat that they have ever eaten. It was first rate, no mistake. One mans horse fel with him while on the run in the persuit and turned a summerset on to the rider and hurt him bad. No bones broke. We passed t[w]o graves, no inscription. Appeared to be one or two years old. At night misquitoes very troublesome, but the wind rose in the night and blew hard which drove them away so that few returned.

Although this was a small buffalo herd, Mattes found that when herds numbered in the thousands, "blackening the earth and making it tremble, the emigrants were transfixed and overawed, for nothing they had read or dreamed of had prepared them for the spectacle."[32] In 1850 William McBride described how frightening it was to hear a herd passing in the dark: "Our company was much alarmed last night by a herd of buffalo rushing by our encampment. . . . As the vast herd was coming up they sounded like distant rolling thunder and grew louder and louder until they passed."[33]

Washington's complaint about troublesome mosquitoes echoes through many diaries, but most complaints were far stronger. Henry Stine, who

[30] Ibid., 79.

[31] Holmes, *Covered Wagon Women, 1840–1849*, Vol. 1 (Journal of Keturah Belknap, 1848), 223; and *Covered Wagon Women, 1854–1860*, Vol. 7 (Journal of Sarah Maria Mousley, 1857), 170–71.

[32] Mattes, *Great Platte River Road*, 253.

[33] Ibid., 256.

was traveling on the south side of Platte on this day, wrote, "Day and night they swarm around completely covering the horses and mules." One day he ventured off the main wagon track into the grass to see what would happen "and I had got some distance off when they arose in a solid mass and completely covered me and my horse." The horse rolled on the ground, then both he and his horse ran full out toward the wagons.[34]

[June] 18 Tuesday. *Roads dry, but some rough in concequence of the great number of teams that went before the ground got dry in the Spring, making deep ruts. Crossed several creeks, none very bad to cross. Saw a company of ox teams on the other side of the river. The low lands is so impregnated with salts that in many places the surface is white with it. Day cool and pleasant for traveling. At night camped by the river, which is about a mile wide. The depth we did not assertain, but at low water it may be waded in most places. Very little timber in these parts. It is difficult in many places to get enough to make fires with. Three young men left the road to hunt near night and brought in an antilope. Passed Grand Island, which is 57 miles long and from one to five wide.*

Washington mentioned the ruts caused by the wagons, but ruts running crosswise to the wagon track made the road even rougher. Mattes explained that as the buffalo ran across the trail, they followed behind each other in single file cutting ruts that were twelve to fifteen inches wide by four to seven inches deep. This created a washboard effect that jolted the wagons fiercely, frequently breaking axels.[35]

Although Washington saw wagons across the river, that would not be possible today because the Platte is lined with trees. By comparison, in 1850 the Pecks could hardly find enough wood to build a fire. Most emigrants had to rely on buffalo chips for the next stretch of the trail. Although using animal dung was initially repugnant to the women, they found it burned well. Since it was mainly dried grass, though, a great deal was needed because it burned so fast.[36]

[June] 19 Wednesday. *Rained before. After sunrise cleared up. Day warm and fine. Road a little rough in the fore part of the day. Afternoon road as good as could be wished. Prospect beautiful. The river running near*

[34] Stine, *Copy of the Letters and Journal of Henry Atkinson Stine,* 16, July 5, 1850.

[35] Mattes, *Great Platte River Road,* 243–44; and Conner, *Confederate in the Colorado Gold Fields,* 45.

[36] Kimball, *Mormon Trail, Voyage of Discovery,* 17.

the south side of the vally, which is from ten to twenty miles wide, with high bluffs on the south, the north so far off that we cannot tell the hights, and just timber or bushes enough to mark the place where the bed of the river is. Grass very poor on the dry prairie, although the land appears to be first rate. Prickly pears are quite plenty. Saw one grave, Inscription Jno D N Ward of Wiskonsin. Died June 2, 1850, aged 26 years. The man that got hurt at the buffalo hunt is getting worse. We have some fears of the result.

The injured man was not mentioned again, so he apparently survived his injuries.

[*June*] *20 Thursday. Morning rained for about two hours. Started late. The bluffs on the north side come near the river. Here we saw four stray horses on the bluffs. Quite a number of our company went after them but could not catch them. Two of them continued the persuit. Flies troublesome. Afternoon met two men looking for the horses. Here the river comes to the bluff. On assending an eminence, we had a view of the river for about ten miles. It is near two miles wide, dotted with more than a hundred islands, the vally about four miles wide. High bluffs on the south side. Road sandy. Heavy wheeling in some places.*

[*June*] *21 Friday. Started early. One of the company killed a fine deer close by the road. Crossed a beautiful creek, the handsomest that we have seen for a thousand miles, about ten feet wide. Dined by an exelent cold spring, very large. No timber. Drove to the last point of timber that we find for 200 miles and camped. Here is a grave with this inscription:*

E T Williams June 10 1849
Aged 23 years Residence Detroit Mich
Died with Cholery.

About dark, the men that went after the horses seen yesterday returned with them. The owners went farther looking for others. Two young men of our company that went out hunting did not return.

It was easy for the excited young men to get disoriented and lost when they tore off after buffalo. They often went much farther than they realized. By the time they finished the hunt and looked around on the flat featureless prairie, the white canvas covers of the wagons would be nowhere on the horizon. Others simply traveled too far to return before dark.

[June] 22 Saturday. Concluded to stop and rest our teams and hunt. We dug out a nest of wolves in the morning. The young men that stoped out last night returned about noon. They had been astray and slept on the wet grass without supper. Got breakfast with a company a little ahead of us. Two of the young men waded the river about a mile. Found the water [k]nee deep the most of the way, not more than four feet at any place. The water is high in the river at this time. We do not know how much higher than its real stage, but we suppose a foot and a half at least. Hunters returned. Brought in two antilopes and wounded a buffalo. Thunder shower at night. Found a grave a half a mile to the west of our camp with this inscription:

To the memory of
George Washington Jordan
who Died May 1st 1850 of Congestion of the brain aged 27
Resident Dubuque County Iowa

[June] 23 Sunday. The mammoth wagon came up and drove past without stoping even to speak. Done some washing. Intended to rest til Monday, but two ox teams and three horse teams came up and informed us that three teams was coming that had the small pox, so we thought it best to hitch up and drive on a few miles and keep ahead of them. Drove six miles and camped. Six men that went out to hunt did not return. At this place the flats is very wide. It is caused by the junction of the South Fork, which pours its water in a few miles below. Not enough timber in sight to build a big fire.

Washington was insulted at being snubbed by the men with the Mammoth Wagon, but they may have been distracted. Mattes wrote, "The endless shimmering valley had a hypnotic effect upon the emigrants." Rebecca Ketcham (1853) reported, "We are all afflicted with drowsiness, partly in consequence of having so little time to sleep. . . . This morning every soul in the carriage was asleep at once, and the horses going along as they pleased." James Evans, on the trail in 1850, reported that when he was overtaken by a company of pack mules, "I never so much as turned my head to look at them . . . for such is the unsocial habit of nearly everybody after they have been on this monotonous and stupefying trip."[37]

This is the second time the Pecks have encountered smallpox. Their fear was strong enough to make them travel even on a Sunday.

[37] Mattes, *Great Platte River Road*, 244.

[June] 24 Monday. The hunters returned this morning, reported that they killed two buffaloes and one antilope, but they had been led by the buffaloes to such a distance that they walked all night before they came to the road, and we had breakfasted before they came up. Poor fellows. They looked used up. The distance was two great to go for them, so we drove on. Roads good most of the day, some heavy sand. Dined nearly opposite the point of bluffs between the South Fork and the river, a pretty place. A great many islands in the river. No timber, nothing but grass to be seen on the islands. Crossed a stream 6 rods [100 feet] wide and two feet deep, then down over a point of high bluffs. Land sandy but would be productive with good cultivation. Here we was hit by a heavy thunder storm, some hail. Drove to a small clean stream called Bluff Creek and camped.

[June] 25 Tuesday. Rained heavy before day. The roads very heavy. In some places loos sand and others wet and swampy. We drove too far, 20 miles, worse than 40 on good roads. Two horses gave out. A few days more [of] such management and we must be defeated in our enterprize. Passed the mammoth wagon and returned their compliment of Monday. The Bluffs come near together and has the appearance of some rocks, a thing that we have not seen for four hundred miles. Opposite our incampment the bluffs are high with some few cedar bushes scattered up and down its side. Saw several buffaloes in the morning but got none. Light[en]ed our load a little by throwing away a few things and selling a pair of boots for what they cost in Detroit and expect to lighten more in the same way. Night clear and cool. Appearance of fine weather. Egerton and myself is quite unwell with diherrea. At night the mammoth passed as before.

Becoming ill with diarrhea was especially worrisome because it was also the first symptom of cholera, a bacterial disease contracted from contaminated water or food that could kill within hours.

[June] 26 Wednesday. Morning drove on. Found the roads wet and sandy, but not so bad as the day before. Drove fifteen miles and we stoped. The rest went on about two miles. The captain came to us and said that he would not leave us, and if the rest are not satisfied, they may go on. We passed a grave with the following inscription: To the memory of Amos Fisk who died June 22 1849 with an old diseas of the lungs Aged 50 years.

Captain Duncan's offer to stay with the Pecks in spite of their sickness speaks of his respect for Washington and his family and maybe concern over leaving Mercy, one of the few women on the trail, with a sick husband and son.

[June] 27 Thursday. Morning Egerton and self better. Came up with the company after which we had good roads all day. Passed the lone Tree. It is a red ceder, 2 ft in diameter, stands 70 m west from anything that can be called a tree and about 130 miles East from any that is on the north side of the river. Their is a few trees once in a long distance on the south side. The company is determined to drive slow. Our most impatient man, Mr Tillet of Michigan, drove on and left us. Found a grave, inscripton: Hiram E Shackelford of Adams Co Ill, Died June 17 1849 of Cholery, member of the Ill. Independent Co, Dr. Wells Capt.

The hunters killed an antilope. At night camped by side of the river. On the opposite side their was t[w]o companies of wagons and two of Packers. Thundered and light[ning]ed and wind blew in the night.

There were a number of Lone Trees along the trails, but historian Mattes noted that "like all Lone Trees, it was gradually hacked and dismembered even as it was being admired, and by 1866, it was only a memory."[38]

[June] 28 Friday. Found the roads soft and bad. Drove eleven miles. Found the company determined to go on, as usal, so we fell behind. Was overtaken by three horse teams and camped together at Crab Creek. Passed some romantic places on the south side. Bluffs on the north side low. Passed two graves. One, no inscription, died last year. The other, Margret Hawk, Died May 16 1849, aged 46 years. Thundered and lightened almost all night. Rained a little. Misquitoes troublesome. Any quantity of old man [wormwood] grows in these parts and wild sunflowers.

The contrast of this scenery after days of prairie landscape was a welcome change commented on by many diarists. Many described the scenery as "romantic," a term that was in common use.

[June] 29 Saturday. The Bluffs is getting higher and more rocky. We visited Bluff Ruins, so called from their appearing like the ruins of ancient castels and fortifications. We injoyed ourselves for two hours among them and would have been delighted to have spent as many days. Saw a great

[38] Ibid., 133–34.

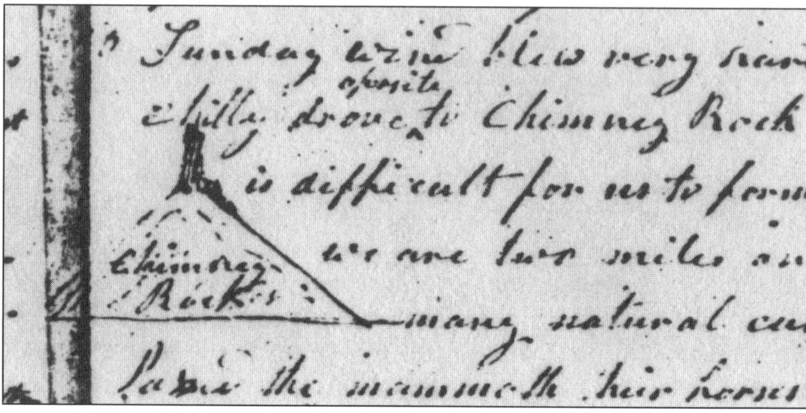

Washington Peck's sketch of Chimney Rock
was drawn in the page margin of his 1850–51 diary.

many strange plants, some very handsom. It is all together a romantic place and would [be] pecularly [particularly] interesting to the geoligist. Here we overtook our company again. Near night we was met by a tremendious storm of wind, thunder, lightning, rain, and hail. We prepared our wagons as well as we could so that our covers were not any of them torn. Got sight of Chimney Rock, a distance of more than thirty miles.

John Udell's travels paralleled the Pecks throughout many of the next eight years. At this time he was two weeks ahead of the Pecks on the same trail. When Udell climbed two hundred feet to the summit of the Bluff Ruins, he saw "the road on either side literally covered with the teams of California emigrants as far as the eye could reach above and below."[39] This is an example of how diarists recorded different observations. Washington makes no mention the heavy traffic on the trail, just comments on singular wagons passing by.

[June] 30 Sunday. Wind blew very hard from the north west, cold and chilly. Drove oposite to Chimney Rock. It is said to be 300 ft high. It is difficult for us to form an opinion of its highth as we are two miles or more from it. Their is a great many natural curiosities in this vicinity.

[39] Udell, *Incidents of Travel,* 17.

Chimney Rock, on the south side of the Platte, was one of the most famous landmarks on the trail. It was 325 feet high in total, with the spire being about 120 feet. Mattes noted that "More enthusiasm and more diary space were devoted to this particular landmark than to any other of the covered wagon migration." Thirty-five travelers made sketches, most of which have been published.[40] Although many emigrants predicted that the column would be eroded away in a few years, the stone was harder than it appeared and today is only forty-five feet shorter.

Passed the mammoth, their horses done out. Poor creatures. Never saw horses so used up. Their shoulders galled horridly and tired out, so that they could only make them move by whipping all the time. They can go but little further.

Galls were terrible sores caused by chafing of the harnesses. This is the last mention of the Mammoth Wagon. What happened to it remains a mystery.

July 1 Monday. Passed some High bluffs, romantic scenery. They drive so fast that we are forced to stop. One team gave out today, a man and his wife from Joliett, Ill. He has been one of the most clamorous for driving fast. He now sees his folly when it is too late. Hard is their fate. They had better return.

[July] 2 Tuesday. Drove alone, except the team that gave out yesterday. Drove 19 miles. Mr. Cruthers team stood it pretty well, so he drove on, which left us all alone 28 miles from Fort Larime. We have determined to risk falling into the hands of the Indians rather than over drive our team and render them unfit to perform the journey and finaly be left in worse circumstances. Found the roads very good today. Thunder and lightning with a slight sprinkling of rain.

[July] 3 Wednesday. Road good. Found a mistake in the guide, the distance being 8 or 10 miles more than the guide called it. Overtook an ox team and camped. Thunder and lightning with a little rain.

The Pecks were entering what would later become Wyoming. The error in the *Emigrants' Guide* noted by Washington was later discovered and recorded by Stanley Kimball: "The longitude reading . . . is incorrect by about 22 minutes, or nearly nineteen miles to the east."[41]

[40] Mattes, *Great Platte River Road*, 378, 416–18.

[41] Kimball, *Latter-Day Saints' Emigrants' Guide*, 57.

[July] 4 Thursday. Arrived at the ford, 522 miles from the Missouri, about noon, a mile and a half from the Fort. The Fort is a beautiful location almost surrounded with hills. Larime Fork running close to the Fort on the south, a fine stream, swift current with plenty of fish in it. It has been a trading fort til a year and a half ago when it was given up to government and about 150 soldiers stationed in it. They are building new barracks and are paying sixty or seventy dollars per month to mechanecks. We hear of a great many deaths on the south side of the river among emigrants.

Passed a grave. James Cox, Died June 7 1850, Age 29, and another at the ford, Stephen Moss, 1850.

Fort Laramie was originally a trading post built in 1834 by William Sublette and Robert Campbell and then sold to the American Fur Trading Company in 1836. When the large westward migration began in 1849, the federal government bought it and established Fort Laramie to aid the flood of emigrants in various ways. The high rate of pay was needed to keep the men from defecting to the gold fields.

Although Washington did not record it, the soldiers at the fort celebrated the 4th of July, which diarist Henry Stine, who arrived the same day as the Pecks, described thus: "In the evening sky rockets were sent up from the Fort."[42]

[July] 5 Friday. Bought a light wagon for $25 and left our heavy one. Flour at the fort $20 per cwt, other things in proportion. Ancient spirits very high. Our captain sold a pint of Brandy for three dollars. Decided to continue on the north side of the river. By so doing we shun coming in contact with those sickly companies that are on the south side. Some companies have gone on the north side and the road is said to be good. Afternoon drove on. Thunder, lightning, wind, and rain at night. Found some choak cherries and a few wild goose berries, the first wild fruit that we have seen since we left Missouri.

Although not apparent from Washington's brief entry, the fort was a beehive of activity with more than a thousand people a day swapping, repairing, and adjusting their equipment.[43] Washington went to the post office in the sutler's store and paid ten cents to mail a letter home to his

[42] Stine, *Copy of the Letters and Journal of Henry Atkinson Stine*, 16, July 4, 1850.

[43] Mattes, *Great Platte River Road*, 513–15.

daughter Mary Ann and her husband, George Banghart, which he mentioned in a letter he sent from Salt Lake to his son David.

People lined up to sign the emigrant register, which listed the names and number of people and animals in their party, and to look for the names of friends and family ahead of them on the trail. To the dismay of trail historians everywhere, the registers at Fort Laramie and Fort Kearney have long since disappeared.[44] Fortunately, some trail diarists, such as Henry Stine, copied the register's figures into their diaries, thus preserving some of the statistics. As of July 5, 1850, 37,171 men, 803 women, 1,094 children, 7,472 mules, 30,616 oxen, 22,742 horses, 8,998 wagons, and 5,270 cows were ahead of the Pecks on the road. Deaths, presumably on the trail, were listed at 237.[45] And these were only the emigrants who registered. Some did not register. Entries from other dates reflect the same percentage of women—about two percent, or one woman to fifty men. Even in an organized company, Mercy had few women with whom to visit.

The soldiers at the fort told the emigrants that the northern route was impassable, but a few parties, who were three weeks or so ahead of the Pecks, had discounted the stories as scare tactics designed to keep travelers on the south side where some of the soldiers had lucrative side businesses operating private ferries. Even legendary frontiersman Kit Carson put in his two cents: "the Devil himself could not get through on the N. side." Carson and Timothy Goodell had brought forty to fifty horses and mules from Santa Fe to sell to California emigrants whose worn-out animals needed replacing. Carson's comment was recorded in B. N. McKinstry's diary on June 21–22, 1850. Carson arrived at Fort Laramie in June and spent a month there, so he may have been present when the Pecks arrived. Carson's memoirs recall that a number of emigrants, excited at the prospect of meeting him, approached other mountain men at the Fort, misidentifying them as Carson, some of whom went along with the charade. So Carson himself may not have made all the statements attributed to him in pioneer diaries.[46] What Carson did not mention was that he too was operating a ferry on the south side.[47]

---

[44] Faragher, *Women and Men on the Overland Trail*, 35; and Mattes, *Great Platte River Road*, 502.

[45] Mattes, *Great Platte River Road*, 502–503.

[46] McKinstry, *California Gold Rush Overland Diary*, 131–32; and Peters, *Kit Carson's Life and Adventures*, 355–56.

[47] Holmes, *Covered Wagon Women, 1850*, Vol. 2 (Journal of Margaret A. Frink), 100.

McKinstry and his party had decided to stay on the north side, perhaps the first in 1850 to do so, and his journal documents the opening of that route. Washington's guidebook stated that the south side was "much better traveling if the river was fordable," but the river was high.[48] Washington decided to stay on the north side of the river for three reasons, which he detailed in a letter home: the river was so high they would have had to take two expensive ferries; they could avoid the sickly companies on the south side; and those who had gone that way ahead of them had not returned, thus they were presumed to have gotten through safely.

[*July*] *6 Saturday. Morning saw quite a number of magpies. One or two was killed by the company. Drove over a very hilly road, rocky in some places. Broke our hind axeltree of our heavyest wagon. Went back about half a mile and picked up an old one, a first rate hickory, and took it with us to the camp. The country is very high hills and deep ravines. The face of the hills is mostly rocky, the sides doted with scrubby pitch pines and red ceder bushes, which is of so dark a green that at a distance they appear almost black, which is the reason, I suppose, of their being called the Black Hills. When we assend some of the high hills, we obtain a delightful view of the surrounding country. We saw a scull and horns of a mountain sheep, which had not been long killed. The horns are about four inches diameter and about 2½ ft long forming about two thirds of a circle. Judged them to weigh at least 30 lb. That part of the horn that comes in contact with others in fighting was worn away and* [*an*] *inch deep. It appeared to be very old.*

[*July*] *7 Sunday. Morning got two young men to put in my axeltree. The company, their promises to the contrary, notwithstanding, seem determined to travil on Sunday, so at eleven oclock we started. The captain said that we would drive 8 or 10 miles to water and grass and stop. We found exelent water and grass at that distance, but no stop. Drove on over a tolerable level country with the best of grass and some water til almost sun set and camped on a sand nobb with scarsely grass enough to feed a dozen sheep and the worst of feeling prevailing in the company, having traviled about 18 miles without feed and almost none at night. Got rid of the man that we were taking through.*

Captain Duncan's company obviously had adopted a rule about resting

[48] Kimball, *Latter-Day Saints' Emigrants' Guide*, 84.

on Sunday, but the stopovers became less frequent due to the necessity of finding forage and water. Helen Stewart (1853) explained it this way: "It was not our intention to travel on the Sabbath but we find that we do more harm by stopping than moving on."[49] The Pecks have been with Captain Duncan for a month, but the comment on ill will in the company indicated that the organization might be starting to disintegrate. Washington expressed clear irritation at driving past good feed for his horses only to stop where there was nothing.

[July] 8 Monday. Morning at break of day we and two other teams hitched up and drove on about a mile to where we found grass and stoped to breakfast and feed our horses. Here we passed a grave inscribed L C Williams, Died June 7 1850 of Cholery, Aged 26 years. Drove about 18 miles over a Hilly country, the road winding among the hills so that the assents were not very steep and part of the time on the flats of the Platte. Road hard and good. At night we and three other teams stoped by a large dry creek. Found plenty of good water by diging a small hole. Grass first rate. No thunder and lightning, a thing uncommon in this country. Dew very light. Used the last of our butter. We have had plenty, but now we are forced to bid a long farewell to this luxury.

The Pecks endangered their health by digging a seep well—a hole dug two-to-four feet deep that water quickly filtered into. Historian J. S. Holliday explained that emigrants dug many seep wells beside the trail, because they usually camped quite a distance from the river. It was easier than packing water to camp. What the emigrants did not realize was that the thousands ahead of them had contaminated the water with human and animal wastes, so the seep wells helped spread cholera and other illnesses.[50] Back in the United States, cholera was sweeping the nation. President Zachary Taylor died of cholera in the White House on this date, and in St. Louis nineteen hundred people died in the month of June.[51]

[July] 9 Tuesday. Drove over a hilly barren country. In many places it would require ten acres to support one sheep. At the same time, the land appears to be good, mostly clay. The sandy land is more productive. Some of the flats of the river is as barren as the hills. In crossing some of the

[49] Faragher, *Women and Men on the Overland Trail*, 96.

[50] Holliday, *World Rushed In*, 161.

[51] Mattes, *Great Platte River Road*, 71.

highest ri[d]ges, we obtained a delightful view of the surrounding country. The pines and ceders have nearly disappeared. Iron ore and stone coal is abundant. Was in sight of the company part of the day but did not overtake them at night. Found midling feed by turning from the road half a mile. Drove about 20 miles. We are about 80 miles from Fort Larime.

Ironically, Washington's concern for the health of his animals, which led him to feed them a half-mile from the road, helped safeguard their health by removing them from the contaminated water nearer the trail. The Pecks also drank coffee, which provided an added measure of protection because the water was boiled.[52]

[July] 10 Wednesday. Morning drove on. Saw several buffaloes bearing down towards us. We equipped and started to meet them. They turned to the north at full speed. Found they were persued by several hunters belonging to the company. We left and drove on a short distance and found the company incamped where the feed was good, so we concluded to stop and rest ourselves and teams, which we felt to be much required. Dined on green peas and bacon, quite a rarity hereabouts. The hunters continued out all day and killed six buffaloes, one calf, and two antilopes. We sent a four horse team out towards night to bring in a load. The distance was farther than was expected and the road so hilly that they were obliged to leave the wagon and ride the ponies in. Arrived at three oclock in the morning. As the wagons (four) did not arrive with the meat some time after dark, the fifth started with a tent, some beding, and provisions to meet them and spend the night, but in the dark they missed each other. In course of the night, three of the teams arrived. Two left their wagons loaded with meat. The other did not find the meat and brought in their empty wagon. The other one and the one with the tent stoped out til morning. The nights have for some time been quite cold, increasingly so as we approach the Rockey Mountains.

Sometimes large buffalo herds calmly grazing across the trail forcing the wagons to halt until they had passed, but other times, as Washington described, the herds came rushing toward them. They were lucky that this herd turned when the men rushed at them. Another wagon train was unable to stop a stampede, which Mrs. Ferris (1852) described: "We suddenly came upon an immense herd of these monsters of the Plains.

[52] Erickson, *Daily Life in a Covered Wagon*, 39.

They started to run in three mighty streams, two of which went directly through the gaps of our trains. As they thundered past in blind fear, shaking the very ground beneath their feet, it seemed to me as though everything must be dashed to pieces."[53]

Daniel Ellis Connor, traveling about 1858, observed a singularly amazing spectacle as a herd passed in front of him:

> On and on they sturdily marched in compact single file for more than five hours ... until their leader became opposite. Back toward the rear ... their proportions gradually decreased until the individual animal was lost in the blended dark streak, which extended and dwindled out of sight in the horizon where the line could not be seen to move at all. It was the most grand and extensive sight I ever witnessed.... The whole line came gradually to a halt and each member thereof quietly changed ends and just as orderly as ever, took up their countermarch back the path which they came. And as far as we could see they were all moving back, while we still sat and looked until they were quite gone from view.[54]

[July] 11 Thursday. Spent the day in camp washing and jerking buffalo meat. A large portion of the meat killed spoiled before it could be taken care of. The men that was out hunting saw three horses in good condition, supposed to be straid [strayed]. Got hold of one, but it broke away. Thousands of buffaloes in this vicinity and as many large wolves.

Many diarists reported at length on the size of the buffalo herds, but Washington is one of the few who mentioned that wolves were also numerous. Historians Arnold and Wiener reported that wolves caused a lot of problems. They stampeded livestock and "chewed through the rawhide trail ropes that secured the horses," setting them free, another cause of strays.[55]

[July] 12 Friday. Ourselves and the three teams that has been with us drove on, the company having to stop to finish jerking their meat and do some repairs to a wagon. Found the road good and the most of the way levil, being on the river bottom most of the way. Grass scarse. Found a good place to camp having drove about 13 miles. A heavy squall of wind near night. We were sheltered by a small grove of timber in the edge of which we had camped. Three or four of the company went out to ketch the three horses seen the day before. We wish them success for they need them. Here we found a grave. M. Richardson, died June 23 1850.

---

[53] Mattes, *Great Platte River Road*, 256–57.

[54] Conner, *Confederate in the Colorado Gold Fields*, 45–46.

[55] Arnold, *American West*, 21.

Jerking meat was done by cutting it in thin strips, then drying it in the sun or over a slow fire. Some emigrants hung the strips to wagon bows to dry as they rolled along, unconcerned about the inevitable dust from the moving wagons. Helen Carpenter (1857) saw the scene as almost cheerful: "Tonight the wagons are decorated with slices of meat dangling from strings . . . along the side of the wagon, looking very much like coarse red fringe."[56]

[July] 13 Saturday. Passed the lower ferry, a large train crossing. They were from Missouri. Found the feed cut off very short. Drove fourteen or fifteen miles and camped. Grass rather poor. Saw a horse on the opposite side of the river, we supposed to have [been] left by some train. An old man in our company of 57 wanted to cross to get it if of any use so he strip[p]ed and swam the river accompanied by a yong man on horse back, the yong man carrieing his shirt and shoes. The water being deeper than he expected, his horse swam and wet the old mans shirt. They got the horse and made several attempts to swim the horses back, but in every instance got back to the side they started from, by which time it was dark and we knew not what became of them, but feared that they would try to cross in some other place and get drownd. At all events, they are in an uncomfortable situation, both wet, and the old man nothing but his shirt and shoes. Today a horse was left by one of the company, and one a few days before, being unable to travil. Bad omin at this stage of the journey. Passed a grave: † Joseph P Gratny from Dubuque Co Iowa, Died July 7 1849.

Washington is guessing that the horse was left behind. Whether intentional or accidental, leaving animals behind was a painful experience that many emigrants faced. When Charles Adam's ox, Sukie, became too lame to continue during their crossing in 1852, he explained to his pleading children that if they left her in a place with food and water, she might have a chance to recover and be exchanged by someone else who had to leave a lame animal.[57]

Washington noted that there were fifty-seven in the company, but did specify whether that was the number of people or wagons.

[July] 14 Sunday. Morning no account of the men on the other side of the river. Examined the islands up and down the river to see if we could see the

[56] Mattes, *Great Platte River Road*, 48–49.

[57] Bliss, *Mary Vowell Adams*, 118–19.

horses or any sign of them. About nine oclock they came. They had gone to another incampment 2 miles and stoped by the fire. The horse is considerable of an animal. Grass being poor we drove on and found it worse. Dined by where some teams were crossing. Here the body of a young man came floating down the stream, was taken out. No papers by which anything could [be] known about him. The company that was crossing were going to bury him. Crossed a very high ridge. Had a pleasant view of the surrounding country. Mountains appearing in the west rearing their lofty peaks towards the Throne of him who created them. Road good, except some loose sand. Lightning, thunder, and wind in the evening and night.

At least ninety drownings occurred in 1850. Historian Unruh, in his analysis of deaths on the trail, concluded that there "was an extraordinarily high incidence of drownings . . . during the course of the trip. . . . Drownings commenced at the crossing of the Missouri River even before the trip had fairly begun, and continued at virtually every stream and river crossing on the entire length of the Oregon-California Trail. Most . . . occurred in the Platte River."[58]

Although the Pecks experienced numerous thunderstorms, Washington mentioned them without much comment, whereas other diarists, such as Helen Carpenter (1857), described storms in fearsome detail: "About four o'clock a terrific storm broke on us. . . . The cattle refused to obey the drivers or face the storm . . . and had to be well guarded by all the men to keep them from running away. The thunder crashed at our very heads and the guards said the lightning circled the wagon tires and ran on the log chains."[59]

[July] 15 Monday. Morning passed a new grave and the upper ferry of the Platte. Here all the roads come together. Not a blade of grass as long as your finger to be seen. According to our guide book, we are to expect no water for 28 miles near the road. Drove 13 miles without feed or water. Road good but crooked. Here we came up to the company that was a little ahead of us baiting [feeding] their horses, about sixty, where the grass was hardly sufficient for half a dozen sheep and no good water. Their was a large mineral spring which our guide pronounced poisonous. We turned out and went in search of grass, which we found in abundance a mile

---

[58] Unruh, *Plains Across*, 409.

[59] Myers, *Ho for California* (Diary of Helen Carpenter), 126–27.

and a half from the road, and a clear stream of water, a little brackish, where we and one more train spent the remainder of the day and night, our horses injoying themselves first rate. The rest of the company drove on 13½ miles further without water or grass. Poor horses. We fear that they will not all go through. Their masters appear to think that the whip will answer every purpose of meat and drink. Afternoon very squally with thunder, lightning and a sprinkling of rain. We were informed by an intelligent candid man that came up the south side that they counted more than 200 graves of persons that died on the fourth and fifth of June. He thought that 800 was a moderate estimate of the number that had died on that side of the river this summer. They had seen the graves of eleven Doctors and one minister. While on the north side, we saw only seven new graves up to the uper ferry and twelve old ones, if we remember right, however, they are all noted on this journal. The sickness is abaiting owing probably to the nights being cool as we near the mountains and the air dry. No dews for some time past. It requires constant attension to wedgeing our tires and wetting our hubs to keep our wagons together.

The roads from both sides of the Platte came together at the Mormon Ferry (present-day Caspar, Wyoming). On June 29, 1850, diarist Byron N. McKinstry had found four ferries in operation that "cross people very fast." By taking the north side, McKinstry estimated that they "gained about two days on most of those that took the South side, had as good a road, better grass, and kept clear of the sickness."[60]

For the next fifty miles the *Emigrants' Guide* described the road as having "much bad water, poor feed, and few good campsites," which is ominous considering that the number of travelers on the road is significantly higher than in 1848 when the *Emigrants' Guide* was written.[61]

The Pecks were learning how severe the cholera epidemic had been on the south side of the Platte. Mormon Orson Hyde reported in Salt Lake that by the end of July there were five hundred graves from cholera on the south side and only three on the north.[62] One indication of how virulent cholera could be comes in Ezra Meeker's 1852 diary in which he wrote that "in one wagon train forty people died in a twenty-four-hour period."[63] Mattes reported that some cholera victims died so quickly that

[60] McKinstry, *California Gold Rush Overland Diary*, 146–48.

[61] Kimball, *Latter-Day Saints' Emigrants' Guide*, 67.

[62] Stegner, *Gathering of Zion*, 209.

[63] Adams, *Sunlight and Storm*, 284.

people who became sick in the morning were buried in the evening, and sometimes graves were being dug alongside people not yet dead, but in the last stages of death.[64] Unruh concluded that although numbers vary greatly, at least hundreds, if not thousands, died in 1850 along the trail, the majority from cholera.[65] Washington's observation that the deaths were declining because of the cool nights and dry air reveals that the emigrants had no idea what caused cholera or how it was spread.

Wedging their wheels was only one aspect of keeping the wagons in good repair. Wooden wheels continued to shrink as they dried, so to prevent the narrow metal rims from falling off the wheels as they rattled over the rough roads, buffalo hide or something similar was wedged between the rim and the wooden felloe. Various methods were used, such as Margaret Frink (1850) reported: "The hubs [were] sometimes wound with wet rags to keep the spokes in."[66] When possible, wagons were driven into creeks where the wood would swell and tighten as it soaked up the water.

[July] 16 Tuesday. Drove on ten miles and found the company incamped. Their horses had, several of them, tired out the day before, so they stoped to rest and alter their loads. Hearing that their was no grass ahead for 12 miles, we stoped for the day. The company shortened their wagon boxes, left some of their stuff and two wagons, and prepaired to start next morning, intending to drive to Sweetwater River, 27½ miles, ten of which is loose sand, a heavy drive for teams in good condition. I intend to take two days to go through, and my team is fifty percent better than the best of theirs. It would seem as if they were determined to destroy their teams and bring upon themselves the greatest suffering, if not death, in its worst form. Poor fellows. If they were idiots, they are to be pittied, and yet, they manage no better. Astonishing. We passed 25 head of dead cattle in 10 miles after passing the poisonous spring, the effect of drinking the water, and great numbers are said to lie off the road, 15 in one hollow.

Washington had found out, perhaps from someone who turned back, that there was no grass ahead, and the *Emigrants' Guide* warned of the heavy sand, thus his caution in avoiding a long drive with his horses. Washington was not alone in his shock and disgust at the abuse of teams by so many. Ezra Meeker (1952) wrote that many "ruined their teams

[64] Mattes, *Great Platte River Road*, 86–87.

[65] Unruh, *Plains Across*, 516, n. 75.

[66] Holmes, *Covered Wagon Women, 1850*, Vol. 2 (Journal of Margaret A. Frink), 143.

by furious driving, by lack of care, and by abuse. There came a veritable stampede to see who should get ahead." Whole trains would attempt to pass each other, "frequently with drivers on each side of the team to urge the poor, suffering dumb brutes forward."[67] David Lee Campbell, who was three weeks ahead of the Pecks in a horse-only company was observing the same recklessness: "There is a heavy crowd behind. Some of them are rushing to get ahead and there by killing their teams. We don't travel on Sunday, but some do. We are now ahead of a great many that started when we did and they travel all the time."[68] The days of rest were as important for the animals as for the travelers.

After this day, Washington did not mention the Company again. By taking an extra day to go through the heavy sand, they apparently lost contact with them.

[*July*] 17 *Wednesday. Drove 14 miles, the road as good as can be most of the way, hard and smoth as a floor, hilly and very uneaven, but the road winds among the hills so that the assents are gradual. A few short steep pitches. Passed over a very high ridge from which we had a pleasant view of the surrounding country to a great extent. Here we could view hills on hills and mountains on mountains piled up in the wildest confusion. But there was one circumstance that detracted from the pleasure we felt while beholding grandier* [*grandeur*] *and sublimity of the scenery before us which was that their was not a fertile spot on which the eye could rest for a moment. The whole face of the country was either bare clay or rock mountains or sand hills and the more levil land covered with wild sage or wormwood of the most dwarfish kind, which gave it a grayish appearance. So little vegitation on the high lands that it would starve a grasshopper. There is some grass in the vallies and that of the best kind, but it is so fed off near the road that it is hard work to get enough for our horses. Cattle and horses are suffering for want of food. Such vast numbers have gone to California and Arizona. We are informed that over twelve thousand wagons crossed the upper ferry of the Platte alone. A moderate allowance for those that kept the north side of the river and that forded and crossed the lower ferry, which was in opperation a part of the time, would make at least 15,000 teams that traviled this road this summer, and at least 1,000 more are on the road.*

[67] Adams, *Sunlight and Storm*, 283.

[68] Jackson, *Direct Your Letters to San Jose*, 79.

There is 500 teams of Mormons on their way to Salt Lake. I shot a Buffalo and wounded it very bad, but could not get it.

Washington's figures were not an exaggeration. In fact, 1850 had the second highest number of emigrants on the road, an estimated 50,000 people, twice the number that crossed in 1849.[69] Donald Dale Jackson, author of *Gold Dust*, concluded, "Never again would the suffering on the trail be as terrible as it was . . . in 1849 and 1850. Before 1849 there had been so few wagon trains that the water and grass remained plentiful. After 1850 trading posts and primitive settlements would spring up to help them pass the most difficult places."[70] Many had reached the end of their endurance by this point and turned back. On July 23, Lucena Parsons, whose wagon train left Council Bluffs a few days behind the Pecks, observed that at this place on the trail they were meeting teams almost every day on the back track.[71]

[July] 18 Thursday. Drove over a levil loose sandy road 15 m. Crossed the Sweetwater and passed Independence Rock and camped about 2 miles from Devil's Gate. Their has been abundance of grass about the river, but it has gone. Such is the rush for California that the very grass has emigrated.

Independence Rock was one of the major landmarks on the trail, but the Pecks did not stop, probably because of the lack of forage. Francis Sawyer described it in 1852 as "a great curiosity standing . . . on the level plain, single and alone, hundreds of miles from any companion."[72] Kimball noted that it was "an oval-shaped outcrop of granite 1900 feet long, 700 feet wide, and about 130 feet high."[73] Hundreds of emigrants carved or painted (with tar) their names on this rock. John Udell, who stopped three weeks earlier, reported that his company climbed the rock and played music at the top that "sounded beautifully in the vallies below."[74]

[July] 19 Friday. Morning spent a few moments in examining Devil's Gate. It is a chasm in the mountain. Near its end where it is tapering off of about 2 rods [30 feet] wide and 400 ft high, nearly perpendicular,

[69] Unruh, *Plains Across*, 120.

[70] Jackson, *Gold Dust*, 295.

[71] Holmes, *Covered Wagon Women, 1850*, Vol. 2 (Diary of Lucena Parsons), 252.

[72] Holmes, *Covered Wagon Women, 1852*, Vol. 4 (Journal of Francis Sawyer), 97.

[73] Kimball, *Mormon Trail*, 37.

[74] Udell, *Incidents of Travel*, 20, June 24, 1850.

through which the Sweetwater River passes with a rush. As to its name, we think inappropriate. If the Devil ever had a gate there, it has long since been thrown off the hinges and gone down the stream. Found the grass good in some places. Road quite levil but sandy.

Perhaps Washington took time to look at Devil's Gate because of Clayton's comment in the *Emigrants' Guide* that it was "a curiosity worthy of a traveler's notice." Author Aubrey Haines describes it as "a gloomy place, and violent also when the water was high." It is a narrow channel about 1500 feet long where the Sweetwater River rushes through a rocky ridge, carving walls 370 feet high.[75] A number of emigrants also carved and painted their names here. Levida Hileman, author of *In Tar and Paint and Stone,* lists all the names deciphered on Independence Rock and Devil's Gate, but she did not find Washington Peck or his family among them.

[*July*] 20 *Saturday. Road good, except loose sand. The vally of the Sweetwater is very pleasant and would be fertile with sufficient rain or irrigation (seldom any rain here in July and August). It is* 2 *or* 3 *miles wide, surrounded with mountains of various highth, most of them bare rock. Some of the highest we saw the clouds run foul of them. The stream is clear, the only one of much sise* [*size*] *that we have seen since we left the Missouri that is so.*

The year 1850 was a dry one, which added to the emigrants' problems. Mattes wrote, "The prairies are parched and oxen . . . die by the thousands."[76] In great contrast to the stereotypical movie scene of a small wagon train alone on the prairie, John Udell (1850) wrote that "within one and a half miles of us there are encamped one thousand men." He mentioned that the road was so full of teams that it was difficult to pass between them. "At some of the encampments there are so many in one place, that it resembles a small village."[77] Washington focused on the scenery and never mentioned the crowds.

[*July*] 21 *Sunday. Drove a few miles in the afternoon. Saw a Buffalo chase by a man on a mule of a mile and a half. Don't know which beat as they went through a pass in the mountain and we lost sight of them. The road continues to be strewed with dead cattle and now and then a horse.*

[75] Kimball, *Latter-Day Saints' Emigrants' Guide,* 70; and Haines, *Historic Sites,* 207.

[76] Mattes, *Great Platte River Road,* 16.

[77] Udell, *Incidents of Travel,* 19–20.

Road good today. We are now 743 miles from the Missouri, having made 97½ m this week. Thunder, lightning, and wind. Sprinkling of rain.

[July] 22 Monday. Morning the first thing that arrested our attention was a distant view of the Rocky Mountains called Wind River Mt at Freemont Peak, 13,570 ft high, which with many others had their proud heads lifted almost to the skies, capt [capped] with eternal snow. Had to drive 16 miles without water. Found some grass on the way on which we baited our horses and gave them about two gallons of water each that we took with us and they went through without suffering. Found the road good today, a little loose sand. Passed 28 head of dead cattle and four horses. Their cannot be less than 200 cattle dead on the road for a hundred miles back, chiefly caused by their drinking alkali and other poisonous water. Their is many springs and ponds of it here, some so strong as to skin the toung [tongue] if touched with it. Some of them are now dried up and the bottom is crusted over, salerates [saleratus] half an inch thick. Other places the low ground is covered with saltpetre and other places with salts. The cattle that drink strong alkali water will sometimes die in half an hour. Others will live a day or so. They are scattered all along the road, many of them in the road. The smell is very offensive. At night found some goose berrys, the first wild fruit that we have had, except a very few wild currants of inferior quality.

The scene of dead animals was a sad testimony to the number of emigrants who did not keep their animals from drinking at the alkali springs, which contained caustic soda or lye. As the water evaporated, the concentration of alkali increased. There were simple methods that some emigrants used to protect their animals, such as forming two lines of wagons with the loose stock in between them or by tying loose stock to their wagon.

Charles Adams, when traveling on this part of the trail in 1852, told his children to put on their heaviest shoes because the alkali dust would eat through thin soles. The dust burned the emigrants' eyes and faces and throats, and the animals suffered along with them. As they passed the dead animals, Mr. Adams told his sons to cut hide from them to make *ox mocs*, boots to tie over their cattle's feet to protect them against the sharp rocks in the road ahead.[78]

---

[78] Bliss, *Mary Vowell Adams*, 83, 119, 129–30, 145.

Saleratus was the common name for baking soda. Many who were running low on their supplies picked some up, as did Henry Stine, who was here on the same day as the Pecks. He gathered enough to supply his train and wrote that it made "better bread than that which we had been using."[79]

[*July*] 23 *Tuesday. Crossed a high ridge of land. Assent and decent gradual. Road good. Grass scarse. Drove ten miles. Rested in the afternoon on account of it being a little too far to the next feed to drive on, such feed as we have. Camped by the Sweetwater. Very rapid first rate water powers along here, the land a little more fertile than it was before we reached this stream. Their is a little very short fine grass on the high lands in the valley. Good if not fed off.*

[*July*] 24 *Wednesday. Morning drove over a succession of hills and hollows, some of them very high, the assents and decents gradual. Road hard and good all but a few places that was rockey. Two or three places presenting favourable opportunity for breaking wagons with car*[e]*less driving, but with care, there is no danger. The remainder of the day found the road tolerable levil, hard, and smoth as if macadamised. Grass more plentiful. Cool and squally with a little rain. Dined at Strawberry Creek. Here we saw some strawberry vines, the first that we have seen for 778 miles, some of them in bloom, none ripe. Passed the nearest point that the road approaches the Wind River Mountains, about ten or fifteen miles, but much further to the highest peak. Our view was obscured by the clouds imbracing them and folding them in their arms for several thousand feet below their summit. Camped at Willow Creek.*

The *Emigrants' Guide* warned that the rough rocky ridges they were coming to were "dangerous to wagons, and ought to be crossed with care."[80] For those who needed them, there were plenty of replacement parts from the abandoned wagons. Dee Brown, author of *The Westerners*, wrote, "From Fort Laramie to Bridger's Fort . . . the road was strewn with articles that had been discarded. Broken wagons and dead oxen lay along both sides of the trail."[81]

According to Father Pierre-Jean de Smet, most Indians called the Oregon Trail the Great Medicine Road of the Whites because they applied the term "medicine" to whatever they found "grand, religious, mysterious,

[79] Stine, *Copy of the Letters and Journal of Henry Atkinson Stine*, 18, July 22, 1850.
[80] Kimball, *Latter-Day Saints' Emigrants' Guide*, 72.
[81] Brown, *Westerners*, 125.

or incomprehensible. . . . They filled their pouches with knives, forks, spoons, basins, coffee-pots and other cooking articles, axes, hammers, etc. . . . Earthenware with any figure or inscription" was used to make ornaments for their necks and ears.[82] Although Washington did not note the goods they passed along the road in his diary, he mentioned them in the letter he wrote home from Salt Lake City.

[July] 25 Thursday. Crossed the backbone of North America 800 miles from the Missouri. Found the road good, not as hilly as in many other places. If our guide book had not particularly noted the place, we should have passed it with[out] knowing it. The land is not near as barren as it is a hundred miles back. Reached the Pacific Spring where we expected to find plenty of grass, but all that could be got at was eaten up, a part being soft and very miry. A great many dead cattle and horses in and about it, so we took a road leading off to the north supposing it would lead to grass. Followed it about a mile til it ceased to be a road, but no grass, only what little grew among the wild sage, and the rain forcing down, we concluded to stop and spend the night all alone, notwithstanding we lacked three very essential elements of comfort: wood, water and grass. Thus we passed our first night in Oregon.

Forenoon some rain, cold and chilly. Required overcoat and mittens. Saw a snow bank in a hollow, north side of the bluff beside the Sweetwater. Took it to be white rocks. Afterwards was informed that it was quite a body of snow. Passed 8 new graves. D Burns shot himself accidentialy, one of cholery, one a lady. Since the roads came together, we have seen quite a number of graves, but few in comparison with what there is below Fort Larime on the south side. Those that have died since are lingering cases.

The Pecks had arrived at South Pass, the continental divide, and a milestone for most because it marked the halfway point and the beginning of Oregon Country. Many emigrants commented that the 7,550-foot South Pass was unremarkable because it was a gentle incline over a broad open meadow. Maps of Oregon Country for 1850 show that the eastern boundary extended into Wyoming.[83]

Washington's observation on the fewer number of graves, and implied reduction in cholera deaths, was accurate. Mattes wrote that most deaths

[82] Adams, *Sunlight and Storm*, 280.

[83] Haines, *Historic Sites*, 234; Kimball, *Latter-Day Saints' Emigrants' Guide*, 73; Wexler, *Atlas of Westward Expansion*, 98; and Beck, *Historical Atlas*, 104.

occurred between the Missouri River and Fort Laramie,[84] and Unruh pointed out that the estimated number of deaths from cholera for different years did not include the hundreds of Indians who died from cholera and other contagious diseases, such as measles and smallpox, which were brought by the emigrants.[85]

Washington's notation of the man who shot himself was reflected in Mattes conclusion that accidental shootings accounted for many deaths among the emigrants, who had come west armed against what they perceived as a great Indian threat, but with little knowledge of how to handle firearms.[86] As early as 1841, diarist John Bidwell reported the death of a young man who shot himself when he pulled his loaded gun from the wagon, muzzle first.[87]

In fact, when Unruh analyzed data for deaths on the trail, he concluded that far more emigrants died from disease and accidents—drownings, gunshots, and being run over by wagons—than were killed by Indians, and emigrants killed more Indians than vice-versa. In 1850 Indians killed forty-eight emigrants, while emigrants killed seventy-six Indians. From 1840 to 1860, Indians caused fewer than 400 of the 10,000 emigrant deaths.[88] Michael L. Tate's study of interactions between emigrants and Indians noted that "patterns of cooperation, mutually beneficial trade, and acts of personal kindness clearly outnumbered the cases of contentiousness and bloodshed" and included a number of emigrants whose lives were saved by Indians after they had become lost, injured, or had run out of food or water.[89]

[July] 26 Friday. Morning drove 1½ miles to Pacific Creek. Fed and breakfasted, intending to drive 9 miles and camp for the day, but when we arrived, we found the water bad and the grass worse, so we had to drive 13¾ miles further to Little Sandy Creek, which we reached after dark, two late to hunt for grass, so we watered, tied up our ponies, and went to bed. Thundered and lightened, rained and blew most of the night. Had good roads, the land rooling until after we passed the junction of the California and Salt Lake roads (we taking the Salt Lake

[84] Mattes, *Great Platte River Road*, 84–86.

[85] Unruh, *Plains Across*, 395.

[86] Mattes, *Great Platte River Road*, 90–91.

[87] Unruh, *Plains Across*, 412, 517, n. 86.

[88] Ibid., 185, 408.

[89] Tate, *Indians and Emigrants*, x, 76–81.

road) a short distance when we entered on a very extensive valley of levil land with here and their a singular looking mound until we reached the creek. This day compleats my 49 year.

For some reason Washington ignored the information in Clayton's *Emigrants' Guide*, which clearly stated that "the water was brackish and not fit for cattle,"[90] as well as the information that there was very little grass here in 1848, which was a light travel year. Everything would have been long since eaten off this year.

This junction was called the Parting of the Ways. Washington is not quite accurate in his trail identification, which noted that the other fork was the road to California. In fact, it was continuation of the main Oregon Trail. After the road passed Fort Hall, a branch split off to the southwest, which was the California Trail.

[July] 27 Saturday. Up at break of day. Turned out our horses. Made a roaring fire. Baked some bread. Had a powful breakfast. Hitched up and moved down the creek to where we found good grass. Spent the day washing, cooking. In the evening was overtaken by a family of Mormons which we passed day before yesterday with whom we intend to travil to Salt Lake. Took our ponies and moved down the creek about 3 miles further, the creek running nearly parrellel with the road. Had first rate feed. Made 84 miles this week. We are now 200 miles from Salt Lake.

[July] 28 Sunday. Observed as a day of rest.

This day of rest Mercy would spend baking and washing, but the high altitude made it even more difficult. Mary Vowell Adams (1852) explained that "everything took a most unreasonable time cooking, and they all had sore backs from being so long at it."[91] The amount of stooping the women had to do in their chores was an ongoing complaint. Ester Hanna (1852) explained: "Have to wash without either tub or board but get along very well with a large bucket and pan set on an ox yoke. Still it requires me to stoop considerable. All our work here requires stooping. . . . It is very hard on the back."[92] And Ester was a young woman of eighteen compared to Mercy's age of forty-four.

[90] Kimball, *Latter-Day Saints' Emigrants' Guide*, 72.

[91] Bliss, *Mary Vowell Adams*, 145.

[92] Allen, *Canvas Caravans*, 37.

[*July*] *29 Monday. Morning passed two ox teams at Big Sandy. They were diging a grave to bury a man that died the night before. Found the road good, some loose small flat stones in some places. The country as we proceed becomes gently rooling, the banks of the creek higher. Passed better and more grass than we have for a long time.*

Washington's diary is one of very few that did not include burial of a member of their party. Burials along the trail were especially difficult because emigrants realized that wild animals often dug up the graves, and they feared that Indians did too. David Cartwright (1852) wrote, "While we were in the midst of a funeral service the coyotes were on a knoll . . . fighting and howling so dismally it was difficult to hear the preacher."[93] Emigrants tried disguising graves by building campfires over them or driving their wagons over them as they rolled out in the morning, but to no avail. Mariette Foster Cummings (1852) reported coming upon a man who had been "exhumed by the Indians for his blankets," and diarist Catherine Haun (1849) noted that the Indians spread cholera and small pox "among themselves by digging up the bodies of the victims for the clothing," but neither of these diarists actually witnessed the event they recorded.[94] Author Michael Tate refuted Indian involvement and concluded that "natural erosion and desecration by wild animals accounted for virtually all of the [disturbed shallow graves] discovered by passing emigrants.[95]

[*July*] *30 Tuesday. Drove over a beautiful road to Green River. Here is a ferry, price $5 a wagon. This river can be forded only at low water. The water is two high to ford now, so we were obliged to ferry, but we ascertained that their was opposition, so we concluded not to til morning. Drove up the river a short distance and camped. Grass good. This river is a fine stream, 16 rods* [*250 feet*] *wide 2½ ft deep at low water. Current swift, water clear and cold, its margins skirted with small patches of cotton wood.*

Running a ferry was so profitable that there was a great deal of competition between entrepreneurs at various crossings. Here at the Green River crossing, larger operations of a few boats were estimated to earn as much as $50,000 in a single season, which Unruh concluded was reasonable. He also reported that the "Green River crossing was another particularly

[93] Mattes, *Great Platte River Road*, 89.

[94] Holmes, *Covered Wagon Women, 1852*, Vol. 4 (Diary of Mariette Foster Cumings), 161; and Schlissel, *Women's Diaries* (Catherine Haun, 1849), 182.

[95] Tate, *Indians and Emigrants*, 153–54.

treacherous stretch of water which claimed at least thirty-seven victims" in 1850.[96] Washington was willing to wait until morning to cross the Green River so that he and those traveling with him could save a few dollars.

[July] 31 Wednesday. Morning got our wagons over for $2 per wagon. Drove down the stream 9 miles and camped. That is two miles below where the road leaves the river in order to find grass.

Aug 1 Thursday. Laid by all day. Nothing worthy of note occurred.

[Aug.] 2 Friday. Drove on. Found the road tolerable good, land rooling, and in some places hilly. Reached Blacks Fork, a branch of Green River, 6 rods [100 feet] wide 2 ft deep. Here we drove 15½ miles without water. Carried water with us. Stoped to feed and water. 14 wagons passed us here, a part of a train of 75, which started laden with provisions for the garrison at Fort Hall, but [the train] met an express [a military dispatch] at Fort Larime to stop, as every man at Fort Hall had run away and gone to the gold diggings, so he got his pay at Fort Larime, full price $14 per cwt amounting to the nice little sum of $42,000. He then returned rich and well pleased, and the trains above mentioned kept on for California. When within a few rods of our wagons, one of their oxen laid down, and they drove on. Never tried to get him up. They have plenty of teams, 5 yoke to a wagon and 80 loose oxen to repair losses. We gave him about three gallons of water and a little grass we had in a bag when he got up and went to feeding and drove on well. If we get him to Salt Lake, he will be worth something.

Diarist Byron McKinstry had arrived at Fort Hall five days earlier. He was told that the post commander had abandoned Fort Hall in the spring because they ran out of provisions and he had marched his three hundred men to Fort Vancouver. This was confirmed by the Secretary of War annual report in 1850, which noted that Fort Hall had proven to be unsuitable for military purposes.[97] If the government express (letter) to the packer redirected the supplies without explanation, the packer's comments to Washington may have been speculation based on military desertions to the gold fields taking place elsewhere.

Henry Stine, traveling near the Pecks, reported that John Brown, the

[96] Unruh, *Plains Across*, 273, 409, 483, n. 25.

[97] McKinstry, *California Gold Rush Overland Diary*, 221–22; Utley, *Frontiersmen in Blue*, 103 n.28; and Unruh, *Plains Across*, 206–208.

leader of the government freight train, sold some oxen to the emigrants for a hundred dollars per yoke.[98] Washington had a sharp eye for opportunity, so in contrast to those who overworked and abandoned their animals, he applied his excellent husbandry skills to revive the abandoned ox. The Pecks were only ten days from Salt Lake, so Washington had obviously decided it was worth driving his horses at a slow enough pace to allow the ox to keep up.

[Aug.] 3 Saturday. Mr Wixom, the Mormon that we was in company with, was sick, so we laid by all day.

[Aug.] 4 Sunday. Drove on 5 miles to Hams Fork, a fine clear cold stream 2 rods [30 feet] wide 2 ft deep. No timber but Rose Willows. It emtys into Blacks Fork. Here we ascertained that they were waiting for another object. Two Mormons that were going to Salt Lake from Green River and their son that had gone back for a cow that straid and would probably wait til Tuesday, so we drove on and left them. Found the roads good, tolerable, levil, a few steep pitches. Met some men from Salt Lake. They say that provisions are plenty, but prices exorbitant: flour $25 per cwt, beef 12½ do [ditto]. Camped by Blacks Fork near some singular looking hills and mounds 16 miles from Fort Bridger.

[Aug.] 5 Monday. Found the road pretty good to Fort Bridger, which is a traders fort composed of four log houses (we do not know where the timber is) and a small incloser for horses. It is in the valley on Blacks Fork a few miles north of a range of high mountains clad with perpetual snow. Drove on ten miles. Crossed a very high ridge of land, assent gradual, some coble stones. Decent very steep, crooked and over coble stones, the worst hill in all our rout to Salt Lake, at the foot of which we camped by a small stream of pure spring water.

Washington's question about timber arises from seeing Fort Bridger sitting on a flat grassy plain, but this is the second Fort Bridger, which Jim Bridger and Louis Vasquez built about 1843. Historian Aubrey Haines noted that the log buildings might have been moved from the first fort. It was a small trading post where emigrants could get a little blacksmithing done and pay a few dollars and exchange their worn-out animals for ones that had been restored to health by rest and good feed.[99]

---

[98] Stine, *Copy of the Letters and Journal of Henry Atkinson Stine*, 19, July 30, 1850.

[99] Kimball, *Latter-Day Saints' Emigrants' Guide*, 75; Hurn, *Pioneers*, 104; and Haines, *Historic Sites*, 271–72.

[Aug.] 6 *Tuesday. Found the road very crooked, but exelent, hard, and smoth with few exceptions. Country very mountainous but no steep assent or decent in the road. Crossed the dividing ridge between the Colorado and the great basin, which raised considerable in the world, being 319 ft higher than any former posision. Passed through some deep ravines with huge mountains on each side, but not steep and rocky in but very few places. Camped on Sulpher Creek, a nice place. Strong sulphur springs, oil or tar spring, with an exelent spring of the purest water and if not surrounded by the everlasting hills, we never will be in this wourld. Sprinkling of rain at night.*

[Aug.] 7 *Wednesday. Morning crossed Bear River, a beautiful stream 6 rods [100 feet] wide, 2 ft deep. Water clear and cold, very rapid, with more timber, cotton wood and some fir, than we have seen on any stream since we left the Missouri valley. ¾ of a mile wide, very rich. The soil is generally much better west of Fort Bridger. Afternoon crossed some high ridges. Land rich. Grass abundant. Well watered with springs and small streams. Entered a deep valley to Ec[h]o Creek where we camped. Road hilly, some very steep, but hard and smo[o]th.*

The Pecks were passing from modern-day Wyoming into Utah. Clayton called the valley Deep Ravine, but it was also called Echo Canyon. Historian Stanley Kimball wrote, "The Pioneers were fascinated with the sounds of animals and ammunition and musical instruments in this canyon," and in 1848 William Clayton described how "gunshots reverberated over and over and horses and oxen found the echoes of their own sounds very unsettling."[100]

[Aug.] 8 *Thursday. Road continued down the creek for 17 miles. Crossed it 8 times. Some of the crossings bad, very steep in and out. Some bad mud holes and rocky in some places. The valley narrow, mountains on each side. We do not mean hills, but mountains, the real genuine article, no mistake. The creek enters the fork of Weber River. The mountains are very high near and at the river. Rocky on the north side of the creek. The river is a fine stream of clearest water, very swift. Valley narrow. A great many rose willow bushes. Drove down the river 2 miles and camped after driving 19 miles over the worst road that we have passed. Found yellow and black currants on the creek, both sower*

[100] Kimball, *Latter-Day Saints' Emigrants' Guide*, 78–79; Kimball, Mormon Trail, 49.

[sour] and flavoured like the Eastern red currents. Saw some oak bushes, the first oak that we have seen for 872 miles.

[Aug.] 9 Friday. Crossed Weber Creek. Drove over high mountains, up and down deep narrow ravines. Reached Canyon Creek, a rushing stream one rod [16 feet] wide, 2 ft deep. Followed the stream up about 5 miles. Crossed it 7 times and camped alone, surrounded by huge mountains. The soil generally good with considerable small shrubbery and weeds with but little grass. Made about 17 miles, the road better than we had yesterday.

Although the 1848 *Emigrants' Guide* stated that the numerous crossings over Echo Creek were not difficult, perhaps by 1850 the immense number of wagons on the trail had broken down the banks.[101]

As the Pecks neared Salt Lake, Washington seemed grateful to have good road so that they could go faster. Although his diary is different from all others because of his unique experiences, it also has a commonality—a continuing record of how many miles they have traveled. Historian Norman Wright, in an article about odometers on the trails, concluded, "It is not surprising . . . that distance traveled each day appears almost universally in the overland journals of western emigrants." Novelist A. B. Guthrie (*The Way West*) expressed it poignantly: "Miles. Distance. Distance was the enemy, not Indians or crossings or weather or thirst or plains or mountains, but distance, the empty, awesome face of distance, the miles on wrinkled miles of it, the levels and hills and hollows and bluffs, unconquerable by the slow turn of wheels or the creaking step of oxen."[102]

[Aug.] 10 Saturday. Continued our course up the creek [Echo Creek] for three miles. Crossed the stream 4 times, then entered a deep narrow ravine with a small creek running down it and commenced the assent of a high ridge, being 4 miles to the sumit following the windings of the road. Most of the way a forest of small timber. Several bad mud holes at some of the crossings of the creek, so that we may say that the road was mudy, rocky, stumpey, crooked, and sideling. Altogether we found it an up hill affair. When we reached the sumit, we obtained a view of the southern part of that valley in which the anchor of the Mormon hope is cast for this world. Whether it is sure and steadfast, time alone

[101] Kimball, *Latter-Day Saints' Emigrants' Guide*, 78.

[102] Guthrie, *Way West*, 169–70.

will tell. The decent was very steep. We had to lock both hind wheels of our heavyest wagon for at least half a mile in a streach and in several places after. Drove down another ravine 4 miles and crossed another high ridge, one mile to the sumit, very steep both sides. Came to the last creek and camped. But when on those high ridges, we were not at the top of the mountain, their lofty peaks were towering in awful grandier above us, streaked with perpetual snow.

The summit of Big Mountain was 7,400 feet, about 300 feet lower than South Pass.[103] The descent dropped over 3,000 feet from the summit to the valley floor, a rough trip for the wagons, which the emigrants had to lock and slide down the steep slope. Historian Houston Hurn described the method in detail: "At the crest of the hill men would lock the wagon wheels by chaining them to the wagon boxes, then slowly skid the wagons by ropes down to the bottom," which prevented the wagons from running over the teams.[104] John Udell, who passed by four weeks earlier, described this last descent and stretch of road into Salt Lake as twenty-five miles of the "roughest road we have yet seen."[105]

[Aug.] 11 Sunday. Drove down the creek 5 miles. Crossed it 19 times, very difficult in many places. Then 5 miles more brought us to the Temple Block of the city of Later Day Saints. We hartily wish that they were all what their name indicates. The city is well laid out, the streets wide running at rite angles with water running through all the streets. Drove through the city and crossed over the River Jordan and camped.

Washington's wish regarding the Saints can be interpreted two ways. He is either indicating that his dealings with them in the past had been tainted—whether on the trail in 1850 or earlier when the Pecks and Mormons lived in Illinois—or he is hoping that future interactions will provide evidence of their goodness.

[Aug.] 12 Monday. Spent the day in looking for a house to rent. Found several empty, but their owners were out of town.

Henry Stine described his party's arrival on August 12: "All the talk and desire was to arrive safely in the City, to enjoy the luxuries of civi-

[103] Kimball, *Latter-Day Saints' Emigrants' Guide*, 79.
[104] Hurn, *Pioneers*, 98.
[105] Udell, *Incidents of Travel*, 24.

lized life, after a long and toilsome journey." At first glimpse, it seemed to consist of a few mud huts, "but on approaching nearer we saw that it was a beautiful place, resembling a large garden laid out in regular squares, each house occupied one and a half acres of ground. . . . The houses are one story high and built of unburnt [adobe] brick in cottage style, making a very good appearance."[106]

[Aug.] 13 Tuesday. Ranged over the town again. The buildings are not compact, the lots being 1¼ acres each. The buildings are mostly small, one story high and only one room, made of logs or unburnt brick. It is not quite two years since they commenced building. The first winter they lived in a fort, a large square with a row of buildings around it, which are now mostly abandoned. They have only a temporary place of worship called a Bowery. They intend to build one next year. Money is plenty. Wages high, from two to five dollars per day. Flour $15 per cwt. Beef $10.

When the Mormons arrived in 1847, they built a fort with small rooms side by side that provided protection from the Ute Indians.[107] It had been expanded as needed, but the Indian threat never materialized, so that by the time the Pecks arrived, most Mormons were living in houses outside of the fort. The bowery where they held church services was an open air shed with a thatched roof made of branches that provided shade.

"There was plenty of money and all kinds of work to do," wrote David W. Cheesman, who arrived at the same time and who would be traveling to California with the Pecks. His first job was to haul adobe bricks from where they were being made to a building site. He then began cutting hay, which he sold in town for ten to twelve dollars per ton.[108]

[Aug.] 14 Wednesday. Swaped part of our ponies and light wagon for a heavy wagon and 13 head of cattle.

[Aug.] 15 Thursday. Moved into town and camped by a house that we are to have on rent on Saturday. Swaped the rest of the ponies. Got 5 oxen and wagon.

Washington had decided to use oxen to pull his wagons for the rest of the trip.

---

[106] Stine, *Copy of the Letters and Journal of Henry Atkinson Stine*, 21, Aug. 11, 1850.

[107] Marks, *In a Barren Land*, 112, map locating western Indian tribes.

[108] Foy, "By Ox Team from Salt Lake to Los Angeles, 1850, A Memoir of David W. Cheesman" 274, hereafter cited as *Cheesman Memoir*.

[Aug.] 18 Sunday. Went to meeting. Bowery crowded. Some good speakers.

The Bowery had been expanded as the population increased; Cheesman estimated that it could seat from 1,500 to 2,000 people.[109]

[Aug.] 25 Sunday. Found no entry since the 18th. Spent the week in harvesting, threshing and moveing. Being disappointed of the house we expected to get, we bought a room in the fort. Paid $40, a small, but comfortable room, so we have secured a dwelling place while we stop. Crops as far as matured are exelent. Wheat, I think, cannot be beat on this earthly ball. Corn and potatoes have not come to maturity. There is not much corn raised in the valley. What there is promises a middling crop. Potatoes promises an abundant yield. We think provisions will be sufficient for the wants for the people with prudence. The Mormon emigration will be heavy, about ten or twelve thousand. The foremost trains are expected in a few days.

There had been a major change during the past week. The Pecks had decided to stay in Salt Lake for a time. In a letter to his son, Washington revealed that he was influenced by a story in the August 17 issue of the *Deseret News* which reported that a party lost their way and wandered in the desert for over four months, then lost four members to starvation and arrived in California on foot, having lost everything—wagons, horses, and cattle.[110] In addition, the Mormons needed his coopering skills to make kegs, barrels, washtubs, and the like. Henry Stine wrote that he "came very near staying myself having been offered a very fine salary and free trip to California in the Spring," but in the end, after resting for a week, he continued on to the gold fields.[111]

Sept 1 Sunday. Spent the week threshing a little and preparing to commence coopering. Bought a few staves. Made a horse and pair of jointers and some other fixings. The foremost train of Mormons arrived on Friday. Hard wind on Saturday night.

There is a gap in the diary from this date until the Pecks left for California in the fall.

---

[109] Ibid., 284.

[110] *Salt Lake Deseret News*, Aug. 17, 1850.

[111] Stine, *Copy of the Letters and Journal of Henry Atkinson Stine*, 21, Aug. 11, 1850.

Stopover in Salt Lake

The Pecks had arrived in Great Salt Lake in time to help with the summer grain harvest, which was critical to Brigham Young, who needed enough flour to feed the large number of emigrants enroute as well as the current residents. The supply during the previous winter had been so scarce that in a recent Sunday sermon, he had reminded the brethren of their obligation to provide for the Saints who were coming. A warning in the *Deseret News* admonished Mormons who were rumored to be selling flour to travelers at half price, which was in contradiction to Young's sermon. And they were taking names.[112]

Washington earned a substantial amount of money during this time, according to family history, and he was one of the first coopers in Salt Lake City, if not *the* first, producing barrels, tubs, and buckets, amongst other items.[113] No coopered items were mentioned in the stories of travelers trading goods, animals, or wagons with residents during this time nor were coopered items included on the lists of items available from local merchants who advertised in the *Deseret News*. Two years later Lucy Rutledge Cooke reported that coopered items were still selling for a premium and a local man told her, "You can stay one winter and get quite rich."[114]

Washington wrote a detailed letter to his eldest son, David Peck, who was running the cooperage back in Kilworth. He told the family how and where they were and their plans for the fall. He included many details of the sights they had seen on the road that he did not include in his diary entries. Families often loaned interesting and informative letters to the local newspapers to reprint, which is how this letter was preserved. It was published in the *Canadian Free Press* of London, Ontario, on January 17, 1851.[115]

Sept. 8, 1850

Dear Son,

I wrote to George Banghart [his son-in-law] from Fort Laramie, in which I gave a short account of our journey to that place; we will continue the narrative from that to this place. Fort Laramie lies on the south side of the river Platte and most of the emigrants that come up to the north

---

[112] *Salt Lake Deseret News*, Aug. 10, 1850.

[113] Peck, Montzheimer and Miller, *Past and Present of O'Brien and Osceola Counties, Iowa*, 715.

[114] Holmes, *Covered Wagon Women, 1852*, Vol. 4 (Lucy Rutledge Cook's Diary), 260.

[115] *London* (Ont.) *Canadian Free Press*, Jan. 17, 1851, 2:6–7.

side of the river Platte, cross there and travel up the south side and travel for one hundred and twenty-five miles, then cross over to the north side again, and see the Platte no more. We found that a few companies had continued up the north side of the Platte, so after much enquiry and deliberation we determined to follow up the north side of the river for two reasons: first, the water was so high that we must ferry at both crossings of the river, which would cost $7 per wagon, and second, we avoided coming in contact with the sickly companies of the south. Now for 120 miles our printed guide was of no use, and all our information amounted to was that a number of companies had gone that route and had not returned. The inference was that they had succeeded in getting through.

We found the road much better than we had expected, only one bad hill to descend, and ascend, in crossing a creek, which was deep, but our heaviest loaded teams went up without doubling. Here, too, the grass is more plentiful, not being eaten up as it is on the south, but when we came to the upper ferry of the Platte, and all the travel comes on the one road, then, for the first time we really felt the want of food. Here for fifty miles the country is more barren than any we have passed, there being no grass only on the flats of the creeks and some springs and swamps. Where our guide spoke of abundance of grass, it was fed off until it was as bare as the streets of Kilworth.

Here all the companies broke up that had not previously done so, and everyone looked out but for himself. There was another difficulty, the water was bad. After driving twelve miles without water, we came to a mineral spring of poison water. Those who suffered their cattle to drink lost more or less. Then there were strong alkali springs, very fatal to cattle; saleratus lakes, around which large quantities of saleratus could be gathered. Almost all of the low lands where the grass grew is covered with salts, saltpetre, or saleratus, all of which rendered it an unhealthy place for stock. Our guide pointed out all these places, some that had no guide lost all their cattle, which [while] others sustained heavy losses. We drove very slow, going off the road 2 or 3 miles in some places to camp, and kept our teams in good condition.

After we reached the sweet water, we found better feed, and when we passed a junction of the California and Salt lake roads, we had good feed with very few exceptions in that place. As to the roads, I just say that they are much better than I had expected. At the south pass of the "ridgepole of North America," the road is excellent except the crossing of the streams, which in some places are steep in and out. There are no steep hills to cross around so that the grades are not steep. The bed of the road is generally hard and smooth. Many places for miles at a stretch they are incapable of improvement by [——] being as hard and much smoother than any macadamized road I ever saw. The Wind River mountains, some fifteen miles north of the south pass, are very high, broken and rugged, their peaks penetrating far into the clouds, capt [capped] with eternal snow; those on the south are neither high nor much broken. The worst part of the road is the last hundred miles before we reach this place, which is a very mountainous country; here we rise higher in the world than at any place. Some of the descents are very steep, requiring both hind wheels to be locked, but the teams loaded with merchandise for this place bring 40 cwt [4,000 pounds] to a wagon.

The destruction of property is great on this road, tons of wagon irons are strewed along the way, (the wagons are generally burned for fuel). Rifle and shot guns, double and single barrel are scattered about in profusion, also beds, bedding and clothing of every description, and chains almost without end. Of live stock, it is said that a machine has been invented in Texas for rolling the fat out of cattle. It works in this way: the cattle are taken to the place and put in one at a time, and the machine set in operation and when sufficient fat is rolled out, the animal is taken out and another put in and so on until the whole has passed through the mill, then the tallow is packed up and is fit for market. Now, I assure you that it is no fiction when I say that a great number of machines are in full operation on this road that as effectually roll the fat out of cattle as any machine in Texas. With some difference it is true. There one animal is put in at a time; there [here] the whole team is put in at once; there the fat when rolled out is said to be fit for market, here when rolled out it takes wings and flies away. There it is said that the fat can be rolled out twice in the summer. Here once answers for the whole season; there it operates only on cattle, here it works equally well on cattle, horses and mules; there when the surplus fat is rolled out, the animal is let loose, here many continue to roll out not only the fat but the flesh itself is gone, and in many instances life is extinct. Overdriving and bad management have used up and killed a great many animals. After we passed the first poison water, the road was literally strewed with dead carcases, many of them on the road, and many others close by the side in every stage of decomposition which rendered it very unpleasant travelling on account of the smell. For more than 200 miles it was difficult to find a camping place where we could breathe the pure air.

With good management teams can go through in good condition 100 miles per week on an average, but for the sake of gaining one week, many run down their teams, so that when they get here, they have to give two for one after losing part on the road; others bring them in good order, which is always practicable with [——].

As to ourselves, when we found that the feed was so eaten up, and all the roads coming together for 500 miles this side of the diggings and reports coming back of much [——] suffering on the road, we concluded to winter in this place. Notwithstanding our ponies were all in good order, we swapped our horses for cattle. Got five yoke of good oxen and 4 yoke of cows which are worth at least $700, and at the mines, each ox or cow is worth as much as a horse.

Provisions were very high in this place when we arrived, flour was $25 per cwt. [hundred], beef 12½, pork, none, potatoes $4 per bushel, butter 50 cts [cents] per pound. Wages were high also, a man could get as much flour and meat for two day's work as would last him to the mines. Cooper work is very [——]. We sold the three kegs we brought with us from Kilworth for [——] (worth in Kilworth 5 shillings each). We prepared for working at it and bought a few tools of an emigrant very cheap. Paid $52½ for a little less than a thousand pine staves, dressed, more than half of them being wash-tub staves, and have commenced work. Washtubs bring from $4–$5, barrels without covers $3, barrel and a half $4. Provisions have fallen. Flour is worth $10 per cwt., meat the same, other things in proportion. We suppose at the lowest point, the Mormon emigration will be near ten thousand, but what the number of gold diggers that intend wintering here is not known, probably two thousand, which is a heavy emigration to be supported. This being only the third harvest in the valley, and the whole population, (exclusive of this year's emigration) is but ten or fifteen thousand. Notwithstanding crops are great. Wheat will yield 50 bushels per acre, and potatoes can't be beat on this earth, corn good but little planted, in short the earth has yielded abundance to the seed sown. There was much less sown and planted than otherwise would have been, so that, all things considered, there is cause to fear a scarcity before harvest. Therefore it is thought best to go on this fall on the southern route, as near as we can ascertain it, is the Mormon route to the diggings. But sinners (as all are called here that are not Mormons) have not been permitted to pass that way. They have not shown them the road, for by letting them go the old road, four or five men could tend *the ferry at Bear river for three months at a time, and make from $25 to $30,000; quite an inducement for withholding knowledge. But now circumstances have so far changed, that it acts as a safety valve to let off the surplus population, and an experienced mountaineer has offered to pilot a company through. He will strike the diggings 100 miles south-east of Sacramento City. He says that the road is good and grass plenty. The mountains he will pass are not high, but course gently. But little grass ever on them—One day's travel will cross them in that place. We are determined to go with him, and are now in a great hurry to work up our stuff, and be ready to go with him the first of October. He says that it is nearer than the northern route which is 800 miles to Sacramento City, this being 700 miles. As to the people of this city, we have no fault to find, many of them are very kind. As to Mormonism we think that it can never make the comers thereinto perfect as its tendency appears to be not to elevate and perfect the human character but to sink and debase the morals and highest branch of knowledge. Notwithstanding they present a beautiful illustration of the principle that "Union is strength."*

This is a beautiful valley, surrounded with mountains, some of their peaks streaked with perpetual snow. The land is of the best quality and yields abundance with irrigation, without which it will produce very little. There being very little rain during the summer season and no dew, which is the case all the way after we pass Fort Laramie, but the valley is so situated that it can all be irrigated. Timber is scarce, consists of fir, spruce, and some pine in the mountains, very difficult to get out. Lumber is worth $4 per foot, very scarce at that. Firewood $5 per load.

The city is laid out in square blocks of ten acres; each block is divided into eight lots. The streets are eight rods wide and cross at right angles. The buildings are all built of sunburnt bricks, mostly small, but it is improving rapidly and will become a large place, abounding in riches.

To all that intend to go this way to the mines, I would say, that Indian or French ponies are equal to mules, but never take large horses, better to stay at home.—Those coming this way to the mines had better start as early as we did, the 22nd or start the middle of May if you take the southern route to this place. Drive steady, make no large drives, be diligent but never in a hurry. Rest every Sabbath if feed will permit, do your washing every week and be sure to go to the north side of the river Platte. Use no water but running streams; the river water if possible, muddy as it is. Take light two horse wagons for 4 horses, and good one horse wagons for two horses. For each person take 100 lbs of flour, 50 lbs of hard bread, 25 lbs of bacon, 25 lbs of sugar and 10 lbs of rice when you leave Council Bluffs, and only two or three persons to a four horse team. Make no waste of provisions, and take water casks, 3 gallons to a horse, and don't be too lazy to fill them when wanted, and ten to one but you will go right through to the mines without coming to this valley, by which you will save 120 miles and experience very little difficulty.

Our health is as good as usual through the summer. We are all well except your mother who is rather unwell. We think it a long time without seeing or hearing from any of you.

You may put the distance to the place at 2000 miles, it is 1043 from Kanesville measured, then add 57 to the 900 that I called it to Kanesville, which I think moderate, and we have 2000 miles.

WASHINGTON PECK

With all that advice on what to take and how to travel, Washington appeared to be well aware that people back in Kilworth, who were thinking of making this trip, would be wanting just such information.

This letter contained the first reference to Mercy since they left and the description of her being "rather unwell" was vague and worrisome news to send home to the children.

This letter revealed another change of plans. Three weeks after deciding to stay over, Washington feared that a food scarcity would arise, so he decided to continue to California after all, but on a more southern route. He also revealed that previously the Mormons had been unwilling to show the "sinners" (non-Mormons) the southern route, but with the expected food shortages, the Mormons realized that they needed to encourage some of the sojourners (temporary emigrants) to move on.

The day after Washington wrote his letter, the Pecks were present for a major historical event in Mormon history. Although the State of Deseret proposed by Brigham Young was cut back to half its size, on September 9, 1850, the Territory of Utah was established. President Fillmore appointed Brigham Young governor but also appointed a number of non-Mormon eastern men as officials, which resulted in dissension, both inside and outside the territory. Statehood would not be granted for almost fifty more years.

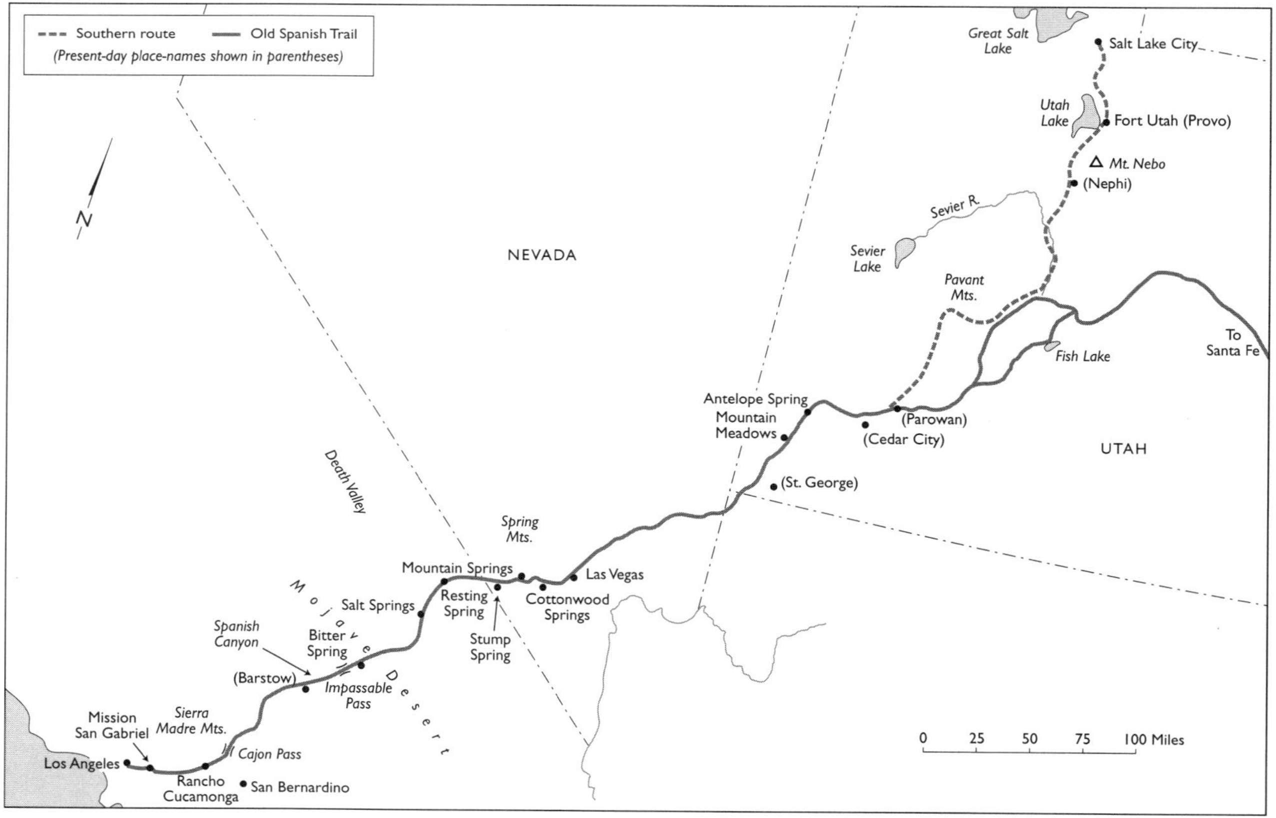

In the fall of 1850 the Pecks took the Southern Route from Salt Lake City to pick up the Old Spanish Trail near Parowan, Utah, and traveled to Mission San Gabriel, California. Adapted from Hafen & Hafen, *Old Spanish Trail. Courtesy Arthur H. Clark Co.*

3

1850–1851 Wagon Trail Diary: Salt Lake City to the California Mines

THE NEXT PART of Washington's diary covers the Pecks' short stay in Salt Lake City while they made arrangements to continue to California. It follows them back onto the trail as they head south to pick up the Old Spanish Trail, the so-called Southern Route, which crossed southern Utah, the deserts of Southern California, and then carried on to Mission San Gabriel, about ten miles east of Los Angeles. After a three-week rest at the Mission, they herded their cattle westward toward the coast and arrived at present-day Ventura. They traveled up the California coast, turned inland to Stockton, moved on to Sacramento, and finally arrived in the gold fields at Nevada City, California.

In spite of the money to be made by coopering in Salt Lake City, Washington's fear of a food shortage over the winter caused him to take notice of an advertisement placed in the *Deseret News* on September 7 by Elijah Barney Ward.[1]

CALIFORNIA EMIGRANTS.
TAKE NOTICE!!

> ELIJAH WARD, (generally known by his mountain name, Barney Ward,) intends leaving Utah Valley, on or about the first of October next, for the SOUTHERN MINES in California. Mr. Ward is thoroughly acquainted with the SOUTHERN ROUTE, and will pilot Emigrants through to said mines for ten dollars per wagon; and ten dollars for every company of five persons with packs, or pack animals. As fast as Emigrants come in, and can get ready for the journey, they will pass through Great Salt Lake City, and Utah Valley, and encamp on Hobble Creek, about ten miles south of the Utah Settlement, where they will find GOOD FEED AND WATER TO RECRUIT THEIR TEAMS. Any

[1] *Salt Lake Deseret News*, Sept. 7, 1850, 1:1. Typescript.

further information wanted, can be obtained by calling at my dwelling in Utah Settlement.

ELIJAH WARD, Pilot.

N. B. No one will be permitted to travel in the train, until his fare is paid to the Pilot.

The contemplated route to the Southern Mines, is no worse than the usual route from the States hither, so far as rocks and mountains are concerned; although the deserts are more extensive.

We expect to leave the old road, near the foot of the mountain, and near Mahave (or Mahawbee) Creek. I will pilot the company either to Williams' Rancho, or to the Gold Mines in that region, just as a majority of the company shall decide, for their convenience. E. W.

Barney Ward was a forty-year-old mountain man who had lived in the Rockies from the age of fifteen until 1847 when the Mormons arrived. He became a convert and served as an Indian interpreter, trader, and guide. Ward claimed that he had found a shortcut that turned due west through the region that Fremont had marked as unexplored in 1844.[2] An additional story in the September 14 paper highly recommended Mr. Ward's ability and the southern route. It encouraged additional families to leave before winter.[3]

Washington was planning to go with Ward on his shortcut, but was unaware of the 1849 disaster that had occurred the year before when Jefferson Hunt, a Mormon Battalion captain, had been sent to Los Angeles to buy supplies for Salt Lake.[4] Hunt signed up about a hundred wagons of emigrants to travel along the Old Spanish Trail to Los Angeles. Hunt wrote that "after several days travel, a packer, O. K. Smith, consulted a map he had obtained, which showed a shortcut that would supposedly save 20 days and 500 miles," a map attributed to Barney Ward. All but seven of the wagons went with Smith. Hunt told them that although packers might make it, he doubted that wagons could, and then ended with, "If you want to follow Captain Smith, I can't help it, but I believe you will get into the jaws of hell." After three days of travel over rough terrain, most returned to the southern route and were, by then, a week behind Hunt. In his study of the event, Brigham Madsen wrote that the

[2] Hafen and Hafen, *Journals of Forty-Niners* (Flake-Rich Company), 35, 227–28.

[3] *Salt Lake Deseret News*, Sept. 14, 1850.

[4] Lyman, *Overland Journey*, 41.

rest struggled along what was called Walker's Cut-off, "suffered terribly," and all became lost. Historian George Koenig described how "the wagon train began to disintegrate. Individually and collectively they began to scatter in search of water." Some died after they wandered into the desert now named for them—Death Valley.[5]

Along with the Pecks, the Macy-Cheesman party, who had arrived in Salt Lake four days after the Pecks, signed on with Barney Ward. The party included Dr. Obed Macy, his wife, seven children, his son-in-law, David W. Cheesman, and David's very pregnant wife, Urania. The party had suffered a difficult crossing to Salt Lake, including a cholera attack that killed fourteen-year-old Charles Macy. They planned to stay over until Mrs. Cheesman delivered her baby and recovered. Their son Randolph was born in mid-September.

As the departure date of October 1 approached, the emigrants made their way in small groups to the staging area at Hobble Creek to wait for Ward, but the night before they were to leave, according to Cheesman, Brigham Young ordered Ward north where his translation skills were needed to help resolve a Snake Indian dispute.[6]

A committee of those planning to take the southern route, including Cheesman, met with Brigham Young and requested a copy of a report that detailed the route, grass, water, passes, etc., which had been written by Mormons that had returned from California that August. After trying to dissuade them from traveling so late in the season, Young promised to give them a copy, but he never did. Whether the meeting with Brigham Young took place before or after they had learned that Barney Ward would not be guiding them was not stated. Fortunately, one of Cheesman's neighbors, a Mr. Hudson, also a California returnee, provided him with a "memorandum of the watering places and our camping places on that route which was the only guide we had, and this was very meager."[7]

A cautionary note regarding the Cheesman Memoir: Mary E. Foy, Cheesman's niece, believed that the memoir was written shortly before his death in 1884,[8] thirty years after the events occurred. Thus it would

[5] Hafen and Hafen, *Journals of Forty-Niners* (Flake-Rich Company), 38; Madsen, *Gold Rush Sojourners*, 113; and Koenig, *Beyond This Place*, 51.

[6] O'Gorman, "Foy and Allied Families," *Americana* (*American Historical Magazine*), 25:250; and Foy, *Cheesman Memoir*, 273, 283.

[7] Foy, Cheesman Memoir, 283, 273–74.

[8] Ibid., 272.

have been subject to all the tricks memories play, including lost details and confused sequences. That said, the annotations for the next part of Peck's diary draw heavily on that memoir because it is the only other known record of the journey, and its additional information more fully explains the events that occurred.

Old Spanish Trail

[Oct 2] *Wednesday. Afternoon took our departure from the City of Great Salt Lake. Drove about twelve miles. Found no grass. Bought some straw for our cattle and camped.*

After trading their ponies, the Pecks were driving two ox-drawn wagons and herding the rest of their cattle, which included some pregnant dairy cows. Washington had fifteen cattle in all.

There were two travel schedules for those going to the gold fields. Those who traveled west from Salt Lake City to California needed to leave during the summer so they arrived before the winter snows in the Sierra Nevada Mountains, whereas those who took the southern route, such as the Pecks, left in the fall to avoid the worst of the summer heat in the deserts.

[Oct.] 3 *Thursday. Drove about ten miles to Willow Creek. Found abundance of grass and camped.*

[Oct.] 4 *Friday. Passed a boiling spring. Crossed a point of a mountain that divides the valleys of Salt Lake and Utah, assent very steep with loose sand and gravil. From the summit we had a fine view of the Utah Lake and valley. Decent gradual. Some exelent land in this valley and well watered. Reached a fine stream called American Fork and camped, having drove 15 miles.*

[Oct.] 5 *Saturday. Drove about 13 miles to the settlement, which consisted of fifteen families. The buildings so arranged as to form a kind* [of] *fort for defence against the Indians, which place has received a large increase of numbers within a few weeks past.*

Fort Utah, now Provo, was one of many small outlying communities founded under the direction of Brigham Young. Not only did this disperse the population to lessen the drain on the resources of Salt Lake City, but it also helped settle Utah Territory.[9]

[Oct.] *6 Sunday. Drove 7 miles to Hobble Creek, the place of rendevous for the Emigrants bound for the gold diggings. Expected to find 3 or 4 wagons but they were gone. Here the Mormons are going to make a settlement. About 20 families are encamped here prepairing for winter.*

Hobble Creek was the place set by Barney Ward for the wagons to meet. The settlement was later called Springville.

[Oct.] *7 Monday. Laid by waiting for the company. Only two wagons arrived at night.*

[Oct.] *8 Tuesday. The wagons came in fast so that in the afternoon we formed an organisation. Elected a captain and two assistants. Mr Peck capt. Mr's Brown and Fanvalkenburgh assistants.*

Someone brought word that Barney Ward was not coming, so the emigrants organized themselves and elected Washington Peck as captain of the wagon train. *Parsons Guidebook* of 1859 gave this advice on how to organize a company:

> Three officers are needed—wagon master, assistant wagon master, and captain of the guard. You should select a man of experience with teams—a man of promptness and undoubted courage—a man who will do a thing when he has said it, and make others do the same. Select him with care, and when you have selected him, OBEY IMPLICITY [*sic*] every order which he may give, without questioning its correctness. . . . The success and safety of your train will in a great degree depend upon the encouragement and support which you give this officer.[10]

[Oct.] *9 Wednesday. Morning some rain before day. Cold and chilly. At daylight we discovered the mountains covered with snow for more than half way down. Started about nine oclock. Continued cold and some rain. Hard wind all day. Drove about 7 miles to Spanish Fork and camped. Found the company to consist of 29 wagons and two carts, 92 men, 9 women and 28 children. Appointed a guard and arainged for the night. The cattle broke away from the guard and scatered among the bushes.*

---

[9] Bancroft, *History of Utah*, 308–309.

[10] Hafen, *Pike's Peak Gold Rush Guidebooks of 1859* (Parsons Guidebook), 173.

As captain of the wagon train, Washington surveyed the wagons and took count. Cheesman wrote that ninety wagons signed up under Barney Ward, and noted that the party did not leave in a body, but over two or three days so that they would be "within reaching distance for protection and at the same time not to be in each other's way on the road, and especially at camping places, but to travel in detached parties."[11] The number of wagons and people was in constant flux as people went ahead or were overtaken.

Although Washington did not list names in his diary, many who traveled with the Peck Wagon Train have been identified. Spellings were often phonetic, which led to interesting variations, especially with the wide number of accents being spoken—northern, southern, and European. Washington named the following people in diary entries: Mr. Brown, Mr. Fanvalkenburgh, Mrs. DeMasters and baby daughter, Mr. Pepper, Mr. Heath, C. Rumsey, H. Dwinger, Asa Carrico, Mr. Moseley, Mr. Blodgett, and Mr. Fancher.

Cheesman named all those he could remember, including Washington Peck, and added some personal details. Cheesman family descendants added a few more details. Cheesman's list: Mr. Pepper (a man from Missouri, who was traveling with his slaves and considerable stock), Mr. and Mrs. Samuel Heath, Mr. Mosley, Hiram Mendenhall and his son Amos, a violist named Burke, James Knight, James Glover, Jimmy Cyrus Adams, an English couple, Mr. and Mrs. Mellett, their two children, and a man named Borse from Memphis, who was murdered in Angels Camp in the gold fields a year or so later.[12] The Cheesmans were a day or so behind the main wagon train and caught up on October 27.

Historian Will Bagley further identified the Fanchers listed by Peck: Alexander and Eliza Fancher, their seven children, his brother John Fancher, his wife, their four children, and a large drove of cattle.[13]

[Oct.] 10 *Thursday. Morning storm over. Calm and pleasant. Found the cattle. Drove twelve miles, road good, and camped.*

[Oct.] 11 *Friday. Crossed the ridge between Utah and Yoab* [*Juab*] *valleys. Latter is a beautiful valley about six miles wide and 30 long. Drove*

[11] Foy, *Cheesman Memoirs*, 286.

[12] Ibid., 286–87, 307.

[13] Bagley, *Blood of the Prophets*, 58–61.

about 21 miles, road good, and camped at Salt Creek. Days warm like summer while the higher mountains are clad in the Habiliments of winter.

Salt Creek is today's Nephi.[14]

[*Oct.*] *Saturday. Drove 15 miles. Roads good to Rattlesnake Creek and camped. In the evening some Horses and mules straid away.*

[*Oct.*] *12 Sunday. Very hard frost. Found the animals that straid last night. Laid by for rest.*

[*Oct.*] *13 Monday. Crossed the dividing ridge between Yoab Valley and the Sevire* [*Sevier*] *River, a stream about 6 rods* [*100 feet*] *wide and three feet deep, a little rily. We think it is caused by the late rain. Found the road good. Made twelve miles and camped on the bank of the river. Good grass.*

[*Oct.*] *14 Tuesday. Crossed a range of low mountains from the river to Increase Valley, so named by us on account of their being a birth in the company. The valley is ten or twelve miles long and 4 wide surrounded by mountains. Drove 14 miles. Found good water and grass about a mile East of the road and camped at the foot of the mountain. Had good roads.*

This was Round Valley, where today's Scipio is located.[15]

[*Oct.*] *15 Wednesday. Morning very cold. Froze hard. Found Mrs DeMasters and her young daughter doing well, so we started at the usal time and went on our way rejoicing. Drove over a mountain (assent very gradual and decent also) into Sevire* [*Sevier*] *Valley, a large beautiful valley. Passed Ceder Spring about two miles and camped by a small creek. Evening warm and pleasant. The road rockey in a few places.*

[*Oct.*] *16 Thursday. Drove 17 miles. Passed two creeks. Road good. Camped by a small creek surrounded by willow bushes. Poor grass. One of the company traded a gun for a horse with an Indian, contrary to a rule of the company.*

[*Oct.*] *17 Friday. Got up our cattle to start. Three head was missing. Searched the bushes in vain. At last the tracks were found followed by an Indian. Twelve men were armed and mounted and sent in persuit.*

---

[14] Lyman, *Overland Journey*, 3.

[15] Ibid., 4.

Returned in night with two oxen. The cattle were not found. It was ascertained that they were driven away by the Indian that traded for the gun and [——] [——] to which he belonged. By which strategem he [——] [——] [increased] the value of his horse. The company suffering notwithstanding.

[Oct.] 19 Saturday. Drove about 25 miles. No water on the way. Fore part of the road deep dust or sand, the latter part very mountainous. One long steep decent with two short steep assents. After dark came to Willow Spring. Good water and grass. One ox gave out. The rest stood it well. Some dissatisfaction in the company, a part wanting to drive faster than the others. Passed pumis stones in several places.

[Oct.] 20 Sunday. Morning 8 wagons left the company and went on. We which remained laid by for rest.

Stopping on the Sabbath may have been a rule decided upon by the company, to be maintained whenever practical. Certainly it was one that Washington preferred, which is evident by his comments earlier in the diary. Although one of the most common rules, it was also one that led to much dissension. In their anxiety to cover more miles, many emigrants did not see the value of resting their animals—even after one ox had given out the day before.

[Oct.] 21 Monday. Drove 8 miles to Walkers incampement. Found the Indians very friendly. They urged us to stop and trade. Omommah a yong chief, Walker's son, speaks English tolerable well. So we spent the day and traded for Deer Skins and some meat. At night they gave us a war dance. Exhibited two scalps taken from the Snake Indians with whom they are at war. All retired to rest a little after 10 oclock.

Washington had met famous Ute Chief Wakara, also called Walker, and apparently his son at their camp on Willow Creek. There were some obvious language difficulties between the parties. The name Washington wrote looks more like Ammon, Wakara's half-brother, who succeeded him as chief.[16] The Macy-Cheesman party arrived shortly after the Peck train, and he also reported meeting Wakara's son, but he interpreted the name as Como, and said Como had learned English when he lived for a time with Brigham Young. Wakara's relationship with Brigham Young

[16] Ibid., 113.

began on good terms when he initially helped Young establish the community of Manti. Problems from earlier in 1850 had settled down, so at this particular time, the situation was peaceful. Wakara had a reputation for stealing horses in California from the Spanish Ranchos and for selling captured Indian children as slaves. By 1853 the deteriorating relationship with the Mormons led to the Walker War, which broke out after Wakara realized that Young's settlements throughout Ute lands were eventually going to destroy the Utes' ability to survive.[17]

During the meeting, some of the men in the Peck wagon train traded for horses, but Cheesman declined, and after a visit to Wakara's tent, which contained a number of Snake Indian scalps, he also declined their offer to stay overnight, preferring to catch up to the rest of the train.

[Oct.] 22 *Tuesday. Drove out to the creek and camped. Feed poor. Country very rough and mountainous. Road good. No very steep places. Very dusty. The cattle being disposed to ramble on account of the feed being poor, we had to put all hands on guard two hours each.*

[Oct.] 23 *Wednesday. Morning drove up our cattle at break of day and drove to Beaver Creek, a fine stream, one rod* [16 *feet*] *wide and one foot deep, 3 miles and stoped to breakfast. Plenty of grass. Was visited by a number of Indians. Traded with them for some deer skins. About noon we started. By our* [*written*] *guide we had to drive 27 miles without water. But we expected to find a spring at 17 miles. Crossed a high ridge, the assent gradual for 6 miles to the sumit, then crossed several ravines, some steep places and the road rockey. Pumis stone in abundance all along through the mountains. Hard on Cattles feet. Stoped at sun set and camped. Good grass and plenty of wood. Held our election at Beaver Creek. Resulted in the reelection of the same officers.*

The Indians hunting in the area were some of Wakara's band. The Utes wanted to trade for flour and ammunition. Cheesman reported seeing the Ute smoke signals, which told them that the wagon train was being watched. He wrote, "We were telegraphed through as we passed through different valleys, by fires built on mountain points and answered by others in the distance. At night we were especially watchful lest they might raid our camp."[18]

[17] Foy, *Cheesman Memoirs*, 288–89; and Bancroft, *History of Utah*, 474.

[18] Foy, *Cheesman Memoirs*, 289.

Crampton and Madsen, authors of *In Search of the Spanish Trail,* identified the dry stretch through which the party passed as the Parowan Valley where the route from Salt Lake intersected with the Old Spanish Trail that had originated in Santa Fe.[19]

The guide Washington referred to may have been the *Mormon Way-Bill* written by Joseph Cain and A. C. Brower, who had traveled the route in 1849.[20] It was promoted by the *Deseret News,* which stated flatly that it was not safe to go the southern route "without written instructions, unless you have a pilot, on account of the deserts, diverging tracks, etc."[21]

[Oct.] 24 *Thursday. Morning intended to start at break of day but was bothered in finding our cattle so that the sun was up when we started. Drove over some rough rockey places and down some deep ravines to the valley of the Little Salt Lake. But when we came to the spring, it was so low that it would have taken about two hours to water our stock. We were obliged to drive on without water to a small stream to the left of the road about a mile and about two miles before we reached the creek spoken of on our guide. Camped at 4 oclock, having drove about 25 miles over the roughest road that we found since we started without water. Hard fare, no mistake. A Horse straid during the night. It had been got in a traid with an Indian about 30 miles back. Two young men went back in search of them.*

The route that the wagon train has been following would later be called the Mormon Corridor. A string of Mormon communities was established along the corridor over the next ten years, extending from Salt Lake City to San Bernardino.[22]

[Oct.] 25 *Friday. Morning found that the Indian's had stolen two horses during the night, one of very little value, the other a good one. Drove on to the South Kanyon Creek and camped, having made 12 miles. In the evening the young men returned with the stray horse.*

[Oct.] 26 *Saturday. Laid by. Our hunters went out, some to the mountain and some to the Lake. No game to be found in the mountains. At the lake fowl very plenty but difficult to get at. A few ducks brought in.*

---

[19] Crampton and Madsen, *In Search of the Spanish Trail,* 69–70.

[20] Hafen and Hafen, *Journals of Forty-Niners,* Appendix, 321.

[21] *Salt Lake Deseret News,* Nov. 2, 1850, 149.

[22] Wexler and Braun, *Atlas of Westward Expansion,* 105; and Beck and Haase, *Historical Atlas,* 39.

[Oct.] 27 Sunday. Observed as a day of rest. Was overtaken by six wagons. Dr Macy, Pepper and Co was admitted into the company. They had 21 men, four women and five children.

The Macy-Cheesman party had caught up to the main wagon train.

[Oct.] 28 Monday. Drove on over a low ridge to a spring. Stoped to dinner, after which we continued on to near Muddy Creek. Found water and exelent grass and camped. Two wagons and three men was ahead which wanted to lead the company on faster than they wished to go and they drove onto the creek about two miles ahead of us. At 12 oclock a messenger came in great haste stating that the Indians had got all their horses, but one, and feared that all hands would be killed. A company of ten armed themselves and went with all haste to the place of combat. Found all the horses on the way, but to the great disappointment of the [men], no Indians were to be found, and we very much dout their being any near. All it amounted to was that their horses being used to a large company, when left alone, were uneasy and took fright and ran off a short distance, when the men (poor fellows) thought that they were surrounded with Indians. However, we hope that it will cure them.

[Oct.] 29 Tuesday. Crossed Muddy Creek, which we had to make a bend in the road of about four miles to find a ford and drove on to Antilope Springs. Where we left the valley of Little Salt Lake, a beautiful valley of more than 40 miles long, but a large portion of it cannot be irrigated, their not being sufficient water in the streams. The mountains are not so high as they are further north, but few of the peaks are streaked with snow. A little cottonwood timber on Muddy Creek. Large quantities of oar [ore] in the vicinity of Antilope Springs, pronounced by those that profes to be judges, very rich silver oar.

Cheesman wrote, "At Antelope Springs, we were apprehensive of trouble from the Indians. This is one of the places that we were cautioned to watch closely by Mr. Hudson at Salt Lake."[23]

The ore that Washington described was iron ore, which led to the founding of Parowan within a few months.[24]

[Oct.] 30 Wednesday. Morning started on a drive of 28 miles without

[23] Foy, *Cheesman Memoirs*, 289.

[24] Bancroft, *History of Utah*, 316.

water through a beautiful valley 15 or 20 miles wide. Very little grass. No stream that we could see. Surface a little rooling [rolling]. We found ourselves agreeably disappointed by finding a spring about half way and a little beyond, bunch grass. Found a note posted up for our benefit by the company ahead stating that the Indians are bad. The company before them had two head of cattle killed by the Indians arrows. A little rain in the afternoon and evening.

Crampton and Madsen's study of the trail noted that this was where Barney Ward's shortcut left the Old Spanish Trail and turned west toward Death Valley.[25] Following a track across this desolate region was extremely difficult, even on the main trail. Jefferson Hunt's son recalled that "we found the directions very hard to follow, and lost the trail so often and spent so much time hunting it again, that we finally ran out of provisions before we . . . reached . . . Las Vegas."[26]

In spite of having been warned by those ahead of them that the Indians in this area were "bad," some members in the train were remarkably naïve in dealing with them. Cheesman related that after meeting a group of Indians, some of the young men in the company were having such a good time with them that they invited a couple of "young bucks" to come along with the train and spend the night in their tents. In the middle of the night the Indians went to the guns stacked outside a wagon and took two or three, only those belonging to the young men. This encounter could have had tragic consequences. There were no further invitations issued for sleepovers, nor did the young men get any sympathy.[27]

Cheesman's story is an example of the details Washington omitted from his diary. With the responsibility for the train on his shoulders, Washington had to resolve day-to-day problems and listen to concerns and complaints, which left him less time to write in his journal.

[Oct.] 31 Thursday. Drove on to the creek. Road exelent with a little sprinkling of rain. Heavy shower in the night.

Nov 1 Friday. Road heavy. Quite muddy and hilly near the divide. Several showers of rain. Day unpleasant. Reached the spring on the rim of the Great basin of California having drove 14 miles.

---

[25] Crampton and Madsen, *In Search of the Spanish Trail*, 72–73.

[26] Hafen and Hafen, *Journals of Forty-Niners*, 25.

[27] Foy, *Cheesman Memoirs*, 291.

The wagon train had arrived at Mountain Meadows, site of the infamous 1857 Mountain Meadows Massacre during which Mormons and Indians killed over 120 people during the conflict and turmoil of the Utah War.[28]

[Nov.] 2 *Saturday. Having good feed, we stoped to rest. Heavy shower before day. Morning cold. Showers of rain through the day. Snow in the afternoon.*

[Nov.] 3 *Sunday. Morning about three inches of snow and more coming. Prospect gloomy. Concluded that we could not better our condition by going on, but on the contrary, we might not find wood and grass. Sage would be very poor fuel in the snow, so we decided to remain another day.*

Cheesman recorded that they got a foot of snow and he was quite anxious to cross the Great Basin before they got snowed in.[29] The wagon train remained for three days in the rain, then snow, waiting for a break in the weather.

The miserable weather was insignificant compared to what lay ahead for Alexander and Eliza Fancher and their seven children. Seven years later, the entire family was murdered here in the Mountain Meadows Massacre. Two younger Fanchers who were born after 1850 were among the seventeen small children who survived.[30]

[Nov.] 4 *Monday. Four inches of snow. Weather fine. Drove on. Roads bad. Deep mud in places. Made 5 miles.*

[Nov.] 5 *Tuesday. Morning very cold. High wind from the south. Held our Election for officers. Resulted in the reelection of the same officers. Drove over some high ridges and decended into a deep ravine. Road exceeding good for the country through which it passes. No snow except on the highest mountains. Our incampment is very unfavourable for defence against the Indians, being surrounded by hills and bushes.*

[Nov.] 6 *Wednesday. Day pleasant. Drove over a very mountainous country, our road running down the Santa Clary, a small rapid stream 20 miles from the spring on the divide, crowded between two huge mountains. Which made our road crooked having to cross the stream a*

[28] See Bagley, *Blood of the Prophets* and Juanita Brooks's *Mountain Meadows Massacre* for in depth history of this event.

[29] Foy, *Cheesman Memoirs*, 291.

[30] Bagley, *Blood of the Prophets*, 60, 386–89.

great many times and drove over rocks, loose sand, through thick willow bushes and cottonwood trees, about 14 miles and camped with very little grass. Found wild grapes and squashes or goards in abundance.

[Nov.] 7 Thursday. Continued down the creek 6 or 7 miles. Thick bushes most of the way. Some loose sand. Passed some singular looking sandstone rocks, red and white, yesterday and today, with some curious holes or caves. Camped at a spring 25 miles from where we first came to the Santa Clary. The last 25 miles is the most broken, mountainous, rockey, barren country that we have ever seen. The road remarkable good for the Place. Our cattles feet is getting tender. Bunch grass to the left, a mile south of the spring. At night was overtaken by 6 wagons & 26 men.

[Nov.] 8 Friday. Laid by and shod what cattle we could.

Whatever method the company used to shoe their cattle and oxen, it involved more work than Washington's brief entry implied. Shoeing oxen was quite different from shoeing horses. Cattle do not balance very well on three legs and were usually pulled up into a sling at a farrier's shop. On the trail, others methods had to be devised. One method was to lay the ox on its side with its feet tied. Another, described by Lydia Waters in 1855, involved the men digging a trench and then "somehow the animal was turned upside down into it to get at his hooves safely." Washington did not record whether they had metal shoes, which were made in two parts because of the splayed hooves, or they used alternates, which Mattes described as either nailing sole-leather on the hooves or "after smearing the hooves with tar, buffalo hide boots were fastened on."[31]

[Nov.] 9 Saturday. Morning found our cattle quite refreshed. Soon after we started, we commenced the assent of a mountain up a narrow Kanyon. Assent gradual for about five miles when we reached the summit and decended about fourteen miles gradually to a large valley, then about six miles to the Rio Virgen, a rapid stream about 4 rods [65 feet] wide and a foot and a half deep. Water ryly. The road we found rockey and gravely, very hard on the feet of our stock. Arived at the river at nine oclock at night having drove 24 miles without feed or water. Turned our stock loose and went to bed without placing a guard, quite a risk in this

[31] Mattes, *Great Platte River Road*, 40, 562. Refers to Lydia M. Waters, "Account of a Trip Across the Plains in 1855."

Indian country. When we approached [——] valley, the barrenness of the country was distressing to behold. Mountains instead of being to some extent covered with cedar [——] and oak bushes presented nothing but bald rocks and the [——] entirely destitute of any feed for cattle. There were some small bushes that we have no name for and a very singular shrub or weed growing to the highth of 10 or 12 feet and some of them 12 inches in diameter branching out like a tree, each twig being about 1½ inches in diameter and covered leaves of a beautiful green, six inches long, pointing in every direction, being half an inch wide at the base and terminating in a stiff thorn at the point. Every years growth of leaves, instead of falling off, turned their points downward and remained for years. The trunk was a soft porous substance differing from any wood that I have seen. There is a great variety of the Cactus and Prickly Pear. The Pear grows to the size of large pumpkins and the Cactus to the hight of four feet branching out and forming a beautiful tree.

The company was crossing Utah Hill. The desolate scene before them was desert, which begins at this corner of Utah and extends west into California as far as Palmdale. In 1849 Jefferson Hunt identified the small shrubs as creosote bushes, which grew across the desert to Cajon Pass.[32] The "singular shrub" Washington described was a Joshua tree, which is specific to the Mojave Desert. The trail, as located by Crampton and Madsen, ran through a forest of Joshua trees.[33]

The prickly pear cactus Washington described was another source of problems for both people and animals. Most emigrants wore out numerous pairs of shoes during the long walk, which could rarely be replaced while on the trail. Seven-year-old Benjamin Bonney recalled that during his crossing in 1845: "We children were barefooted and I can remember yet how we limped across the desert, for we cut the soles of our feet on the prickly pears. . . . They also made the oxen lame, for the spines would work in between the oxen's hoofs."[34]

[Nov.] 10 Sunday. Morning found the cattle and all right. Spent the day resting our cattle, washing, etc.

[Nov.] 11 Monday. The company split, eleven wagons and one cart

[32] Hafen and Hafen, *Journals of Forty-Niners*, 83.

[33] Crampton and Madsen, *In Search of the Spanish Trail*, 79–80.

[34] Werner, *Pioneer Children*, 19.

went on and left the company in consequence of some restless spirits that wanted to go faster than the majority thought prudent. Towards night we drove about three miles down the [Virgin] river over very heavy loose sand and found good feed and camped.

[Nov.] 12 Tuesday. Continued our way down the river about nine miles over very loose sand and gravil. Crossed the stream eight times, and drove over a point of bluff by which we avoided two more crossings. One of the wagons in the company that left us that was ahead of us upset into the river and lost a number of things. Found first rate feed on the left of the road by the river and camped.

The trail was crossing the northwest corner of Arizona into Nevada. The southern route basically followed the current route of I-15 from Salt Lake City to Las Vegas.

The missing words in the next few entries are due to excessive damage to the original diary which has corners broken off.

[Nov.] 13 Wednesday. Continued our course down the river over a sandy road about ten miles. Found the [——] [——] [——] we had it yesterday.

[Nov.] 14 Thursday. Proceeded down the river road [——] [——]. We are now near the point where we leave [the Virgin River. We have been] following its windings for forty miles, We have [——] [——] disappointed in finding the feed better than we [have. In] short we have found the feed good on the river. [——] [——] mountains are very high. Several of the peaks are [——] [——] snow. On the right there are high mountains at a distance. [——] flats of the river are more than a mile wide in places. In others the high barren cliffs of conglomerate rocks shut in very near together. The stream, persuing a zigzag course, obliges the traveler to cross it twenty times. The fording is good in most places. In high water it would be very difficult. We find a great change in the climate. The nights are cool but the days are warm and pleasant, very seldom a cloud to obscure the suns rays for a moment. The misquitoes are singing about our ears. Four teams, Dr. Macy and Co. left us today to our great joy. Very little timber on this stream, a few cottonwoods, willows and a shrub called miskeet, resembling the locust, the leaves being smaller and thorns sharper.

The wagon train had arrived at Halfway Wash where the Virgin River turned south away from the Old Spanish Trail.[35]

Washington's joy at the Macy-Cheesman company departure revealed some level of friction between them, but it was also unusual because Washington rarely criticized anyone. Cheesman never mentioned it.

[Nov.] 15 Friday. *Morning left the river taking up a canyon the bed of a dry creek, about six miles over loose sand and gravil, being heavy on teams, to the foot of a very long steep hill. Most of the way up very deep sand. About two hundred feet at the top was an elevation of about forty five degrees. We reached the sumit about an hour after sunset and drove on (the moon being near the full) 6 or 7 miles. Found a little grass and stoped untill day light and then proceeded on to water. Found the road first rate to the brink of a steep long hill, which we had to decend over sharp rocks. Then we proceeded over a sandy road about two miles to Muddy Creek. The Spanish name is Rio de lo Angeles (river of the Angels) twenty miles from Rio Virgen, the hardest road on teams for a dry one that I ever saw. Here we were met by a number of Indians of the Pautah* [Paiute] *tribe. They are a strong robust set of men nearly naked, armed with bows and arrows. Perfectly ignorant.* [——] [——] [——]. *Appear to be very poor. Set a great* [——] [——] *skins, we suppose on account of game being* [——] [——].

Edward Leo Lyman, author of *Overland Journey from Utah to California*, explained that these pioneers now faced "the most challenging long roadway in the history of U.S. pioneering . . . the nation's most difficult wagon road . . . [particularly] the insufficient livestock feed and water."[36] The climb up Virgin Hill was the steepest place on the entire trail.[37] The fact that they did not arrive at the summit until after sunset indicates how difficult it was. Cheesman described how they had to double and triple team their oxen to haul the wagons up onto the first bench and then drove the cattle up the second pitch and just over the summit. There they fastened the wagons, one at a time, to as many as twenty yokes of oxen to pull the wagon over the summit. When they took Dr. Macy's wagon up, one of the chains broke, and "the wagon shot down the mountain like an

[35] Crampton and Madsen, *In Search of the Spanish Trail*, 81.

[36] Lyman, *Overland Journey*, 1.

[37] Crampton and Madsen, *In Search of the Spanish Trail*, 81.

arrow, but cramped and upset and fortunately went no further." Macy's wagon had one of their most valuable goods—his medicine chests—but little damage was done, so they gathered their belongings and tried again and got the wagon over successfully. Cheesman finished the day at "2 A.M. when we got the last wagon up. We were all worn out."[38]

[Nov.] 16 Saturday. [——] [——] in resting our teams and prepairing for crossing [——] [——] 50 mile desert which we expect to s[t]art on Tuesday Our cattle are very weary as well two of our oxen being lame. [——] visited today by the Indians. They appear very friendly.

[Nov.] 17 Sunday. [——] that overtook on the 7th and Dr. Macy & Co that left us on the 14th [——] was overtaken by a company of ten teams. Concluded not to start on the desert till Wednesday morning hoping that our cattle will get well. They appear to be mending.

[Nov.] 19 Tuesday. Drove about two miles. Crossed the creek (a stream of twelve feet wide and 3 ft deep) the last point at which water is to be obtained before entering the Great Desert. Filled our water casks preparatory to starting in the morning. Our cattle is better, but I fear that one of mine will not be able to stand so hard a drive as that before us. Bought 10 lbs of bacon this morning of one of the men that overtook us yesterday for 40 cents per lb. Held our election for officers this morning. Resulted in the reelection of the same officers. One of Mr Peppers horses was not found. It was of no use on the road.

[Nov.] 20 Wednesday. At nine oclock we started. The day was unusually cool. Drove about 20 miles. Stoped at 7 oclock on some bunch grass. Let our stock grase and rest til one oclock [A.M.], then drove until day light about 12 miles. Stoped 2½ hours, breakfasted, turned the stock on some bunch grass to the left of the road. When we hitched up, we dealt out the water that we brought with us, a little over two gallons to each animal that worked. Those that were loose got none. Then drove on without stoping until six oclock when, to our great joy, we arrived at Vegas Springs with all the animals that we started with and only three or four that lag[g]ed. The springs is in a large valley of rich land surrounded with mountains. Water good, a little warm, and abundance of exelent grass with plenty of miskeet bushes for wood, a first rate place to stop and recruit stock. The road, except a very little sand, is hard and good wheeling with, but

[38] Foy, *Cheesman Memoirs*, 293–94.

few hills. No steep one to assend. One high one to decend, not very steep. [——] [——] the road is gravil and sharp rocks. Very bad on the [feet] of cattle. Quite a number appear tender. We found a note left by the company ahead of us stating the time of their arrival by which it appears that they were forty hours in crossing and left one wagon and one ox. The ox was brought in by two of our company. We crossed in thirty three hours and brought all our property and stock safe over.

The wagon train had crossed a fifty-mile waterless stretch of desert that historians Crampton and Madsen described as following "up the wide California Wash for 27 miles and then [it] crosses broken country for about 12 miles to . . . the edge of Las Vegas Valley. . . . [It] was one of the most difficult places on the Spanish Trail for both men and animals."[39]

Washington's comment that the gravel and sharp rocks were hard on the cattle's feet was echoed in Jefferson Hunt's diary from the year before, when he wrote that "they were covered with sharp points and corners, are very hard black and shining. . . . This is the worst days travel we have had for our cattle's feet, those that are barefooted cripple very much."[40] Geologist John Peck suspects that they were quartzite or volcanic rocks that were coated with "desert varnish," which was "a coating of manganese and iron compounds that form over thousands of years on the surface of rocks having a significant amount of silica. . . . The blacker and more shiny the surface coating, the longer the surface has been exposed to arid weather."[41]

[Nov.] 22 Friday and Saturday. Laid by to rest our stock which appear to injoy it well. Saturday night the company in the rear came up after being 48 hours on the desert. Their stock appear very tired. They left 2 head.

The rear company was the Macy-Cheesman party.[42]

[Nov.] 24 Sunday. Moved up to the head of the spring, about 4 miles. The day cloudy with high wind.

[Nov.] 25 Monday. Found the road gravil and rockey and up hill almost all day. Decended near night in to a valley between two moun-

[39] Crampton and Madsen, *In Search of the Spanish Trail*, 87–88.

[40] Hafen and Hafen, *Journals of Forty-Niners*, 91.

[41] John H. Peck, consulting geologist, e-mail message to author, Sept. 29, 2002.

[42] Foy, *Cheesman Memoirs*, 294.

tains. Found good feed between two springs, water in holes. Rained a little in the afternoon. Turned cold and snowed on the mountains. Made 18 miles.

Cheesman identified one of the springs as Cottonwood Springs (present day Blue Diamond, Nevada) where they camped on a grassy place that caught fire from their campfire and they "came near being burned up." They reacted quickly and were able to put it out.[43]

[*Nov.*] *26 Tuesday. Morning very cold wind, high from the north. Drove uphill nearly all day to cross a high range of mountains, some places steep up and down. The country has changed its appearance. The nut pine and ceder has again appeared on the sides of the mountains in considerable quantities. Two oxen in company gave out and one horse. The horse was of no value. Made ten miles. Camped soon after we commenced the decent from the mountain. Very little feed, water good.*

They were crossing the Spring Mountains range, where the elevation of about 5,500 feet was the Old Spanish Trail's highest altitude in Nevada.[44]

Everyone in the Macy-Cheesman party suffered as they struggled up to the summit. All, including the smallest children, had been walking for most of the last hundred miles to lessen the loads, but their cattle were about used up. The situation worsened when they encountered snow at the summit. By then the younger ones were crying from their sore, cold feet. When Cheesman faced the same lack of fodder that Washington noted, he emptied the grass from their tick (mattress) to feed to his cattle.[45]

[*Nov.*] *27 Wednesday. Morning ground froze. Started late. Found the road down the bed of a dry creek for 5 or 6 miles over gravil, mostly hard and good. Continued the decent all day. Camped after dark on a place of hard gravil without sufficient vegitation to support a grasshopper. Road on the whole favourable on the feet of our animals.*

[*Nov.*] *28 Thursday. Started at daylight. Drove about five miles crossing a great number of gullies washed by the rains and melting snows. Passed Willow Spring. Found sufficient water for our stock but no grass.*

---

[43] Ibid.

[44] Crampton and Madsen, *In Search of the Spanish Trail*, 93.

[45] Foy, *Cheesman Memoirs*, 295.

The little that grew around the spring was all eaten up by those companies that had gone before. We expected to find grass and water about five miles to the right of the road, but was sadly disappointed. So we watered and rested till noon and drove on, having thirty miles to go to the next water. Found abundance of grass of an inferior quality at seven miles and camped. Left one of the oxen that gave out day before yesterday. Some of the men in the company of Dr Macy and Heath came up to us at the spring and reported that the teams are very tired and some have gave out, and it is doubtful if they are able to get them all to the water. Willow Spring is in a large valley surrounded by high mountains. In this valley it appears as if the godess of desolation and barrenness has erected her throne and reigns without a rival.

As the wagon train left Nevada and entered California, the Old Spanish Trail crossed the heart of the desert region.[46] Historian Edward Leo Lyman corrected Washington's location. They were at Stump Springs, not Willow Springs, and the valley surrounding them was later named Pahrump Valley.[47]

The men who feared that some of the Macy-Cheesman animals would not survive were right. Cheesman wrote that "we were journeying along slowly all on foot about 10 A.M., when all at once a wheel ox dropped dead. . . . I had regarded this as one of the best oxen in the team, one most likely to stand the journey through. We all collected around him almost with tears in our eyes and saw him breathe his last. Poor Bright was gone."[48]

[Nov.] 29 *Friday. Morning drove on the road assending for several miles where we decended a steep long hill into another valley. Road good till within about two miles of where we left the valley where it has been washed in small gullies, having the rocks and gravil bare to the foot of the mountain which we had to cross. Here we had to assend a long steep rockey hill, very hard on team. When we reached the sumit, we immediately commenced the decent, very steep and rockey for considerable distance when we entered the bed of a dry creek and continued to decend over rocks and gravil for about five miles where we decended into a narrow valley and soon found good grass and water a little after dark.*

[46] Crampton and Madsen, *In Search of the Spanish Trail*, 97.

[47] Lyman, *Overland Journey*, 9.

[48] Foy, *Cheesman Memoirs*, 296–97.

We have traveled, according to our guide, 90 miles in five days, crossed four ranges of mountains with only one place of good feed and but three watering places interveining. Our cattle tired, their feet tender, and their sides almost meeting for the want of food. This place is called by the Spainyards Archilite. Fremont called it Hernandez Spring on account of two men being killed by the Indians and their wifes taken prisoners a day or two before he arrived at the place, one of the men being of that name. Here we rested four days. Saw a man from Salt Spring from whome we assertained that a gold mine had been discovered at that place and two companies formed which are bringing on machinery for grinding the rocks and in a few days will be in operation. From this place three men of our company, C. Rumsey, H. Dwinger, and Asa Carrico shouldered their packs and went on to the settlement, distance about 200 miles. While incamped at this place we were overtaken, Dr Macy, Heath and company. Their in very bad condition, some left on the way and seven others died after their arrival here.

After their exhausting past few days and this day's crossing of Emigrant Pass, the company stopped for four days to rest themselves and their cattle.

Washington had time to write extra notes in his diary. His reference to an incident during Fremont's trip in 1844 implied that he had some knowledge of Fremont's report, or perhaps some time to visit with others in the area that knew the history. This spring was also called Resting Spring.[49]

Dec 4 Wednesday. Morning concluded to move on about 8 miles to Saleratus Creek and spent two days in exploring the mountains to see if anything could be discovered in the gold line. Found the road assending for about three or four miles over sand and loose gravil, then decended a very steep rockey hill to the creek. Continued down the creek about two miles and camped.

This was likely the Armagosa River, which was so alkaline that it was not safe for the cattle to drink. It had saleratus deposits along the bank.[50]

[Dec.] 5 Thursday. Three teams drove on, Mr's [Misters] Moseley,

[49] Crampton and Madsen, *In Search of the Spanish Trail*, 98–99.
[50] Ibid., 100–101.

Blodgett and Fancher, we being out of danger of Indians. Day cold with high wind from the north.

The perception that they were out of danger from the Indians was false. They were likely shadowed every step of the way across the desert. Ongoing thefts of horses by Wakara's Utes and Mojave Indians were bitterly and loudly denounced by the owners of ranchos in the areas south of Cajon Pass, who lost thousands of horses and cattle, and occasional lives to them, before, during, and after this year.[51]

[Dec.] *6 Friday. Made no discoverys in the gold line. Are prepairing to start on the morrow. Day warm and pleasant. Nights cold.*

After the Pecks spent one day looking for gold, they moved on. It is unclear whether they had illusions of being able to find gold nuggets easily or whether Washington had allowed Egerton and Edmond a chance to look for gold as more of a day's entertainment. After being so long on the road, the boys would have been anxious to start prospecting.

[Dec.] *7 Saturday. According to appointment, we started. Continued down the creek about six miles, most of the way over rocks or gravil. Left the creek and commenced an assent which we have to continue for forty miles. Had several miles of loose drifting sand to cross. Very hard on teams. Arived at Salt Springs about sunset. Found the grass nearly all eaten up and the water very salt[y]. Here are two companies commercial mining, with what success we know not. But certain we are that it must be a rich mine that will pay for working in this place 220 miles from Publo de Los Angeles, the place from which their supplies must come, with a desert of 80 miles to cross. Provisions and labour very high. It looks to us like a poor prospect.*

Lyman identified the mine at Salt Springs as the Amargosa Mine.[52] Addison Pratt had discovered gold here in 1849 while traveling with Jefferson Hunt. It fueled a small gold rush early in 1850, which is what Washington was describing, but Gwinn Harris Heap of the Beale Survey reported that by 1853 it had been abandoned. He wrote, "A fortune had been sunk by men who were sufficiently deluded . . . to abandon the rich mines of California, travel across 150 miles of desert, and live . . . in

[51] Cleland, *Cattle on a Thousand Hills*, 64–71; and Hafen and Hafen, *Old Spanish Trail*, 236–57.

[52] Lyman, *Overland Journey*, 205.

a spot so desolate and forlorn that there is actually not sufficient vegetation to keep a goat from starvation."[53]

[Dec.] *8 Sunday. Morning started about 8 oclock. Found the road good through the day with a light assent. In the evening had the road more stoney and washed in small gullies. Drove till ten. Stoped and coraled our cattle till four in the morning when we rolled on. Found the road rough, the assent increasing for several miles. When we approached a pass in a low mountain when we found the road smoth and graviley, which continued till we passed the mountain about a mile. Here we had one short hill. When we reached the summit, our cattle tired, hungary and thirsty, no water and not a blade of grass, nor have we seen any since we left Salt Spring. Here we stoped and rested our cattle a short time and got breakfast and then drove on two or three miles and, to our inexpressible joy, found water in some holes in a flat to the left of the road and grass about two miles in the same direction. Never did our cattle need it more.*

The wagon train was climbing up to Silurian Lake, a dry white playa (the flat central floor of a desert basin) two and a half miles long before coming to Red Pass. The bright reflection off the white surface was blinding in intensity.

When Heap came through here in August of 1853 with Beale, he described the heat as almost unbearable. "Their guns became almost too hot to touch, and the wind, laden with sand, blew in their faces."[54] The intense August heat is the reason the emigrants had not left Salt Lake until October. Crampton and Madsen wrote that this stretch of the Spanish Trail remains "remote and isolated from the world at large . . . deep in the Mojave Desert."[55]

[Dec.] *10 Tuesday. Stoped and rested our teams. Here we met a man by the name of Brown, a citizen of Salt Lake, on his return home from the mines, alone with 5 horses and mules. One of his horses feet was very tender. He offered five dollars for two shoes putting on. We had no blacksmith in company. I had a few shoes and nails, so I undertook the job and succeeded to his satisfaction and received five dollars for it. Also*

[53] Crampton and Madsen, *In Search of the Spanish Trail*, 102–103.

[54] Ibid., 107.

[55] Ibid., 104–106.

met some packers with supplies for the mining companies. The accounts from the mines are not very flatering for minerals, but the prospects for keeping a boarding house is good.

[Dec.] 11 *Wednesday. Drove on to Bitter Spring, 8 miles, and water[ed] our stock. Filled our kegs and drove a mile and a half to some grass on the left on the foot of the mountain and camped.*

Bitter Springs was the first sure water after leaving Salt Springs. The bitter taste came from the high sulphate content.[56]

In researching for his book on this route, Edward Leo Lyman noted that Washington Peck's diary is "virtually the only trail diary detailing travel down Spanish Canyon and across the next stretch." They were facing a grade "long afterward known as Impassable Pass."[57]

[Dec.] 12 *Thursday. Morning drove our stock to the spring and watered them and then started on the desert, 35 miles. Heavy sand for about 3 miles when the sand was changed for gravil, rather soft in places. Our road was a steady assent for 14 miles, rising at least 150 ft per mile, and much of the way the wheels sinking half the depth of the fellow in the sand or gravil. Sun shined hot and our cattle felt it miserbly. We were obliged to rest often and drive slow. Reached the summit about 8 oclock* [P.M.]. *Here we had a steep hill to decend and drove about 2 miles and camped. Corralled our cattle. Started about four oclock in the morning. Road soft and sandy. At 8* [A.M.] *we stoped a short time for breakfast. Turned our cattle on a little course bunch grass, the connecting link between grass and shrubbery. Then continued our march until two oclock when we reached the long wished for Mohave River, a point greatly to be desired as it is the termination of the Great Desert. When we arrived at this point, we felt like the mariner that had long been tossed on dangerous and almost unknown seas when he arrives into port after all the dangerous points are past and the place of his destination near at hand. We have traveled 683 miles from the City of Great Salt, in which we have crossed a desert of 260 miles with only ten watering places intervening and a great part of the water salt bitter and strongly impregnated with alkali, the grass mostly of an inferior quality and scarse. The remnant of the company that remains had sixty cattle in the start, five*

[56] Ibid., 106–107.

[57] Lyman, *Overland Journey*, 12, 79.

of which has perished on the desert or one twelveth. One large company last year lost one fourth on the same desert and some has lost more than that this year. I have 15 head, not one of which has tired, and they all look nearly as well as they did when we started. The reason that I assign is that I have traveled lighter, whipped less, and always attended to my cattle to see that they had as good grass and water as their was to be had. We are now 98 miles from the settlement, with grass and water every few miles, except one place of 25 miles without water. The road from the sumit to the river decending all the way and good, except a little too much sand in places. This river sinks in places. Here is no water, only in holes, some cottonwood trees and willow bushes with a good supply of grass and some deer.

The wagon train had successfully avoided one of the most serious dangers of this desert crossing, getting lost. In 1848 Orville Pratt reported that they missed the trail in this area, became lost, and then could not find water.[58] From Washington's reference to the "remnant of the company," he revealed that most of those in the original wagon train had gone on ahead.

[Dec.] 14 Saturday. Laid by and rested our teams. Our hunters were unsuccessful. Day warm and showery. This morning Dr Macy, Heath, and company came up, their teams badly used up. They were ten hours longer on this desert than we were and their cattle came in 20 percent worse.

Cheesman wrote that "the poor oxen . . . were so worn out that they would scarcely go one-half mile, till some of them would tumble down. We would let them rest a few minutes, when one of the women would hold out . . . a bunch of grass, just far enough, so he would have to struggle to his feet to get it, in this way we would get them up again, and so move on a little distance further." They stopped to rest at the river for several days, thinking that their troubles were over.[59]

[Dec.] 15 Sunday. Our stock of provisions is so far exasted [exhausted] that we were obliged to keep doing [going], notwithstanding our cattle required more rest. Drove on 12 miles over a levil sandy road, part of

---

[58] Hafen and Hafen, *Old Spanish Trail* (Diary of Orville Pratt), 357.

[59] Foy, *Cheesman Memoirs*, 298–300.

the way heavy wheeling, but very favourable to the feet [of] our stock. Camped where the grass is abundant.

[Dec.] 16 Monday. Drove on a few miles when it came on to rain. Waited till it held up, then drove on again a short distance and camped when the rain poured down again, having made about seven miles. Road much the same as yesterday.

[Dec.] 17 Tuesday. Drove about sixteen miles. Crossed a low ridge to cut off a bend in the river. While on the sumit, we had a view of the Siery Nevada in a northwest direction, clad in garments of the purest white. Also some peaks of the east range in a south and south East direction, all white with snow. While partly surrounded with snow, it is mild here.

[Dec.] 18 Wednesday. I went ahead of the teams to hunt for deer. Saw abundance of tracks, but no deer. Made about ten miles and camped where there is very little grass, but what there is, is of the best quality.

[Dec.] 19 Thursday. Drove to the point where we leave the river. We have traviled what is called fifty miles up this river (long ones they are). It is a bold running stream at this place, six rods [100 feet] wide and one foot deep, and in about ten miles, it sinks [Mojave River Sink]. Then there is no water, only holes, as far as we have seen it, and, we suppose, much farther. There is some good land on the flats, but no water to irrigate, therefore it cannot be very productive. It might produce wheat, oats and barley without irrigation. The road is good most of the way and feed plenty, except in a few places. Very little timber for any purposes except fuel. The country on both sides is a barran desert.

Before leaving the river, Cheesman realized that two cows he had brought from Kansas were so weak they could go no farther, so "one I shot, the other I turned away and left. I had not the heart to shoot her." As they started on, the party found that the heavy sands slowed them and soon made it apparent that the few days rest had done little for their worn-out animals. Just before starting the day's climb to the summit of Cajon Pass through the San Bernardino Mountains, their best oxen, Bill, got stuck in a quagmire. Although they got him out, he was too weak to travel, so they had to leave him behind.[60]

[60] Ibid., 301.

While losing an animal at any time was difficult, it was heart breaking when it occurred near the end of the trail. Ester Hanna (1852) described her feelings when the mule she was riding "appeared to fail at every step and finally lay down on the roadside. . . . This noble animal that had been of so much service to us and worth so much to us if we got her through, laid down to die! I went on ahead with the mules. . . . Finally I saw them coming carrying her bridle. I knew then that it was all over with her. I burst into a flood of tears."[61]

[Dec.] 20 Friday. *Was delaid in finding our cattle till nine oclock. Drove until two oclock, then stoped and let our cattle grase an hour and a half on some bunch grass, the best that we have had since we left the rim of the basin. Then continued on expecting to reach the sumit in fifteen miles from the river, which would be a little after dark. The night was very cold. Froze hard, which made us more anxious to get over the sumit before we stoped as it would not freze so hard on the south side as we had a great decent to make in a short distance. So we continued on until 12 oclock [midnight] and stoped, turned our cattle loose on good bunch grass, supped, and went to bed.*

[Dec.] 21 Saturday. *Morning ground froze hard, so we waited til nine and started. Found it two miles to the sumit. This is the last range of mountains that we have to cross and expect that a few miles of travil will bring us into perpetual summer. As we approach the mountain, it is thickly wooded with live oak, small, scrubby, crooked, fit for no valuable use except fuel and to produce acorns, which they do in great abundance. Up to this point, the road is good. Here we make a steep decent to a narrow ridge, being only wider than the wagons, and the decent very steep on each side for three or four hundred feet, a frightful looking place. We followed this ridge for ten or fifteen rods [150–225 feet] and then made a long very steep decent of several hundred feet into a canyon which continues to decent for miles at a rapid rate. Reached the water in the afternoon. The patch of grass around it was nearly all eaten up. Our cattle was tired, so we concluded to stop til morning, having traviled 35 miles without water, being ten miles farther than we expected. After we crossed the mountain, we found a great variety of shrubs that we were not acquainted with and many of those that we had seen on the desert was much improved in size.*

[61] Allen, *Canvas Caravans*, 117.

This was Cajon Pass. Cheesman described the final few feet to the summit as so steep that they all helped to push the wagons up. At the top the ridge was so narrow that the front wheels were on one side and the rear wheels on the other. Cheesman unhitched all but one ox, locked the hind wheels, and "for a distance of fifty or sixty feet, it was so steep that the cattle and all slid down."[62]

Behind them, Wakara's Utes were on the trail. In January of 1851, Utes swooped down Cajon Pass, raided nearby ranches, and drove a band of 800 to 1,000 stolen horses back over the Old Spanish Trail. Although the owners chased after them and recovered most of their animals, by March Wakara was selling horses in Utah.[63]

[Dec.] 22 *Sunday. Drove on to find grass, which we can expect to find a little in 8 miles. Followed down the canyon, some of the way in the bed of the stream. Sand deep and heavy wheeling. Other places rocky. Reached a small patch of grass, but short grass, and turned out, dined and Shaved, what we have not done for eleven weeks past. Near night we drove on some four miles to a beautiful valley with abundance of exelent grass, good water and plenty of Sycamore timber for fuel. Here we overtook Mr Blodgett that left us at Alkali Creek.*

The beautiful valley was Sycamore Grove, and Cheesman described the excellent grass as "clover, nearly waist high." The Cheesmans reached here a week after the Pecks. Mr. Sanford, whom they had met a few days earlier freighting equipment to the gold mine, brought in their ox Bill, who had recovered enough to travel.

Here Cheesman saw "large bands of wild cattle. . . . I went out one day and did my best to kill one. I could not get near enough to them. . . . I shot several times but with no other effect than to cause a stampede. I was not aware of the danger I was in."[64] Theodore H. Hittell, author of a four-volume work on the *History of California*, described the old Spanish cattle as "long horned and fierce . . . and no one was safe in going much amongst them except on horseback."[65] In 1847 James S. Brown described being attacked: "On our march out, the wild cattle, which were there by

[62] Foy, *Cheesman Memoirs*, 301.

[63] Hafen and Hafen, *Old Spanish Trail*, 254–55.

[64] Foy, *Cheesman Memoirs*, 302.

[65] Hittell, *History of California*, 3:879.

thousands, became excited and began to bellow and crowd toward us. We could see them for miles coming on the run. They closed in quickly until we were surrounded by them on three sides, with a deep gulch . . . on the fourth." The men stayed in the gulch all night and could not safely leave until the next day.[66] Cheesman had been very fortunate.

[Dec.] 23 *Monday. Laid by to rest. Went on a hunting excursion, but returned unsuccessfull. Wind rose at night. Blew a gale all night.*

[Dec.] 24 *Tuesday. The gale continued. Drove fifteen miles to the Cocomongo Ranch, a beautiful location. Was politely received by Mr Prudon, the proprietor, a French man that got the ranch, five leagues of land or 34,560 acres, as a dowery with his wife. When we approached the house, a tremendious gust of wind came which forced* [us] *to rush into the house in an unceremonious manner. The same gust run a wagon belonging to the ranch over a precipice and smashed it to pieces. Our wagons was in a hollow which protected them. Drove into a hollow by a small stream and camped.*

Washington had brought the wagon train through in about the same number of days as Jefferson Hunt had the year before.[67]

Rancho Cucamonga was a Spanish land grant given to Tubercio Tapia and inherited by his daughter, Maria Merced, who had married Leon Victor Prudhomme.[68]

[Dec.] 25 *Wednesday. Christmas day. Waited to get a quarter of beef, but they made it so filthy in dressing it that I would not take it. Mr Pepper, one of the company, took a quarter and I took a few pounds of his. The beef is exelent, notwithstanding the feed is poorer at this season than at any other period of the year. This is properly the spring in this country. Vegetation is just starting since the late rains. The grass is short, but the Prairie is green and the flowers begin to appear. The weather is mild, but not hot, the nights cool with slight frosts occasionally, not hard enough to injure vegetation, only to retard its growth. This is truly a delightful climate.*

[Dec.] 26 *Thursday. Drove on over a beautiful country and not finding*

[66] Brown, *Life of a Pioneer*, 81–82.

[67] Beck and Haase, *Historical Atlas*, 33.

[68] Hafen and Hafen, *Journals of Forty-Niners*, 108.

water as soon as we expected, we continued to drive until after dark, when we came to a beautiful stream, crossed over and camped. Grass pretty fair.

[Dec.] 27 Friday. Drove to San Gabril Mission and camped. Here we found most of the company that left Salt Lake. This mission was founded about 70 years ago by the Jesuits and was once in a flourishing condition. It was said to contain at one time twenty thousand persons and had 300,000 head of cattle. But Tekel is written upon it. It has been going to ruin about thirty years. There are a few persons about it and 2 grey Friars. The fences are broken down. Vineyards and Pear and Olive orchards are laid waste. The only incloser that remains attached to the mission is an orange orchard. The prevailing opinion is that the land belongs to the United States government but will not be disposed of under the pre-emption law, consequently it offers but little inducement to Squaters. Provisions are very dear. Wheat $10 fanager [fanega, 1.6 bushels], 144 lb Corn 8, Butter $1 per lb, Pork 35 cts lb, No flour to be had at any price. Tea bread 25 cts. Beef cheap, $16 per head for fat cattle.

Washington was referring to the Biblical quotation in Daniel 5:27: "Tekel; Thou art weighed in the balances, and art found wanting." Once considered the pride of the missions, San Gabriel had been famous for its orchards and vineyards and at one time had over 26,000 cattle, 15,000 sheep and 2,400 horses.[69] The Secularization Act of 1833 dismantled the mission system, and the subsequent Mexican governors granted the lands to new owners. When the United States took over California in 1848, the Mexican land grants were exempted from the usual land sale procedure, which is what Washington was referring to. Thousands and thousands of acres were tied up in the courts for years and years while the United States Land Commission heard claims from previous owners.[70]

1 Jan, 1851 Wednesday. All well but we lacked the company of old friends. Day warm and pleasant. Thermometer up to 90 degrees in the middle of the day.

On January 5, the Macy-Cheesman party finally arrived. Cheesman wrote that the women, who had walked the last four hundred miles alongside the men, were sunburnt, "clothes nearly worn out, ragged and hag-

[69] Hafen and Hafen, *Old Spanish Trail*, 234.
[70] Robinson, *Land in California*. For a detailed history of land titles in California, see 100–109, 209.

gard," but the "health of all the company was remarkably good." Cheesman learned from Washington that there had been no deaths in the wagon train.[71] This was the final meeting place before the Pecks and Cheesmans went their separate ways. Whether they met again is not known.

Dr. Macy was delighted with what he saw in the Los Angeles area, so he decided to stay, but Cheesman booked passage on a steamship for his wife and baby and steamed north to San Francisco. When they reached San Francisco, Urania asked David to give up his quest for gold and stay in town to practice his law profession, but Cheesman could not resist the lure of the goldfields.[72]

[Jan.] 16 *Thursday. Having rested our teams and procured our provisions, we started (late in the day, haveing been detained in finding our cattle) intending to go through the Tulare Valley. Drove about seven miles and camped.*

Washington planned to travel along the eastern side of the Tulare and San Joaquin Valleys.

[Jan.] 17 *Friday. Morning found that one of the cows had calved and we had not found it, so we sent the cow and boys back for it. Here the property of Mr Pepper was taken on execution to satisfy a unjust demand, and to give him an opportunity to appeal, I receipted it. Afternoon the boys returned with the calf.*

Mr. Pepper was being challenged by a local rancher for ownership of a horse that Pepper had purchased from Chief Wakara. Wakara had stolen it from the Mexican rancho a few months earlier.[73]

[Jan.] 18 *Saturday. Morning started to drive a few miles to where we would find wood and wait the settlement of Peppers affairs. When we drove up the cattle, one of them was much bloted, having eaten two much clover, and after we started, one after another commenced bloating until we were obliged to unyoke several, and one of our best oxen we were obliged to pierce with a knife to let out the gas or wind, which soon relieved him, and we moved on very slow, letting the cattle rest often until we reached a good camping place, about seven miles, and stoped.*

[71] Foy, *Cheesman Memoirs*, 304.

[72] Ibid., 312–14, 319.

[73] Ibid., 307.

In January 1851 the Pecks left Mission San Gabriel and took the Coast route north to Nevada City, California, in the gold fields. Adapted from Charles F. Outland, *Stagecoaching On El Camino Real: Los Angeles to San Francisco, 1861–1901. Courtesy Arthur H. Clark Co.*

Here we received information that the Indians from the surrounding mountains had assembled in The Tulare Valley and were killing all the whites that fell in their way. So we determined to take the Coast road, which is about 200 miles farther, and avoid meeting these human tigers.

Washington's treatment of his oxen sounds rather drastic—plunging a knife into a bloated cow—but in fact, this treatment was detailed in an 1847 book by S. W. Cole, *The American Veterinarian or Diseases of Domestic Animals, Showing the Causes, Symptoms, and Remedies.* He wrote that bloat "is caused by turning cattle from short pastures, or when empty, upon luxuriant clover. They eat to excess, and as the large mass of food is not readily digested, fermentation takes place, evolving large quantities of carbonic gas; the stomach swells almost to bursting, pressing upon the lungs, and preventing their expansion, and if not relieved, the animal dies of suffocation." One method of treatment involved tapping, inserting a trocar on the left side between the last rib and hipbone, two to three inches deep, in order to reach the paunch and release the gas.[74]

Washington had learned of the Mariposa Indian War, which had erupted in a major fight on January 11 and resulted in Governor McDougal authorizing the formation of a militia unit on January 13 to carry on the fighting.[75]

[*Jan.*] *20, Monday. Egerton killed a deer in the afternoon. Mr Hadly (a man that we are takeing from this place to the mines to help drive our cattle) and myself went out to hunt and Hadly killed one. The deer is very plenty where there is timber or brush. The Indians does not hunt at all and the Mexicans very little.*

[*Jan.*] *22 Wednesday. I killed a deer. We have plenty of venison, which is very tender and sweet but not fat.*

[*Jan.*] *25 Saturday. Mr. Pepper has got his affairs settled and I am relieved.*

After the Mexicans showed their brands to the company, the matter was decided in favor of the Mexicans, but it was left up to the company

[74] Cole, *American Veterinarian*, 209–11.

[75] Hittell, *History of California*, 3:838–39; and Smith, "California and the Indian Wars: The Mariposa War."

as to how they would make it good. The exact details of the settlement were not recorded.[76]

[Jan.] 27 Monday. Drove about 2½ miles near where Daniel Springer of Delaware Canada corals his herd of cattle, as we intend to travil with him to the upper country.

Daniel Springer was from the Pecks' old neighborhood where the Springers were one of the original pioneer families.[77]

[Jan.] 31 Friday. Went up the mountain to hunt. Saw no game, but found the land exelent on the mountains as well as in the valley. Clover grass and wild oats growing luxurently, the oat in many places being [k]nee high.

Feb. 3 Monday. Made another start. Drove eleven miles and camped a mile beyond a spring in Oak openings, mostly white oak. Feed good. Day hot. Road good, some what dusty.

The Pecks were now traveling in a small group that consisted of ten men, Mercy, two wagons, and three herds of cattle. The identified men were Washington, Egerton, and Edmond Peck, Daniel Springer, Mr. Haskel, Mr. Pepper, and Mr. Hadley. Although not clearly described, their route seems to follow along the north side of the San Gabriel Valley, along the southern edge of the Verdugo Mountains (Glendale-Burbank), up the west edge of the San Fernando Valley to the San Fernando Pass (Newhall-Saugus), then west to Ventura.

[Feb.] 4 Tuesday. Drove 14 miles. Part of the day mountainous, road smoth, some hill, the hills beautifully ornamented with various flowers. Camped about a mile South of the road near a ranch in a narrow valley. Water not very good.

[Feb.] 5 Wednesday. Morning foggy. Continued our way winding among the mountains for 14 miles. Soil rather poor, some rockey. Feed indifferent most of the way. More timber than usual, mostly Oak. Considerable live oak, all short and skrubby, but rather improving in hight as we proceed. We saw several today that would make a rail cut each if they would split, which we think doubtful. No steep hills passed today.

---

[76] Foy, *Cheesman Memoirs*, 307.

[77] Militia Land Grant to Daniel Springer, January 1820. Ontario Archives Township Papers, MS658, Roll 61, 268.

[Feb.] 6 *Thursday. Morning decended a very steep mountain into a valley when we saw a storm of rain approaching and camped by some oak and sycamore trees. 8 miles.*

[Feb.] 7 *Friday. Rain over, we drove over a beautiful plain, extending from the mountains on the right to the Ocean on the left. Sand in places, but most of the way, the soil good. Crossed the Santa Clary* [Clara] *River and camped near. Feed good. This stream is capable of irrigating a large tract of land, most of it of the best quality. Here might be a fine settlement. The greatest difficulty is the scarscity of timber. Ducks, geese and sand hill Cranes very numerous. 15 miles.*

By this date the Cheesmans had gone inland from San Francisco to settle in Salmon Falls in El Dorado County on the lower portion of the South Fork of the American River, now covered by Folsom Lake. Mrs. Cheesman had been hired to look after a hotel dining room while David prospected for gold. Wherever she went, miners gathered around her to see the baby, most of them terribly homesick for the babies and families they had left behind. Cheesman wrote, "The miners seeing a woman and babe jumped up from their rockers and came out to the wagon with so many kind words. The babe was passed down to them and around from one to another. . . . The tears would invariable come. . . . 'Oh could I only see my [——],' choke up and turn with a 'God bless you' and return to their work."[78] By taking a steamer from Los Angeles to San Francisco, the Cheesmans were settled in the gold fields two months before the Pecks arrived at their final destination.

[Feb.] 8 *Saturday. Drove about 8 miles to San Buenaventura Mission and camped within a few rods of old Oceans shore. Saw a sail at a distance. Found a few shells.*

The San Buenaventura Mission lands, now Ventura, were in private hands at this time as part of the secularization process, which had begun in 1834.[79]

[Feb.] 9 *Sunday. Observed as a day of rest. Got some clams for dinner. Spent some time on the bank looking at the ocean. Saw several whales spouting at a distance and wave chaising wave until they broke with*

[78] Foy, *Cheesman Memoirs*, 322–23.
[79] Robinson, *Land in California*, 29–30.

fury on the shore. When we felt to appreciate the sentiment expressed by the poet:

> *I love to sit me on some steep*
> *That overhangs the billowey deep*
> *And hear the waters roar.*

After the difficult trek across the hot desert trail, the Pecks were thoroughly enjoying the sight of all that water. Hittell wrote that the most common whale seen on the coast at that time was the California gray whale.[80] The gray whale migration continues to this day.

Washington was quoting from a poem, "Nature," which had been published as early as 1819, author unknown.[81]

[Feb.] 10 Monday. *Drove about 18 miles, part of the day on the beach, some places rockey, very heavy wheeling. Saw quite a number of porpoices, some seals and several whales.*

In later years stagecoaches went along the beach as the Pecks and their large drove of cattle were doing. Joseph O'Flaherty's history of the south coast included a sketch of a six-horse team splashing along in the surf and rocks with a caption explaining that "it was necessary to drive through the surf at one point north of San Buenaventura."[82]

[Feb.] 11 Tuesday. *Road crooked, winding around the points of mountains and sea shore, but smoth good wheeling. Some Hilly. Made about ten miles and camped by a small pond.*

[Feb.] 12 Wednesday. *Morning passed Santa Barbary, an old Spanish town on the sea shore containing about 600 inhabitants, the buildings made of dobos* [adobes]*, one story high, covered with tile. No gardens. Nothing but the bear* [bare] *buildings without any fence or yard, except here and their a coral for cattle. Altogether a desolate looking place. Drove about fifteen miles and camped thirteen miles from town.*

Mission Santa Barbara was suffering the same fate as Mission San Gabriel, and it continued to deteriorate for the next ten years. When William Brewer visited in 1861, he wrote: "The church is in good preserva-

---

[80] Hittell, *History of California*, 2:563.

[81] Taylor, *Literary Panorama and National Register*, 814–15.

[82] O'Flaherty, *End and a Beginning*, photo section following 64.

tion, with the monastery alongside—all else is ruined. It was with a feeling of much sadness that I rode through the old town. Here were whole streets of buildings built of adobes, their roofs gone, their walls tumbling, squirrels burrowing in them—all now desolate, ruined, deserted."[83] In 1853 the Land Commission reduced the size of Mission Santa Barbara from 122,000 acres to 283 acres. Church claims were limited to the area covered by the church buildings, cemeteries, and gardens.[84]

[*Feb.*] *13 Thursday. Drove about ten miles over a crooked and exceedingly hilly road. Camped near the sea shore. Saw a number of whales near shore, Spouting and playing in their native element.*

[*Feb.*] *14 Friday. The road much the same as yesterday. Saw three sail at a distance. Camped in a hollow by a small creek near the sea shore. 12 miles.*

[*Feb.*] *15 Saturday. Drove two or three miles. Crossed several deep hollows and came to a very steep hill. Locked all the wheels and went down first rate, then turned up the creek to cross the east range. Soon came to* [*Gaviota Pass*] *where the mountains were four or five thousand feet high* [*elevation is about 2,500 feet*] *on each side, very steep and rockey. The rocks had rolled down in such quanties for about a mile as to render it almost imposable to pass through with wagons, but after much difficulty and hard lifting at the wheels, we got through safe.* [*Continued*] *our way up the creek for several miles, the road very crooked, rockey at the crossings of the creek, which was a great many and sideling* [*angled sideways*]. *We left the creek, crossed a high ridge, and decended a very long and, in some places, steep hill in to a beautiful little valley with abundance of grass, wood, and water and camped, having made about twelve miles over the worst road that we have had to pass. Passed quite a number of Bay trees, a beautiful tree of a foot in diameter, an evergreen, the leaf somewhat resembling the willow but of a deeper green.*

The road that Washington described as the worst that they had to pass remained in poor condition for at least the ten next years. When William Brewer traveled it in 1861, he wrote, "After leaving Santa Barbara County the roads were again horrible. . . . We crossed gulches down

---

[83] Farquhar, *Up and Down California*, 56.

[84] Cleland, *Cattle on a Thousand Hills*, 21; and Robinson, *Land in California*, 31–32.

almost straight on one side, then 'ker-chug' in the bottom, and then up as steep on the other." Farther north near San Luis Obispo, he continued,

> we had come a longer road because the 'hill was easier' this way. Well, we got to the 'easy' hill. It was about five or six hundred feet high, the sides at an angle or about thirty degrees.... It was very sidling, and very steep at the same time. We chained both hind wheels, and for a time all went well. We had descended about one-third of the way sliding, slipping, dragging, when, quick as a flash, over went the whole concern.... Such a pile! The wagon ... completely upside down.... The mules were tangled in the harness, one on his back.

Luckily, no one was injured.[85]

[Feb.] 16 *Sunday. Continued in camp.*

[Feb.] 17 *Monday. Drove over a high ridge of mountains, the road crooked but smoth. Good wheeling. Exelent pasture on the tops of the peaks. Long decent into a valley to the mission of Santa Iness or San Antiness (St Agness). The mission, like all of the others, in a state of delipidation. Camped about two miles from the mission. 8 miles.*

Washington had begun writing a phonetic pronunciation in parentheses as he struggled with the Spanish spelling and pronunciation for Santa Inés, never quite getting it right. The Pecks were veering slightly inland after crossing the coastal Santa Ynes Mountains toward Mission Santa Inés in today's Solvang.

[Feb.] 18 *Tuesday. Morning a slight sprinkling of rain at day break. Drove about twelve miles. Crossed a high ridge. Hills sandy, not much grass. Entered a beautiful valley, feed only middling, and camped in a light shower. Evening fine.*

[Feb.] 19 *Wednesday. Drove about six miles and took in water and camped in a dry hollow. Feed good. Crossed a high ridge. Road good. Made about fourteen miles.*

[Feb.] 20 *Thursday. Drove about fourteen miles, most of the way a beautiful levil plain road, excellent all, but a little two much sand in places. Camped near a ranch. Good feed.*

[Feb.] 21 *Friday. Road very sandy for two or three miles. When we reached the hills, the road smoth, winding among the hills. One long steep*

---

[85] Robinson, *Land in California*, 79–80.

hill to decend to a creek, thickly wooded with sycamore and rhasbury [raspberry] briers. Camped in a narrow valley, a spring on the right of the road. Slight shower of rain in the night. 16 miles.

Few of the thousands pouring into California settled outside of the gold fields. Again, as on the Oregon Trail, Washington did not record other people traveling on the roads, yet there were swarms of gold rushers crossing the continent on a number of southern trails from Texas and Mexico. The *San Francisco Daily Alta California* reported on April 7 that the roads from the south were filled with travelers, mostly from Sonora, Mexico.[86]

[Feb.] 22 Saturday. Passed through a beautiful valley (but little water), St Louis Obispo, an old mission in ruins, but a few Americans has got in and it now shows signs of returning life. Here [——] beautiful stream coming from the mountains. Drove up one branch of the creek into the mountains, about two miles, and camped, intending to spend the Sabbath here. 12 miles.

In 1840 Chief Wakara and Pegleg Smith, another notorious horse thief, led a band of Indians and whites in a raid on Mission San Luis Obispo and made off with twelve hundred animals. This mission was over two hundred miles from Mission San Gabriel, which shows how far Wakara ranged from southern Utah.[87]

[Feb.] 24 Monday. Drove over a high ridge of mountains [Cuesta Pass] and decended into a valley to Santa Margareeta (Margaret) Mission. Passed it about five miles and camped a little to the right of the road at the foot of a large white oak tree, 20 feet in circumferance. Passed some pine trees of the long leaf kind. The burrs that contain the seed are large. We measured one, which was 8½ inches in length and six in diameter. Edmond killed a wild goose. Grass being short on account of the drouth. Their has been but little rain in any part of California this winter, but between St Louis Obispo and San Whan [Juan] their has been much less than in other parts. The clay land is parched and cracked open. Made 15 miles.

The pine was likely a gray pine, also called a digger pine, Pinus Sabiniana, which is a large airy pine that produces cones six to twelve inches long by five to seven inches in width. Biologist Beverly Gingg observed that "the sparse,

[86] *San Francisco Daily Alta California*, Apr. 7, 1851, 2:2.

[87] Hafen and Hafen, *Old Spanish Trail*, 237, 276.

long gray needles give the pine a pitiful appearance compared to other lushly foliated pines," reminiscent of a "Charlie Brown Christmas tree."[88]

[Feb.] 25 Tuesday. Drove about ten miles over a very poor country of pine and skrub oak plains. The surrounding mountains seasonaly bare, a few fertile spots on the flats of the creek that we traviled down. Camped by another large oak, 22 ft circumference three ft from the ground. Road first rate.

The oak was a majestic Valley oak, *Quercus lobata*, which may be the largest North American oak. They sometimes live for four to six hundred years.[89] The largest living Valley oak at this time has a circumference of twenty-nine feet, a crown ninety-nine feet wide, and a height of a hundred and sixty-three feet.[90]

[Feb.] 26 Wednesday. Drove 21 miles over nearly the same country as yesterday. Passed the Mission of San McGill [San Miguel Arcangel]. Pitched our tent on a beautiful stream nine miles from the Mission. Here one of the Springers oxen puffed up to a great size. We ran a knife into him, but he died in four or five minutes after. We suppose it was two late as we had tried it on two of ours and it afforded instant reliefe.

[Feb.] 27 Thursday. Feed being tolerable fair and fearing that we would find very little for the next 28 miles, we concluded to pass the day here. Mr Haskel, Mr Springers partner, and one of the men went out on a hunting excursion. Near night, the man returned without any game. Soon after Mr Haskel came in with two fine deer and two hares.

[Feb.] 28 Friday. Morning breakfasted on pot pie made of venison and rabbits. Crossed a ridge to another stream. Continued up the creek. Grass poor. Made 16 miles.

March 1 Saturday. Passed the Ojeda (Ohetas) Ranch. Camped about six miles from the ranch. Here we found a little grass. This is in very poor barran country at the best, but this is a pecularly unfavourable season on account of the extream drought. If the drought continues much

---

88 Beverly Gingg, coordinator of Santa Margarita Community Forestry Organization, personal correspondence to author, Nov. 4, 2002.

89 Pavlik, *Oaks of California*, 10.

90 Beverly Gingg, personal correspondence to author, Nov. 4, 2002. *Register of Big Trees* maintained by the California Department of Forestry and Fire Protection and the Northern California Society of American Foresters.

longer, the Earth will not produce enough to support the few cattle that is kept here through the dry season. Made 21 miles.

The Ojitos Rancho (another of those elusive spellings Washington struggled with) was one of the ten stock-raising outposts of Mission San Antonio de Padua. Historian Gary S. Breschini wrote that "in 1823, a large adobe house with tile roof and covered corridor was constructed at Los Ojitos," and part of Rancho San Lorenzo is now King City.[91] The party was traveling north through the Salinas Valley.

[*Mar.*] *2 Sunday. Rested. I read a tract entitled Salvation by faith, holding forth the views of universalists on the subject. One man that appeared to be outrageously orthodox got in a pashion, raved, cursed, swore and tried to quarrel for two or three hours.*

[*Mar.*] *3 Monday. Drove about twelve miles. Crossed a high ridge, road exelent, and camped by the Salinas River, where the brush is very thick at its edge. At about nine oclock, the time of relieving the first watch, Mr Springer was setting at the root of a tree near the herd of cattle holding his horse by the bridle when three Indians came up to him. When he sprung to his feet, they run, he, having no arms, mounted and rode quick to the camp and took a brace of pistols and went in the direction that they had gone and soon came in sight of them. When let fly three arrows at him and he discharged a pistol at them and returned to camp, where quite an excitement prevailed for a few minutes, their being only two guns loaded and two horses saddled. We were all on our feet in an instant and loaded all the guns and pistols and several men mounted and kept on the skout. The rest armed themselves as well as possible. The ax, hatchet, spade, and knives were all placed in readiness. We then moved the wagons a short distance from the fire and hearing or seeing nothing more, we divided the men, five standing the first part of the night and five the latter.*

The Indians of California had plenty of cause for concern when confronted by the new immigrants. The editors of the *Daily Alta California* pointed out that the miners were overrunning and destroying the traditional gathering and hunting lands. They cut down the oak trees, which provided acorns, a staple in the Indians' diet, killed the wild game, drove

[91] Breschini, "Mission San Antonio de Padua," Monterey County Historical Society Local History web site.

the animals from the valleys, and dammed, dug up, and diverted the rivers, which destroyed the fish runs. Nothing was sacred to these newcomers, not even Indian graves, which were dug up in search of gold in the soil below.[92] The Indians' very survival was at stake, which was an underlying cause of the Mariposa Indian War then taking place.[93] The editors were sympathetic to the Indians and pleaded their case in a number of articles: "There is a question of justice, of humanity, of right, of religion. They are the original possessors of the soil."[94]

[Mar.] 4 *Tuesday. Morning found three Indian arrows pointed with flint that had been discharged at Mr Springer. Found that two of the best horses were missing and four head of cattle that they had got that day. After breakfast Springer and one of the men went to look for the cattle and try to assertain which way the horses had gone, we supposing that the Indians had taken them. When we were ready to start, we missed one of our cows that we expected to calve. We hunted all the forenoon without success. We then concluded to drive on a few miles and return next day for the cow. After we drove a mile or two, I told Hadley and Edmond, if they would return and find the cow, I would give them five dollars each. They started and we drove on about six miles and camped at dark. They returned with the cow and the best horse that was lost. The Indians went to a Ranch about five miles from our camp, after failing of success with us, and stole 20 horses and got clear.*

Washington apparently did not fear sending sixteen-year-old Edmond with Hadley to search for the missing cow and calf although he knew the Indians were nearby. Cattle theft was a huge problem at the time. The *San Francisco Daily Alta California* reported: "Throughout the whole range of our state, both north and south, rancheros are suffering large thefts of their cattle and horses.... There is no doubt that a large portion of the beef brought to the San Francisco market is stolen."[95]

[Mar.] 5 *Wednesday. Morning Springer and the man returned. Did not find the cattle but found the other horse. Drove about 16 miles down the river. Road good. Valley broad and handsom but the soil poor. Feed tolerable good since we crossed the ridge on Monday.*

---

[92] *San Francisco Daily Alta California*, Jan. 15, 1851, 2:3.

[93] Marks, *In a Barren Land*, 138; and Hittell, *History of California*, 3:837.

[94] *San Francisco Daily Alta California*, Jan. 15, 1851, 2:3; Jan. 1, 1851, 2:3; and Mar. 17, 1851, 2:2–3.

[95] Ibid., Feb. 11, 1851, 2:1.

[Mar.] 6 Thursday. Morning passed the Saladah [Soledad] Mission. Here we were directed to take the left hand road, the drove of cattle being ahead which put us astray. Near night Springer overtook us and with difficulty we found a ford. Crossed the Salinas River. Met the drove, which has left the road for to meet us and camped near a ranch. Feed rather indifferent. Drove about twenty miles. Made about sixteen. Night foggy.

Horse thieves stole about a hundred and fifty horses from the area around Mission Soledad during that week, and during the following week, nine hundred head of cattle and a number of horses were stolen from another rancho. "We are receiving accounts every day of ranches to the south losing all their horses some by white thieves and others by Indians."[96]

[Mar.] 7 Friday. Intended to drive about twelve miles to a small creek, but when we reached it, we found it dry. Then concluded to go eight miles farther to a larger creek where we would find all the necessarys for camping, but when we arrived near sunset, we found it dry also, so we drove the cattle about ¾ of a mile to a spring where they got a little poor water and we got some from a spring at a ranch no better. Night foggy with a mist. Road exelent.

[Mar.] 8 Saturday. Here we left the Salinas Valley (a beautiful valley ten or twelve miles wide with some good land, but difficult to irrigate, their being no small streams coming from mountains) and crossed a ridge of mountains to the mission of San Juan (Whan). Road bad, their being three high ridges to cross and a great many sideling places and gullies washed with the rains and some deep mudholes where springs break out of the mountains. Made about twelve miles and camped a mile and a half from the mission in a small valley. Good water and grass. Dry wood rather scarse.

Washington does not mention stopping to visit at Mission San Juan Bautista or in the small community that had grown up around it, but he was driving past the door of one of the most famous families in overland trail history. The Breens were living in Castro House, which they had purchased in 1848. Castro House was an adobe built in the 1840s for General José Castro. Patrick Breen, his wife, and seven children were survivors of the ill-fated Donner Party of 1846, who became trapped

[96] Ibid., Mar. 21, 1851, 2:2.

in the snows of the Sierra Nevada Mountains where almost half the party died. Washington would have known their story, which was often repeated as the reason no emigrant wanted to cross the mountains too late in the year. Castro House is now listed as a California State Historical Landmark in the town of San Juan Bautista.[97]

[Mar.] 9 *Sunday. Observed as a day of rest.*

[Mar.] 10 *Monday. Drove about 15 miles. Here we saw some exelent land and quite a number of settlers. Most of them have commenced recently. This bids fair to become the best settlement that we have seen in California, their ranches or farms being much smaller and abundance of redwood, a kind of ceder, very tall and large, and splits first rate, in the mountains.*

The new settlement was Pleasant Valley, which was described by reporter Patricia Loomis as a "redwood shack, which doubled as a wayside inn and stable where the stage between San Jose and Monterey changed horses." Although illiterate, proprietor James Houck nailed a cigar box on the front porch to serve as the village's post office and he became the first postmaster.[98] The town was later renamed Gilroy for John Gilroy, who owned a league of the Rancho San Ysidro where he built an adobe and lived to see it become a town.[99]

[Mar.] 11 *Tuesday. Drove about 13 miles, the land mostly of an inferior quality but few ranches. Feed very scarse. Camped a little off the road at the mouth of a kanyon near a spring. Feed middling.*

[Mar.] 12 *Wednesday. Drove about 12 miles, most of the way in a beautiful broad valley of rich land. Feed much better than we have had for some time past. Camped about three miles from San Jose (San Hoza), a little off the road on exelent grass.*

[Mar.] 13 *Thursday. Laid by to rest our cattle.*

[Mar.] 14 *Friday. Morning drove through the town, a pretty little place, some good buildings. It has been the seat of government since it came into the hands of the United States but has lately been removed, to*

[97] Bancroft, *History of California*, 2:729; and California Dept. of Parks and Recreation, *California Historical Landmarks in San Benito County*, no. 179, Castro House, 97.

[98] Patricia Loomis, "Small Redwood Shack Grows into Gilroy," *San Jose News*, Apr. 26, 1974, 43.

[99] Bancroft, *History of California*, 3:757.

the great injury of this place, which will prevent its growth for some time. There is considerable land cultivated about the town, but the drought has blighted their prospects for the season to a very great extent. Passed the town about five miles and camped.

The Pecks had driven through San Jose, which was the first pueblo (town) established in California in 1777. A pueblo was a civilian settlement where farmers were given enough land for a garden and orchard so that they could provide food for the colonists Spain was trying to entice to California. A pueblo usually contained four square leagues, or about 17,500 acres.[100] A league was 2.4 miles long. Spain's three-part colonization plan included missions, pueblos, and presidios, which were frontier outposts manned with soldiers to protect those at the missions and pueblos.[101]

California became a state in September of 1850, at the same time that Utah became a territory, both a part of the Missouri Compromise. Although the state capitol was first set at San Jose, it was moved several times before being located permanently in Sacramento in 1854.

[*Mar.*] *15 Saturday. Passed San Jose Mission, a romantic place among the hills at the foot of a mountain. Some fine gardens and vineyards fenced with dobos* [*adobes*]. *The fruit trees in full bloom gave a pleasing appearance to the place. Quite a number of Americans has settled here and put up some buildings after the American stile, which gave it more the appearance of an eastern village than any of the old missions that we have seen. Drove about fifteen miles and camped at the foot of a hill in a beautiful valley of rich land. Considerable distance. Poor water.*

Mission San Jose (now the city of Fremont) was separate from the town (pueblo) of the same name. One of the American settlers was Henry Clay Smith, who had converted the abandoned mission buildings into a hotel and had built a general store on one end. His business was thriving because this location was a gateway for miners heading into the gold fields.[102]

[*Mar.*] *16 Sunday. Being so far from water, we concluded to go on. Drove about 15 miles. Road good. Passed the White Hawk Ranch about two miles and camped in a small valley by a spring creek.*

---

[100] Robinson, *Land in California*, 40; and Cleland, *Cattle on a Thousand Hills*, 6.

[101] Robinson, *Land in California*, 24, 33.

[102] Philip Holmes, "The Pioneer Era 1849–1860," in City of Fremont History; and personal correspondence to the author, Sept. 30, 2002.

[Mar.] 17 Monday. As we left our incampment, the land began to be poorer with but little grass until the most of the hills was as bald as a rock, and when we reached the Tulare Valley, large tracts of land that had the appearance of being rich was almost intierly desolate of vegitation, not a blade of grass and as mellow as a fallow. Made about 16 miles and camped on some bunch grass. High wind.

James H. Carson, who traveled the length of the Tulare and San Joaquin Valleys in 1848 and 1849, had the same first impression, but when he re-examined the soil, he concluded that: "There is no portion of this valley that is not all the agriculturalist can desire, when aided by means of irrigation."[103]

[Mar.] 18 Tuesday. Drove about 19 miles to the San Joaquin (San Wahkeen) River. Ferried our wagons and one yoke of oxen, each $5, and swam the balance of our cattle. This is a fine stream of clear water, some twelve rods wide, current not swift. Camped about half a mile from the ferry. As the sun went down, the wind rose and blew a gale for several hours. Near morning had a slight shower of rain.

The Pecks were traveling eastward across the northern end of the San Joaquin Valley.

[Mar.] 19 Wednesday. Drove about two miles. Camped about four miles from Stockton. Very little grass. Six horses belonging to the company straid off. Had a fine rain in the night, which was much needed.

Stockton's original name was Tuleburg, and even had a few tule houses. The tule (pronounced too'*lee*) is a species of bulrush that grows in wet marshy areas to a height of ten-to-twelve feet and at one time covered several thousand square miles in California.[104] Getting lost in the tules would have been no joke.

[Mar.] 20 Thursday. Morning road muddy and slippery. Drove through Stockton, a small seaport town at the head of a slough. Considerable business done in it. But it is the filthiest place we ever saw. Several dead horses and mules lay in the streets roting, the people being two much ingaged in getting gold to attend to such trifles for comfort and health. Found the horses that straid last night. Drove 13 miles.

---

[103] Carson, "Life in California," 62.

[104] Bancroft, *History of California*, 6:465–66; Farquhar, *Up and Down*, 219; and Hittell, *History of California*, 2:558.

Stockton, also called Mudville, was an inland deep-water port connected through an estuary system to San Francisco. Like San Francisco's waterfront, but to a lesser degree, its harbor became jammed with abandoned ships whose crews had defected for the gold fields. At one time a hundred ships were burned to clear the harbor.[105]

[Mar.] 21 *Friday. Drove about twelve miles over poor sandy land to the Calevaris River. Feed middling in a small flat.*

[Mar.] 22 *Saturday. When nearly ready to start, we missed a cow, which we expected to calve. Hunted all day without success.*

[Mar.] 23 *Sunday. Morning renewed the search for the cow, but all in vain. When we offered a reward to an Indian and in a few minutes he brought the cow, we then refused to pay him unless he brought the calf, which he soon did. We then gave him five dollars. We suppose the rascal drove the cow off and concealed her expecting to get the cow or a reward. Here is a toll bridge over the river. They asked ten dollars for three wagons (another wagon having overtaken us) so we examined the ford and concluded to try it. Raised our wagon boxes and drove in. Got safe over. The other wagon got bust on a log in the bottom. Had to hitch to the back end and pull it out and take another start, which proved successful. Drove to the next creek 8 miles and camped.*

By this time Washington had become wise to the Indian ploy of driving cattle off, then waiting to see if a reward was offered before "finding" them. Washington did not object to paying the toll for travel through Indian land for return of his cow and calf, which he valued, but he did object to paying a toll to cross a bridge when he could cross the river himself by doing a little work.[106]

[Mar.] 24 *Monday. Drove fifteen miles over a levil plain, the land most of the way poor and unproductive. Here an attempt was made to drive off three of the horses, but the guard rescued them from the thieves.*

The Pecks were beginning to experience the lawlessness that was taking place in the gold fields. The *Sacramento Transcript* reported, "Within the past two weeks we have received intelligence of many robberies from Nevada [City] in the north to Stockton in the south."[107]

---

[105] Tinkham, *California Men and Events*, 68.

[106] Napton, *On the Santa Fe Trail in 1857*, 13.

[107] *San Francisco Daily Alta California*, Apr. 7, 1851, 2:6.

[Mar.] 25 Tuesday. Arrived in the vicinity of Sacramento. Turned to right and struck the American Fork five miles from the city. We have been eleven months and two days on the way and at last have reached the long desiered haven. Have traviled three thousand four hundred miles, 2000 with horses to Great Salt Lake, 8 hundred to Pueblo de los Angeles and six hundred from their to Sacramento, which we performed with oxen and have had no accidents and have lost no animal.

After the long way around, the Pecks had arrived at their initial destination, 3,400 miles from home. The first 2,000 miles took less than four months with horses, but it had taken over six months to cover the last 1,400 miles with ox-drawn wagons and a herd of cattle. Losing no animals was an astounding accomplishment! In fact, the Pecks saved a few animals that otherwise would have perished, which was a tribute to Washington's incredible husbandry skills.

[Mar.] 26 Wednesday. Visited the city. Received two letters from home. The city, we think, has arrived at the zenith of its prosperity and will wane with the decline of the mines as the country around cannot support a town of one quarter its size.

Like most other arrivals, the Pecks went straight to the post office eager to see if there were any letters waiting. Washington rightly forecast that the gold rush would be short lived, but he was wrong in his prediction that Sacramento would decline as a result.

[Mar.] 27 Thursday. Heavy rain. Also rain Saturday night and Sunday.

[Mar.] 31 Monday. Morning swam our cattle accrossed the American Fork and ferried our wagons over for which we paid two dollars for two wagons, cheap for this country. Drove about 14 miles and camped by a dry creek, a little water in holes.

The Pecks' long journey was not quite at an end. Washington spent five days in Sacramento talking with people to determine where to go in the gold fields. A recent Sacramento newspaper story had reported that: "The richest deposit of gold that has ever been discovered in California is probably in Nevada City."[108] So that is where the Pecks headed.

April 1 Tuesday. Drove 18 miles. Road some what muddy. Feed gen-

[108] Ibid., Mar. 28, 1851, 2:6.

erally good. It is improving since the rains. Camped by a dry creek. It has raised since the rain and is running a fine stream.

[*Apr.*] 2 *Wednesday. Drove 14 miles to Bear River. Feed good. Heavy rain all night.*

[*Apr.*] 3 *Thursday. Rain. Water high.*

[*Apr.*] 4 *Friday. Rain continued.*

The past few days of rain that Washington recorded marked the end of the dry winter of 1850–51 that the miners had been waiting for. Historian Ralph Mann explained that during the dry period, "Miners and investors poured out of Nevada [City]" and headed for San Francisco, Sacramento, or Stockton until the rains began and they could go back to work.[109] Now that the rains had started, the miners were swarming back into the hills, but, as before, Washington did not mention the miners that were sharing the road with them.

Many of those who traveled the trails with the Pecks in 1850 had taken the California Trail directly to the gold fields and had arrived at the diggings six months earlier. Because of the dry winter, they may have gained nothing. John Udell was one example. He spent the winter mining, but made only a pittance and was sick a good deal of the time. By the end of July, four months after the Pecks arrived, he was on a ship heading home.[110]

[*Apr.*] 5 *Saturday. Weather fine. Drove to the crossing of the river. The cattle would not take the water. Drove ours over the bridge. Paid ten dollars toll. Springer drove a few of his over and left Mr Haskel and two of the men with the remainder until he went to Nevada City and try to sell. Drove 8 miles to Round Tent House. At night missed one of the cows.*

[*Apr.*] 6 *Sunday. Egerton went back to look for the cow lost yesterday. Found her at the bridge. Here is a few men mineing in a dry creek. We went to see them. They were washing, their being water since the rain. Saw some specimins. They gave my wife the largest piece that they found today, about 40 cents, because it was the first that she had seen.*

Washington notes that the men were back at work because of the rains. The men may have given the gold nugget to Mercy because she was the

[109] Mann, *After the Gold Rush*, 13.

[110] Udell, *Incidents of Travel to California*, 31–32.

first woman they had seen for a long while. This was the only time Washington directly mentioned Mercy in his diary during the entire year.

[Apr.] 7 Monday. *Drove about 12 miles to Pen Valley. We are now passing in the mountains. Our road was rough and mountainous. The country is mostly covered with skruby timber, oak and pine. Soil generally poor. Feed indifferent.*

The stage route to the mines passed through the Penn Valley, which became a rich agricultural area referred to as the Pantry of the Northern Mines.[111]

[Apr.] 8 Tuesday. *Road rough and rockey. Passed Rough and Ready, a village containing 6 or 7 hundred inhabitants with one street, narrow and crooked. One part of the name at least is appropriate, that is, it has the rough whether it has the ready or not. Here the mines has been worked and are still in some places. Passed* [Past] *the vilage about 3 miles it came on to rain. We went into an empty house. Rain continued heavy all night.*

Captain A. A. Townsend founded the village of Rough and Ready, which he named for his former commanding officer, Zachary Taylor, also known as "Old Rough and Ready." One of its claims to fame was that it seceded from the Union on April 7, 1850, as a separate republic in order to avoid a newly imposed mining tax, a separation that lasted only two months—until July 4, 1850.

[Apr.] 9 Wednesday. *Looked about to find a place where we can get feed for our cattle and sell milk.*

The Pecks knew they could sell milk at a good profit, perhaps from seeing what it sold for in Sacramento. In Nevada City, Phelps Milk Depot was selling milk for fifty cents a quart.[112]

[Apr.] 10 Thursday. *Drove on till within about 2½ miles of Nevada City. Contains from ten to 20 thousand inhabitants including 2 or three miles around it. The town is built in a grove of heavy timber, the tall heavy pines standing in the streets and among the buildings heavy enough to crush them to atoms.*

---

[111] "Penn Valley," *Nevada Valley Gold Magazine*, 25.

[112] *Nevada City* (Calif.) *Nevada Journal*, Apr. 19, 1951, 3:4.

The Pecks had come to a stunningly beautiful place of rolling hills covered in pine forests with grassy valleys in between. Nevada City had grown from a single building—Caldwell's general store—to cover seven hills. Tents, log cabins, brush huts, and two-storied and false-fronted buildings were sprinkled amongst the towering pines.[113]

[Apr.] 27 Sunday. Night our horse was stolen, for which we paid $60 last week, and Mr Hadleys mule.

After safeguarding their animals for thousands of miles, they have had an inauspicious welcome to the gold fields.

[Apr.] 28 Monday. Spent the day in hunting for the stolen animals but found them not.

[Apr. 29 & 30] Tuesday and Wednesday. Built a coral and moved to Gold Flat, one mile from Nevada [City]. From here we can carry our milk to Nevada by hand.

They have found a place to settle in after a year on the road. After securing their dairy herd, they could build a cabin for themselves. Gold Flat was southwest of town where the Phelps family had their dairy ranch.[114] The Pecks had left Kilworth in Canada West on April 22, 1850, and finally reached the end of a very long and unique route to gold fields.

May 16 Sunday. In the 38 days since our arrival, by selling four head of cattle, ten calves and our milk, we have raised a little over eleven hundred dollars.

[May] 20 Tuesday. Bought some claims in co. with Mr Hadley. Paid $1000. I have two thirds and Hadley one.

[May] 25 Sunday. Spent the past week in preparing for mining. Realized about $150 for milk.

These last few, very brief entries revealed an eagerness to start mining and provided more questions than answers. It is unknown whether the Pecks kept their dairy herd and continued selling milk in town or whether their mining claims were close enough for them to remain in Gold Flat.

---

[113] Mann, *After the Gold Rush*, 10, 23.

[114] *Nevada City* (Calif.) *Nevada Journal*, Nov. 29, 1851, 2:5.

4

The Intervening Years

California Gold Rush: Nevada City, 1851

Life in Nevada City during the next few years was chaotic, exciting, and constantly changing. The Pecks lived through rapid population growth, floods, fires, and drought while society evolved to include church services, theatrical performances, and the organization of a local vigilante committee to deal with crime and violence. Miners came and went. Gold production went up, then down.

Nevada City was brand new. On March 11, 1851, a month before the Pecks arrived, an arsonist started a fire in Gates and Smith's ten-pin (bowling) alley. Accelerated by gunpowder stored everywhere, it whipped through the business district, quickly burning the flimsy buildings and destroying the town. Within hours, contracts were let for new buildings, and the town was rebuilt with better buildings and straighter streets than before. Historian Marilyn Starkey wrote that in one instance "a two-story eight-room frame house with a balcony was thrown up and occupied in two days."[1] The *Nevada Journal* published its first issue on April 19 as the Pecks rolled into town.

Federal census takers in 1850 faced an overwhelming challenge as miners poured into California from all over the world. The reported population of 150,000 was only a guess. Miners moved faster than the census takers and were sometimes counted twice in different districts. As the census taker rode out, new arrivals flooded in behind. Around five hundred placer camps sprang up, many disappearing as quickly as they appeared, but Nevada City was one of the largest and it was there to stay. By 1852 its population had grown to 21,365.[2]

---

[1] *San Francisco Daily Alta California*, Mar. 14, 1851, 2:5, Mar. 15, 1851, 2:5; and Mar. 22, 1851, 2:6; Comstock, 150 *Years Ago; A Sketch of Nevada County*, 9–10; and Starkey and Browne, *Sketches of Yesterday and Today*, 30.

[2] Robinson, *Land in California*, 138; and Richards, *Historic Sites of the Mother Lode*, 50.

Mining methods advanced rapidly from the gold pans and rockers to the long tom—an open wooden trough about twelve feet long with a metal sieve bottom. It took two or more miners to operate, but it meant that piles of dirt previously worked could be reworked to recover finer gold dust.[3]

As the number of miners increased and began crowding each other, disputes arose, so mining districts were organized with rules that set out how large claims could be and how they had to be marked, registered, and occupied. Prior to 1860 the courts accepted verbal transfers.[4] If Washington registered the claim that he and Hadley bought on arrival, the records have not survived.

Water was the one essential ingredient required for all placer mining. During summer when the creeks dried up, miners stockpiled dirt dug from the creek bed and banks until the rains began. When rains came, floods often washed out long toms, dams, and dirt piles. To provide a continuous supply of water, miners began digging ditches from the year-round streams to the dry diggings. A ditch that was completed as the Pecks arrived was thirteen miles long.[5]

Working the claims was just that: work, hard work. George Hearst, another 1850 arrival, tried placer mining, but soon found a better opportunity. Hearst and Davis opened a general store in 1851 in Nevada City and then added a reading room upstairs, which they stocked with newspapers from all over the world that had not been picked up at the Sacramento post office.[6]

Cheesman tried rocker mining but soon quit and spent the winter cutting logs for houses. He and a partner built a dam across the American River and floated the logs down to the backwater to wait for spring.

The town grew, and societal refinements began to appear, from churches to theaters, but saloons with drinking and gambling continued to be the main entertainment, just as they were in all mining camps.[7] Added to this were the usual assortment of riffraff committing murders

[3] *Nevada City* (Calif.) *Nevada Journal*, Apr. 19, 1851, 2:2; and Hittell, *History of California*, 3:65.

[4] Robinson, *Land in California*, 136–37.

[5] Comstock, *150 Years Ago; A Sketch of Nevada County*, 15.

[6] Hunt, *California and Californians*, 4:46. This was the same Hearst who later bought the failing *San Francisco Examiner* to give to his son, William Randolph Hearst.

[7] Mann, *After the Gold Rush*, 35–36.

and robberies, and it is apparent that society in Nevada City was nothing like the quiet towns the Pecks had left in the East.

That August the heat was intense. Alfred Jackson, who mined in the area in 1851, wrote, "The weather has been blistering hot for the past ten days and the air is full of smoke from mountain fires. . . . An old dead sugar pine over on the mountain caught fire last night. . . . The flames shot up in the air at least four hundred feet and although it was two miles away I could hear the crackling and roaring plainly."[8]

Like many, Washington did not last long at mining. By the fall of 1851 he was working for a butcher in one of several meat markets in Nevada City. Although an unlikely occupation to produce riches, even the butcher business had a success story in the gold fields. In nearby Hangtown, "Phil, the Butcher," helped bankroll miners who had good prospects but no capitol, and by the end of 1855 he returned east with almost $60,000. Using that money to begin a number of businesses, Philip D. Armour became the multimillionaire owner of Armour and Co. meat packaging, as well as banks and railroads.[9]

The rains returned in the fall of 1851, bringing an influx of miners who filled the deserted cabins on the outskirts of town. Business in Nevada City was so good that by November the Phelps had made enough money at their Milk Depot to add a hotel to their dining room, which they renamed the Express Hotel and Depot. It was the stage stop for alternate day service between Nevada City and Sacramento.[10] If the Pecks were still in the dairy business, they were doing well.

In January Washington wrote to his daughters, Jane and Emma Peck, and married daughter, Mary Ann Banghart, who was looking after the girls, with instructions for his son David Peck. His letter was reprinted on May 6, 1852, in the *Canadian Free Press*.[11] Washington provided a personal and detailed description of the advantages and disadvantages of life in California. By Oregon Country he meant Oregon Territory, which included Oregon, Washington, Idaho, and parts of Montana and Wyoming.

---

[8] Canfield, *Diary of a Forty-Niner*, 82.

[9] Philip D. Armour, biographical information file. California History Room. *California Grizzly* (magazine), Nov. 1907, 57–63.

[10] *Nevada City (Calif.) Nevada Journal*, Dec. 11, 1851, 3:1.

[11] *London (Ont.) Free Press*, May 6, 1852, 2.

California

Is getting rather in the shade, since the discovery of gold in Australia and other places. The following letter from an old inhabitant of this place, will be of interest to many of our readers.

NEVADA, *January 19th, 1852*

Dear Children,—We received yours and David's of the 19th November, day before yesterday, and were a little disappointed to find that you all wanted to come here. We had supposed that you were so well provided for, and David's attachment to the place so strong, that you would all be contented where you are; and were stopping our affairs to return in the summer. But, as your letter was written before you received ours, in which we had mentioned the subject; it convinced us that you were anxious to come, and we think it is of no use to try to discourage you, as we have no arguments that would be likely to prove satisfactory. For it appears to us that when any one gets their mind set on going to California, that they are never satisfied till they have seen the "Elephant."

When we consider California and Oregon simply as new countries, we do not hesitate to say that they possess advantages over every other new country at the present time. First for climate, the most fertile parts near the coast from San Diego to Vancouver's Island, there is no freezing to injure vegetables; such as potatoes and fresh garden stuff may be had all the year, and a great variety of fruit. The South part produces excellent grapes, pears, figs, and peaches; also oranges, but not of the best quality. Farther North, say from Sacramento, apples is supposed to do well. There is no doubt of their doing well in the mountains. For raising Stock, this country excels any part of North America. In the agricultural parts the cattle are fat all the year; it costs nothing to raise them, not even salt. Secondly, we think it a healthy country, especially near the last. In some places in Sacramento valley there are some cases of fever ague; in the mountains the prevailing disease is eryciplas, [a severe streptococcus infection] which in many cases is very malignant. A great many have died this summer, but if men exposed themselves in other countries as they do here, the number of deaths would, in all probability bear a far greater proposition to the whole. Third, its location for trade,—almost in the centre between the two great marts of trade, Europe and the East Indies. The products of the East are cheap here now; tea is cheaper in San Francisco than in any port in the United States. Ready-made clothing is as low here as in London, Canada; boots and shoes about the same. No State in the Union possesses greater advantages for trade than California; add to this its great and numerous water powers, and the vast quantities of the finest timber in the world, (in the North part of California and Oregon) and its extensive gold, silver, and quartz mines; and we must conclude that this country holds out inducements to settle, that no other country can. In short, California has a home market for all its products, probably forever, with the ready [cash] to pay for it. What other country has such a prospect?

But after all, it has its disadvantages; the timber is not equally distributed, the best portions of land is far from timber, and expensive to build where the timber is, and that land is poor. But the great objection to settling here is the state of society. Hitherto there has been very few women, everything has been done by men; cooking, washing, etc.; in this respect there is a rapid change taking place, a great many men have sent for their wives, and every boat that arrives contains quite a number, either accompanying their husbands, or else coming to them. When we first came here, in passing through Nevada [City], it was a rare thing to see a child and if a woman passed through the streets hundreds of men would stop to look at her; now there is quite a number of women in town, and if half a dozen is now seen promenading the street at once, there is but little notice taken of them; and children are frequently seen in groups. A great many families are settling here and many more are going to cross the plains this summer.

If you make up your minds to come, you will want to know the best route. There are two routes by water; the one crosses the isthmus from Chagres to Panama, the other crossing from St. [San] Juan through lake Nicaragua (pronounced Nigeraugur) is called Vanderbelt's Line, it is the nearest and the most healthy; price I believe is about the same. There is one in favor of the latter; you get a through ticket which includes your passage across the Isthmus; the other you must pay extra, which amounts to about $25 per head. It will cost now about $250 from New York to San Francisco per head. The overland route is the cheapest, for if you make a good selection of ponies, like our best, they will sell for as much as the whole cost of the journey. And if you take oxen and cows, you earn double your money; cows work and stand it well—it is best to have a few for the milk on the way. With ox teams, a few horses are necessary to ride. With oxen common two horse waggons are the best.

Four or five yoke per team, and light loads will come through safe, with careful management.

If you come by water, I suppose what money David has collected for us will bring the girls through, and if he can sell, he will probably have nearly enough. How you are situated we know not; we will send a power of Attorney to David to sell the farm in Lobo, and if you or he is short of means use that, and if it will not sell, or will not sell for enough, let us know, and we will send you the ready [cash]. The month of June, or from the first of June to the 20th of July is about the best time to come by water; the most healthy on the Isthmus, and the Boats not so thronged, and fare probably lower.

If you come by land, you will be able to get your teams, waggons, etc., by paying but little money. You will need at least $100 each, after getting your supplies, for ferry's etc. Buy no clothing, unless you have not enough to last you through. Come which way you will, bring no bedding but what you need on the way; sell all your feather beds and furniture.

If you come with horses, our smallest waggon is about the best size you will need. Three waggons, four horses each, and a man or two men that you can depend on. Mind that then if you have two or three extra horses to ride occasionally, and change if needful, then you are fitted out first best. We will give you some particulars in our next, of the road, provisions, &c. The best waggon-covers is tight, thick cotton, put on double without oil. You ought not to be later than we were in starting, chiefly on account of company. You can drive to Louisville [Kanesville] in five weeks if your teams are fresh; we were six. If you cross the Missouri before the 10th of June (we crossed on the sixth) you have plenty of time; it is about 1900 miles, by Fort Hull [Hall] 2000. By Salt Lake, 500 miles per month will bring you through in good time.

I must conclude. We are all in good health—I am with the butcher mentioned in my last, Edmond is working for $50 per month, and grub, and Egerton is mining. The mines are not paying so well this Winter. At last we say, let no man that has a wife come to the country without her; if none, let him get one.

W. PECK

The most surprising news was that the Pecks were ready to go home in the spring of 1852 after being in California for only a year. The letter from the children had taken two months to arrive, so they may have started west before Washington's reply reached them. Washington's glowing report of California would have encouraged not only his children's emigration, but no doubt others who read the published letter. The Pecks decided to wait in case the children were on their way.

Another significant piece of information was the increasing number of women and children living in town and arriving daily. This contradicts some who asserted that "respectable women remained scarce" throughout the first half of the 1850s. But perhaps Nevada City was the exception because of its size.[12]

The weather throughout the spring was miserable. Snow was followed by rain, which melted the snow and caused flooding. By February 10, 1852, it had been raining or snowing almost every day for a month. Alfred Jackson went into town and discovered that the supply teams had stopped coming, which created shortages, so prices had doubled. He feared that "if the rains don't let up, there is a prospect of a famine.... There are eight big team outfits loaded with flour, stuck in the mud, between here and Sacramento.[13] After a brief respite, it began to storm again, and when a snowstorm turned to rain, Deer Creek, which ran through the middle of Nevada City, rose so high that it took out the newly built Jenny Lind Theatre, which tumbled down the creek along with a couple of bridges.[14]

Another casualty of the flood was David Cheesman's dam on the American River, which washed out, destroying his whole winter's work—$60,000 worth of logs. He returned to San Francisco to practice law and later became Treasurer of the San Francisco Mint.[15]

Flooding spread to the Sacramento valley where it washed out sections of the levee and poured into the city of Sacramento, covering everything with three to ten feet of water.[16]

Washington was in a far more comfortable and safe situation working in town as a butcher than his son Egerton, who was the only family member involved in mining by January of 1852.

Crime increased in the gold fields over the next few months. Jackson wrote, "The country above ... [has] been infested with a gang of highway-

---

[12] Mann, *After the Gold Rush*, 37.

[13] Canfield, *Diary of a Forty-Niner*, 120, 122–23.

[14] *Nevada City* (Calif.) *Nevada Journal*, Mar. 6, 1852, 3:1.

[15] Foy, *Cheesman Memoirs*, 324–27; and "The Macy Centennial; 1850–1950," 20.

[16] *Nevada City* (Calif.) *Nevada Journal*, Mar. 11, 1852, 2:5.

men for the past three months and it has not been safe to travel, as they robbed and murdered right and left."[17] In response to the crime wave, citizens organized a vigilante committee in June, which was heartily approved by the *Nevada Journal*, who editorialized that the agents of the law should not be constrained by rules and formalities based on a "more refined state of society." Further, local lawmen should be left to deal with problems when they could, but a "body of good citizens can render them very efficient aid."[18] The citizens wanted justice, as they perceived it, and they wanted it now. Numerous lynchings occurred throughout the gold fields, not always without problem. In one case the "bungling executioners" hung the victim too low and had to hang him again.[19]

Washington finally heard from David. He and thirteen men were bringing a herd of cattle to California, but whether he brought Jane and Emma is unknown. The men started early in the season and were in Kanesville by May 4, 1852, ready to start along the Mormon Trail. The men published a letter in the *Kanesville Frontier Guardian* stating that they were "all in good health and buoyant spirits. Our horses all look well—nothing lost, stolen or strayed on the way."[20]

The men were amongst the 60,000 emigrants that made 1852 the busiest year on the trail.[21] Eliza Ann McAuley wrote in her diary that by May 10 there were thousands of wagons in Kanesville waiting to be ferried over.[22] That meant a wait of several days. That year also saw many cholera deaths. Historian Wallace Stegner cited an estimate of a thousand graves on the south side of the Platte from Council Bluffs to the South Pass by July 4. Unruh's calculation for the year was at least two thousand deaths during 1852.[23]

David Peck's party stayed ten days in Salt Lake City before taking the California Trail across the desert via the Humboldt River. David was on the trail for six months, arriving about September. The September 10 *Nevada*

[17] Canfield, *Diary of a Forty-Niner*, 154.

[18] *Nevada City* (Calif.) *Nevada Journal*, June 12, 1852, 2:1.

[19] Ibid., Mar. 11, 1852, 1:4.

[20] Rasmussen, *California Wagon Train Lists*, 135; and *Kanesville Frontier Guardian and Iowa Sentinal*, May 6, 1852. The other men were W. W. Crouse, William Higgie, Patrick Mee, Henry and Levi Meyrick, Hyram and George Odell, Isaac, Seth, and William W. Putnam, L. E. and M. H. Rowley, and Thomas Woodlock.

[21] Unruh, *Plains Across*, 120.

[22] Holmes, *Covered Wagon Women, 1852*, Vol. 4 (Journal of Eliza Ann McAuley), 45.

[23] Stegner, *Gathering of Zion*, 209; Unruh, *Plains Across*, 409.

Journal reported that there were a thousand emigrants expected shortly and many had stopped in the Carson Valley to recruit their stock.[24]

The peak year for gold production was 1852 at 81 million dollars, twice the 40 million taken out in 1850, but in 1853 production began to decline. Miners began heading home in greater numbers or found other occupations. "By the end of 1854 . . . one third of San Francisco's stores were empty."[25]

David went into the cattle trade in Hangtown (Placerville), fifty miles south of Nevada City.[26] The business probably involved buying used-up cattle that had just come over the trail, recruiting them, then selling or swapping them to arriving emigrants, and also selling them for beef.

Washington and Mercy stayed in California until 1854, eighteen months after David arrived. Exactly when the Pecks sold out in Nevada City is unknown. Fires destroyed all land deed records in Nevada County prior to 1856.

Washington obviously loved California. Perhaps the Pecks felt like Dame Shirley (Louisa Amelia Clappe), who wrote, "My heart is heavy at the thought of departing forever from this place. I like this wild and barbarous life; I leave it with regret."[27]

Water/Overland Route Home, 1854

The Pecks were among 20,000 people in 1854 who took steamers from San Francisco to a land crossing of either Panama or Nicaragua, then boarded a waiting ship on the Atlantic side. Passengers were divided equally between the two very different crossings.[28]

By the time the Pecks headed home in 1854, a railroad was more than half finished across the Panamanian Isthmus: thirty-one miles of track were laid beginning at the Atlantic side with eighteen to go.[29] The crossing time had been reduced from five days to eight hours. The *San Francisco Alta* described the unfinished stretch as "a pleasant mule ride of five

[24] *Nevada City* (Calif.) *Nevada Journal*, Sept. 10, 1852, 2:2; and *Biographical History of Page County*, 643.

[25] Cole, *Short History of San Francisco*, 38, 55.

[26] *Biographical History of Page County*, 643.

[27] Clappe, *Shirley Letters*, 198.

[28] Folkman, *Nicaragua Route*, Appendix B, 163.

[29] Schott, *Rails across Panama*, 27; and Kemble, *Panama Route*, 71.

or six hours along a good road,"[30] but diarist Emmeline Day crossing in 1853 described it as: "a narrow trace, in many places only wide enough for one packed mule to pass at a time. . . . It has been traveled over by mules until they have worn a track in the earth so deep that the . . . level was far above our heads, and the track . . . so narrow that we could touch each bank."[31] Diarist John Udell wrote that some of the passages were "half a mile long; and those entering at one end, continually sound horns to warn travelers not to enter at the other side."[32]

In Nicaragua, Cornelius Vanderbilt had begun building a competitive crossing in 1850, which was to be temporary until he and his partners could build a canal.[33] The 165-mile crossing was mostly by water, different from Panama, but with its own engineering problems.[34] By 1854 the route had improved. The road was macadamized (paved with broken stones) and mule-drawn carriages had replaced the muddy mule ride. The steamer took nineteen hours to cross Lake Nicaragua, which sounds like a pleasant trip, but the conditions were terrible, with no food and no sleeping accommodations. The passengers slept on the open deck, which was usually too crowded for everyone to lie down at the same time. From there the passengers took a series of river steamers down the San Juan River, making three portages around waterfalls, all the while passing travelers headed in the opposite direction. Passengers for California continued to outnumber those returning home via both routes.[35]

Competition between the two routes was fierce. Recruiters for both companies spread lies and promises in order to attract laborers and passengers. Alhough passengers on both routes suffered equally from disease, each company promised theirs was the safer, healthier route.

It was a good time for the Pecks to travel because the best weather in the year occurred from February to April,[36] and the ticket prices were going down and still dropping.[37] The total trip took three to four weeks from San Francisco to New York.[38] Newspapers contributed to

[30] *San Francisco Daily Alta California*, January 13, 1854, 2:3.

[31] Levy, *They Saw the Elephant*, 42.

[32] Udell, *Incidents of Travel*, 90–91, Dec. 30, 1853.

[33] Frey, *Railroads in the Nineteenth Century*, 269–70.

[34] Schott, *Rails across Panama*, 71.

[35] Folkman, *Nicaragua Route*, 50–51, 57–58.

[36] Schott, *Rails across Panama*, 12.

[37] *San Francisco Daily Alta California*, Feb. 15, 1854, 2:1; and Kemble, *Panama Route*, 69–70.

[38] Unruh, *Plains Across*, 402.

the rivalry by publishing ships' notes, which included comments such as "passed Nicaragua steamer *Brother Jonathan*, she having sailed two hours before us, and next forenoon lost sight of her in our wake." It was like a great race. When three ships from competing companies left San Francisco the same afternoon, the passengers made bets on who would get to New York first.[39]

Whichever route the Pecks took, it was a far easier and faster trip than their overland journey west had been.

Middlesex County, Canada West, 1854

Washington and Mercy still owned the cooperage in Kilworth, plus a hundred acres in Caradoc Township. Within a month they had bought another hundred acres in Caradoc near the newly established village of Mount Brydges.[40] (See map on page 28.)

Just before the Pecks returned, in December of 1853, the Great West Rail Road had completed a line to London from Hamilton, a port town at the western end of Lake Ontario, eighty miles due east. Encouraged by success, the company began the next extension and by mid-summer of 1854, construction crews were pounding rails near Mount Brydges, the heart of a rich agricultural district. The new line would move farm products directly to port, quickly and efficiently.[41]

Land speculation was rampant as new railroads sprouted up everywhere. Competition was fierce as they rushed to add new links and extend their lines. Land near existing and anticipated feeder lines quickly escalated in price.[42] The Pecks recognized opportunity when it knocked, so by March of 1855, David, Egerton, and Edmond had all bought property in Caradoc close to the rail line. Between them, the Pecks owned five hundred acres. Apparently, they had not come home from California empty-handed. Now that the entire family would be engaged in farming, Washington sold the cooperage in Kilworth.[43]

---

39 *San Francisco Daily Alta California*, Mar. 22, 1854, 2:2, and May 2, 1854, 2:1.

40 Dean Tiffany to W. Peck, May 25, 1854, Middlesex County Deeds, Caradoc Township, Instrument 577, Lot 20, Conc. 3.

41 Miller, *Century of Western Ontario*, 80–81; and Currie, *Grand Trunk Railway of Canada*, 164.

42 Miller, *Century of Western Ontario*, 79.

43 W. Peck to Arial Towlsey, Jan. 5, 1856, Middlesex County Deeds, Delaware Township, Instrument 650.

The Pecks' cooperage had adjoined the farm of Josiah and Anna Eliza Woodhull. Their daughter Hannah had been ten when the Pecks first moved to Kilworth, which was originally called the Woodhull settlement. By the time Egerton returned from California, little Hannah had grown up. On Christmas Day, 1855, Egerton Peck, age twenty-four, married Hannah Maria Woodhull, almost eighteen.[44]

George and Mary Ann (Peck) Banghart were living with George's parents and three siblings in a log house on a farm a hundred and fifty acres in size. The 1852 Agricultural census reported that the farm had eighty acres under cultivation—fields of wheat and rye—and some pastures for their farm animals—a few cattle, horses, a small flock of sheep, and some pigs—and seventy acres of wild land and woods.[45] It was typical of farms in the area.

From 1854 to 1856 the economy was booming. Railroads expanded rapidly, crop yields were up, and grain exports were high, providing food for troops serving in the Crimean War.[46] In the spring of 1856 the *Treaty of Peace* was signed in Paris, ending that conflict. Few realized how that event thousands of miles away would impact their lives. Throughout the summer, as the demand for grain softened, local merchants ordered record amounts of stock, anticipating continued growth.

On September 4, 1856, Washington ordered the following ad from the *London Free Press and Western Advertiser*:[47]

LAND FOR SALE!
To be Sold by Private Contract,
THREE FARMS OF 500 ACRES
IN THE
TOWNSHIP OF CARADOC,
IN THE NEIGHBORHOOD OF
MOUNT BRYDGES.
W. PECK OFFERS THE ABOVE

Farms on peculiarly advantageous terms. A good portion of the land is cleared and in the highest state of cultivation.

The Farms are beautifully situated, from one-fourth to two and a half miles of Mount Brydges Station.

---

[44] National Historical Company, *History of Holt and Atchison Counties*, 810.

[45] Ibid.

[46] Baskerville, *Bank of Upper Canada*, cxxii–cxxviii.

[47] *London* (Ont.) *Free Press*, Jan. 7, 1857, 4:7.

Intending purchasers will find it to their advantage to make inquiry on the premises from the Subscriber.

WASHINGTON PECK.

Mount Brydges, Sept. 4, 1856

The ad ran weekly from January 1 to February 24, 1857, but it did not bring any buyers, even with the "peculiarly" advantageous terms.

In mid-February of 1857, Washington, and most likely Mercy, went to Woodbridge to sign some housekeeping paperwork on the 1837 sale of his property.[48] It was a chance to visit with old friends and see the bustling village that had replaced the heavily forested wilderness where they had lived twenty years earlier.

Then the economy started on a downward spiral and the bottom fell out of the agricultural market. Historian Orlo Miller wrote, "The whole Western world was on the brink of a post-Crimean-War depression. . . . Few cities on the North American continent and none in Canada were hit as hard as London," primarily because of over-inflated wheat prices.[49] Another historian wrote that when "local land values plummeted and railroad construction ground to a virtual halt," events were set in motion that led to the failure of the oldest and most prestigious bank in Canada—the Upper Bank of Canada. Economic problems in the United States and England resulted in numerous bank failures and then spread even further, becoming the Panic of 1857.[50] The Peck farms began to sell, but they were mortgaged.[51] People simply did not have the money. Washington granted Power of Attorney to his good friend and neighbor William F. Lee for the acres that had not sold.[52]

Washington had made a decision to move back to the United States, a decision that may have been influenced by the economic downturn, but perhaps also because the Pecks were finding life too humdrum, too routine. Life in California had been filled with excitement. J. S. Holliday concluded that many who returned home from the California gold rush found themselves chaffing under the restrictive rules governing their lives

---

48 York County Deeds, Instrument 66458, Feb. 14, 1857.

49 Miller, *Century of Western Ontario*, 104.

50 Baskerville, *Bank of Upper Canada*, cxxii–cxxviii.

51 Mercy Peck to George Moore, Apr. 16, 1857, Middlesex County Deeds, Caradoc Township, Instrument 1393; Edmond, Mercy, and W. Peck to William Kester, May 18, 1857, Instr. 1587; and Egerton Peck to Henry Yeager, Apr. 17, 1857, Instr. 1409.

52 Ibid., Instr. 2325. W. Peck granted Power of Attorney to William Lee, Apr. 17, 1857.

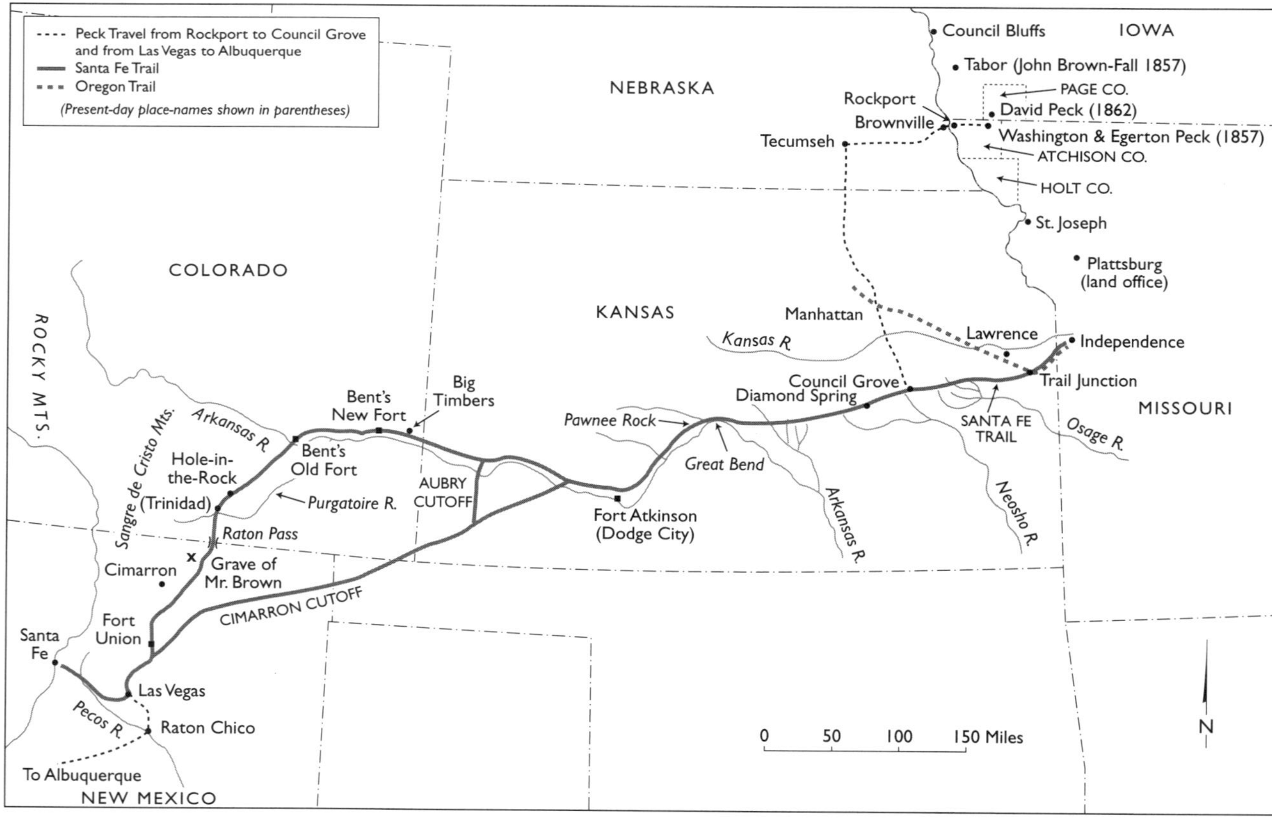

In 1857 the Pecks moved from Mount Brydges in Canada West to Atchison County, Missouri. In the spring of 1858 they started for California by traveling west into Nebraska and then south into Kansas to pick up the Santa Fe Trail. They followed the mountain branch over Raton Pass and then continued on to Albuquerque.

and the slow, measured predictability of daily routines, so much so that many soon packed up their families to return west, this time as settlers.[53]

Financially, they had chosen a good time to go, before the summer's devastating crop failure, but the weather made preparation downright miserable. Miller described the weather that year: "Torrential spring rains came early and stayed late and June was cold and gloomy." The late planting, which was looking fairly good by mid-July, was hit by a late frost that destroyed most of the crop. "Harvest of the remaining poor crop was about to begin when the rains returned" and drowned the rest. By September crop failures were reported throughout North America.[54]

Egerton and Hannah with baby Josiah, and the Bangharts with four-year-old Rosie and baby Flora, decided to go too. George took a small herd of dairy cows that included a yearling heifer that he had raised from a calf and was more like a pet. The little wagon train started off at the end of May, waving good-bye to David and Eliza and their three little ones.[55] It was a final good-bye. Except for Egerton, there is no record that the rest of the family ever saw David and Eliza again.

Atchison County, Missouri, 1857

Once again Washington and Mercy headed west—likely taking some of the same roads that they had traveled twice before—from Canada to Illinois, and then into Iowa. But this time, instead of continuing west, they turned south and planted themselves in Atchison County, Missouri, the northwest corner of the state. They arrived in July of 1857.[56]

Why the Pecks settled here is a mystery. Was this their original destination? What was this place, this Missouri? Oddly enough it was a slave state, which made it a strange choice for an abolitionist.

The families settled in an area with a boundary problem. Conflicting survey lines on the Iowa-Missouri border had created a disputed strip ten miles wide that extended the entire width of the state. There were few settlers and only a handful of slaves in the county.

---

[53] Holliday, *World Rushed In*, 446, 452.

[54] Miller, *Century of Western Ontario*, 108.

[55] Kester to Mercy Peck, May 21, 1857, Middlesex County Deeds, Caradoc Township, Instrument 1604, Mortgage.

[56] Stapel, *Biographical History, Atchison County*, 404.

Maybe it was the appeal of the land itself, gently rolling hills sprinkled with groves of tall trees. The Pecks found land near Walden Grove that had not yet come up for sale. They set to work improving the land to establish a preemptive claim as they had done previously in Illinois.

Although Atchison was quiet farming country, the Pecks were living in the eye of a storm, surrounded by people and events that contributed to the outbreak of the Civil War.

Thirty miles south was the border with Kansas Territory where an ongoing conflict came to be called Bleeding Kansas. The Kansas-Nebraska Act of 1854 had given the residents the right to determine whether Kansas would enter the union as a free or a slave state. As settlers, both pro- and anti-slavery (free soilers), flooded into the territory, hostilities increased. In May of 1856 border ruffians (pro-slavery men from Missouri) attacked free soilers in Lawrence, Kansas. In retribution, radical abolitionist John Brown and his sons hacked five men to death in the Pottawamie Massacre. These events had been extensively reported in the Canadian press, so the Pecks were undoubtedly aware of the volatile situation before they arrived.[57]

John Brown arrived in Tabor, Iowa, just a few miles north of them, a month after the Pecks settled in Missouri, and he stayed through the fall. After fleeing Kansas as a wanted man, he had gone east to drum up financial support to win Kansas as a free state and then returned to Tabor. As he waited impatiently for money to arrive, he developed a grander scheme, a plan to lead an uprising of slaves. When the fall election in Kansas elected a majority of free soilers to the legislature, it punctured Brown's balloon, but he continued to foment problems in Kansas and saved his scheme for a later date with destiny at Harper's Ferry.[58]

Abolitionist activities are not reported in the local histories of Atchison County, but Edgerton Robert Peck,[59] one of Washington's great-grandsons, lived in a house in Rock Port with an out-building cellar that had served as a hiding place for slaves, indicating that some Underground Railroad activity did take place there.

[57] *London* (Ont.) *Free Press*, May 30, 1856, 2:1 and June 5, 1856, 2:1; *London* (Ont.) *Herald*, June 3, 1856 and 3:4, June 6, 1856, 3:1.

[58] Renehan, *Secret Six*, 125–28.

[59] Oral history from Tom Zanna, who saw the hiding place during a visit to his grandfather, Edgerton Robert Peck, in the early 1960s.

Washington Peck's Diary of 1858

At the beginning of 1858 the Peck families were living in three houses. Washington, Mercy, and daughters Jane and Emma lived in one, the Bangharts in another, and Egerton Peck's family in the third. Edmond had gone to Des Moines, Iowa, to work for the winter.

Washington began a new daily diary on January 1, 1858. He reported the weather in great detail—temperatures at morning, noon, and night until the thermometer broke—and not much else except for the number of posts and rails that he, his son-in-law George Banghart, and his son Egerton were cutting and hauling from Walden Grove to build fences in the spring. He made occasional poetic comments about the weather: "In the afternoon the sun peeped out for a few moments to see what affect the storm had produced in these diggings and then hid its face behind the clouds again." As in his previous diary, he rarely mentioned the women. In an entire year, he referred to Mercy four times, but never by name. The only event he recorded was Mercy's visit to nurse a neighbor's sick child.

Keeping warm during the very cold winter was a challenge. The Pecks had the luxury of a stove, not just a fireplace, for cooking and heating, but log cabins were notoriously drafty because they were built of unseasoned logs that tended to shrink and swell, leaving large gaps that needed chinking. On February 21, Washington wrote, "The wind blew very hard all night with a little snow, but it sifted the roof of the house until every thing was covered in the chamber." It was so cold inside their cabin that the snow did not melt.

Entertainment was limited. On January 31, a particularly snowy Sunday, Washington wrote, "We were all at home all day. We read and talked and talked and read. Upon the whole it was rather a long day." Sunday services were held in one of the cabins by either an itinerant or local preacher or the pioneers themselves. Sundays were also reserved for visiting. A steady stream of young men stopped by to visit, mostly on Sundays, and Mr. Cooper came most often of all, often staying overnight on frequent trips north and south. The attraction? Jane and Emma, who were twenty-one and seventeen.

Monday February 22, 1858. We were visited at night by Jim Teague, Odam Zook, Ed Web, and John Smith, and here they sot and sot and sot and sot and sot until about ten o'clock. Jim had good sense enough to leave. Then the others sot and sot and sot until (as the gal said) they tuck-root. Finaly they let their business be known, which was they wanted to get up a party or spree at our house, we of course to furnish the expenses and have the troble. But it's NO GO. *Modist young gentlemen. Wonder what they will want next.*

As the young bachelors sat trying to get up their courage, Washington sensed their discomfort, but let the awkward silence lengthen as he waited them out. As for Mr. Cooper, he was dismissed after an incident on April 5, when Washington went to Rock Port. "Mr Cooper rode with us. Saw Jim Tait. Cooper and he came near having a fight." The next day Washington "wrote to Mr. Cooper to discontinue our acquaintance."

When spring arrived in mid-March, the men began staking off the fence lines so they could begin building. Atchison County historian Stapel wrote: "Before a parcel of land could be cultivated it was necessary to fence it in," to keep the livestock from trampling and eating the crops.[60]

On March 16 Edmond came home from Des Moines with his pay, a span of horses and a wagon. Washington was disgusted. He wrote, "He has made a poor winter's work—worse than doing nothing and paying his board." He set Edmond to work plowing five acres on William Daniel's farm where the Pecks were going to plant wheat. They had not yet cleared enough land to sustain themselves and their livestock.

Tuesday March 23, 1858. Mr Cooper called bring us a St Joe paper containing an advertisement for the sale of the disputed strip, which convinced us that our land has been sold without our knowledge. We are quite discouraged. Think of going to California. Not quite decided whether we will go this spring or next. Would like to go this spring if we could get ready.

This was devastating news. The newspaper story from neighboring Holt County, stated: "Sales of public land in Missouri are advertised to commence at Plattsburg . . . on Monday, March 1st. . . . Pre-emption claimants must establish their claims by proof, and make payment before these sales."[61] The story had been published on March 19, almost three weeks after the sale began. The lost days were critical because land sales drew a virtual stampede of buyers.

---

[60] Stapel, *Biographical History, Atchison County*, 9.

[61] *Oregon* (Mo.) *News*, Mar. 19, 1858.

On March 25 Washington decided to migrate to California. Discussions began amongst the family and neighbors. Who would go and who would stay? On April 14, Washington and George Banghart started for Plattsburgh, a hundred miles away, and camped two nights on the road.

Friday April 16, 1858. We reached Platsburgh. Found that our land was sold. Saw the purchaser and tried to buy it of him, but his terms was so hard that that we left him and thought of California.

Preparations to leave for California started in earnest. Washington and Mercy traded their stove, safe, bedstead, table, and nine dollars for a yoke of three-year old steers. They bought a yoke of oxen from Egerton for seventy-five dollars in gold, which revealed that Egerton and Hannah were not going. No reason was given, but maybe Hannah did not want to go any farther from her family in Canada.

A good deal of trading was reported over the next few weeks as they gathered up the oxen, horses, and food supplies that they would need. They traded or sold whatever household goods they could, including their houses, which would be dismantled and moved. The people who joined their wagon train included Mr. Miller, his wife and child, George Wood, a twenty-five-year old bachelor from Illinois, and Tom Flowers, age eighteen, a native of Iowa.[62] Young men often signed on with wagon trains to help herd livestock in return for food, eager for the chance to go to California.

Mary Ann delivered Mary Jane (Jennie) Banghart on May 16, just ten days before they left.

Washington's entry of May 21, 1858, revealed that he sometimes omitted important events in his diary. He recorded the cold wind and rain, but failed to mention that he had bought ten acres of land for Egerton and Hannah.[63] They now had a few acres to call their own, so Washington and Mercy gained peace of mind knowing the young couple would have a place of their own. There Egerton and Hannah remained for the rest of their lives. They had eight children, one of whom died in infancy. Except for a brief period during the Civil War when Egerton served in the Second Calvary Regiment of Nebraska, they continued to farm

[62] Federal Census, 1860, N.Mex., Socorro County, Rio Bonito Township, 145.

[63] Atchison County Deed Book 4:414.

(*left*) Egerton Ezra Peck and Hannah Maria Woodhull Peck, circa 1860. *Courtesy of Carolyn Dodds Schaeffer.*
(*right*) David Abbott Peck. *From author's collection.*

and increase their holdings, and eventually Egerton helped organize the Farmer's Bank in Westboro.[64]

In 1862, David and Eliza, five children in tow, came down from Canada and settled nearby, but just over the border in Page County, Iowa, because they feared that Missouri land claims might not be recognized after the Civil War. They were three miles apart, close enough for the two families to attend the same Methodist church. David and Eliza had five more children as they built up their farm and improved the land. David served as a minister in the Methodist Church he established, following in the tradition of his father and grandfather.[65]

[64] *Biographical History of Nodaway and Atchison Counties, Missouri,* 375–76.

[65] National Historical Company, *History of Holt and Atchison Counties, Missouri,* 793; and *Biographical History of Page County, Iowa,* 642–43.

5

1858 Wagon Trail Diary

The Santa Fe Trail

The Pecks likely chose to take the Santa Fe Trail for the same reason many other travelers did that year—the turmoil in Utah Territory and along the Great Platte River Road. Military traffic had disrupted travel and consumed rations on the Platte River route. Several thousand United States Army troops, with additional contingents, teamsters, and freight, had marched up the Platte in 1857 to restore federal control to Utah Territory, considered by President Buchanan and his cabinet to be in revolt. Reinforcements were expected in 1858. People were talking about the Mountain Meadows Massacre that took place on the southern route in the fall of 1857, in which a hundred and twenty emigrants had been killed by Mormons and Indians, including the Fanchers who had traveled with the Pecks in 1850. Taking the Santa Fe Trail, then Cooke's route, to California was five hundred miles longer than a direct route through Utah, but it allowed travelers to circumvent the area of the Utah War.

The Pecks avoided the ongoing problems along the Missouri-Kansas border by going west through Nebraska, then south into Kansas to pick up the Santa Fe Trail. Six days before the wagon train left, another incident in the Bleeding Kansas conflict took place—the Marais des Cygne Massacre. Thirty pro-slavery Missourians crossed into Kansas, rounded up eleven anti-slavery men, and shot them in a ravine. Five died, five were wounded, and one was not hurt because he fell with the rest and played dead.

The Pecks took the Mountain Branch of the Santa Fe Trail, which passed by Bent's Fort and over Raton Pass. They continued on to Albuquerque and took Beale's Wagon Road along the thirty-fifth parallel, but they turned back when they met the survivors of the Rose Party, who had been attacked by Mojave Indians at the Colorado River. They were worn out by the time they had retraced their steps to Albuquerque, so after being offered a place to stay, they went south to Fort Stanton, where they took up land claims and set to work building stone houses for the coming winter.

The family members of the wagon train included Washington and Mercy, children Edmond, Jane, and Emma Peck, married daughter Mary Ann Banghart, her husband George, and their little girls—Rosie (four), Flora (two), and ten-day old Jennie—plus a herd of cattle that included the family's pet cow. Other known members of the wagon train included two young men—George Wood and Tom Flowers—and a young couple, Mr. and Mrs. Miller and child. In contrast to the 1850–51 crossing, Mercy had plenty of female company—three daughters, three granddaughters, and Mrs. Miller.

Tuesday May 25, 1858. Rain in the night. Cleared off fine. Wind north east.

Two men came to go with us.

We got our cattle together ready to start in the morning.

Wednesday May 26, 1858. Day clear, calm and hot. Started for California about ten oclock. Drove six miles to Mr Graves and camped. Got a steer from Kimes. Swaped a cow. George Do [*ditto*].

Egerton, James Teague, and Ambrose Daniel went with us until near night when they left for home, the former sorrowfully. In all probability we shall never see each other again in this world (sorrowful thought).

Washington never saw Egerton again. He left his 1850–51 diary with Egerton and Hannah, perhaps not knowing if he and his party would survive or maybe for the more practical reason of limited wagon space.

The Pecks did take one luxury item, a small rocking chair. Whether it belonged to Mercy or Mary Ann, who used it to rock baby Jennie, is not known, but Mercy had been across the open plains before, and she knew the only place to sit was on an ox yoke. That rocking chair has remained in the family. The Pecks were not unique. Diarist Francis Peabody (1865) recorded that after her mother pleaded to take something familiar, "The couple finally agreed to tie her rocking chair on the back of the wagon, and . . . years later, [she] could still recall her mother 'sitting in that chair in the midst of the endless plains when we stopped for the night.'"[1]

[1] Faragher, *Women and Men on the Overland Trail*, 71, 224.

Thursday May 27, 1858. Day warm. Heavy wind from the south east. Drove to the Nishnabotanny and camped. Appearance of rain. Broke a wagon tongue. Heavy squall of wind and rain at night with thunder and lightning. Stoped at Rockport and completed our supplys of powder, lead, tea, sugar, etc.

Friday May 28, 1858. Morning high wind from the north west. Waited till near noon then drove to the ferry and crossed to Brownville. Drove two or three miles and camped on a beautiful prarie. The land is less broken here than on the Missouri side of the river. Some good farms in sight. One cow got her tail cut off on the ferry boat by the geering.

Saturday May 29, 1858. Morning fine. In greasing our wagon, we found a box loose. George wedged it and got the box in wrong. Had to send back to Brownvill for a file to file it so as to get it on. When we started, found two bad sloughs. Got one waggon sloughed pritty bad which detained us some time. Crossed the Little Nemeha on a good bridge. Drove from that three miles and camped by a small gravily bott-tomed creek. Day very pleasant, light wind from the south west. Made eleven miles. Beautiful country. Well settled. Some good farms.

George swaped his dun cow for a dry one and a yearling hieffer.

Sunday May 30, 1858. Commenced to thunder and lighten [lightning] before day and soon the rain fell in torrents. The wind blew and upset the tent. The boys scatered to the waggons but got pritty wet in the operation. Rain over we got breakfast and thought of going on afternoon, but when the time came, it rained again. Continued to drizzle at times. Near night it rained heavy until bed time. The creek rose so as make it difficult to cross.

Georges cow that he traded for yesterday got away. Edmond and Wood went after it and did not return.

The first four days brought a string of problems that could easily have discouraged a less determined group, especially considering that they were heading into the wilderness where they would have to rely upon themselves. There would be nowhere else to buy a file or swap for cows.

Monday May 31, 1858. The boys returned with Georges cow. We had some trouble in colecting our cattle. We found the road slipery in the morning. Crossed two creeks, rather difficult for long teams. Then we had to go round the head of a small creek where the bridge was broken (lost 3 miles). Crossed Muddy [Creek] and passed St Frederic, a town most gloriously small. Drove 6 miles, crossed Spring Creek and camped (made about 16 miles). Beautiful rolling prairie all the way. Day fine. Wind light from the north west. Evening cool.

St. Frederick's town site had been surveyed three weeks earlier. Historians Glen and Evelyn Sheely wrote, "It was not long until they boasted of a store, post office, blacksmith shop, hotel and livery barn," but when the anticipated railroad was located elsewhere, it struck a blow to the town. Then a second blow occurred, literally, according to local history, "when one afternoon in July, 1868, a tornado scattered most of the town over the neighboring fields," It went from "gloriously small" to gone and was never rebuilt.[2]

Tuesday June 1, 1858. A brisk wind from the South East, cool with appearance of rain. Passsed Tecumseth, the county seat of Johnson Co, a pritty site for a town. Crossed the Big Nemeha on a bridge. Had a small creek to cross near the Nemaha. Found the bridge gone. Had to drive round the head of the creek. We took the road west for three or four miles, then struck across the prarie for the road. Found it heavy wheeling, the ground soft with several sloughs to cross. After going farther than we expected it was to the road, we came to a point of timber and camped, haveing drove about twelve miles. At dark it commenced to rain and continued all night.

I swaped rifles with Flowers, got four dollars [to] boot.

After traveling eastward, they turned south toward Kansas. Leaving the main road to cross what appeared to be solid ground caused more than one emigrant regret. Diarist Margaret Frink (1850) described how they had turned off the beaten track onto grass that appeared "firm and solid. To our astonishment, the horses broke through the sod, and, being unable to pull their feet out, they were all soon flat on the ground." They had to be unhitched and the wagon dug out.[3]

Wednesday June 2, 1858. After daylight a squall of wind blew the tent over while the rain was pouring and wet the boys beding. After sun up

[2] Sheely, *History of Nemaha County,* 13; and Stoddard, "St. Frederick—A Lost City," *Beauty-Bounty Nemaha County.*

[3] Holmes, *Covered Wagon Women, 1850,* Vol. 2 (Diary of Margaret A. Frink), 66–67.

a little, the rain ceased and clear sky appeared. We concluded to lay by and wash and let it dry off a little. Day hot. The creeks high and sloughs full with appearance of more. A great deal of thunder and lightning in the night with a little rain.

Thursday June 3, 1858. Morning bids fair for a fine day. Soon after we started, we undertook to drive round the head of another creek and when we were out on the prairie, it came on to rain and we lost our course. Stoped until the sun came out and then proceded, but when we got round one creek, we came in contact with another until we got bewildered so that we did not know which ridge was right, so we took one that lay by in the right direction and drove several miles until we became satisfied that we must cross the creek to the south in order to get on the road. Then we drove down the creek and camped. After super we found a convenient place and made a bridge of sticks and brush ready for morning. The wind came round from the S East to the north west and blew fresh all day and cool evening rain. Very heavy wheeling, being wet & soft.

Friday June 4, 1858. Morning cloudy and cold. Strong breeze from the north. Crossed our new bridge. It proved to be all that we desired. In about three miles we came to another. Bridged it also which detained us about an hour. Then drove on two miles and fetched up against another (which was a creek) and camped. Spent the afternoon in building a bridge. Found the road to be on the next ridge. Saw some Indians. Afternoon clear and pleasant. Evening charming. The boys stood guard. Beautiful location here abouts with timber on the creeks with but few settlers. Have not seen a house for about 20 miles. Saw a man crossing the prarie. He lives on the Big Blue about 5 miles from where we saw him.

Saturday June 5, 1858. Crossed our bridge. One ox got his legs through and we had to unyoke it. Drove three miles to a house. The man put us on a new road to the Vermillion. When we came to where we expected to find a direct road to Fort Riley, we could not hear of any road at all. We were quite disappointed and some were dissatisfied. We thought best to take the course and proceed without a road. Crossed the old California road from Independence. It bears the marks of immence travil for many years. Passed from Nebraska to Kansas. Day fine, wind south west. Saw no game in the teritory except prarie hens and curloos [curlews].

The wagon train seems to be lost in a giant corn maze, going around and around, looking for a way out. For the next two weeks until the Pecks finally got onto the Santa Fe Trail, they lost a number of days going the wrong direction, around impassable bluffs, and seeking out fords and ferry crossings that were not where expected due to heavier than normal rainfall.

Independence was one of many starting points for the Oregon Trail, and it coincided with the Santa Fe Trail for a short distance.

Sunday June 6, 1858. Took a road down the creek 1½ miles to the end of it. Then took the prarie to a branch of the California road. Followed that 2 miles, crossed a small creek, then turned south down the creek on a new road from one house to another. Pritty good most of the way and hear that we will find a road along the creek down to its junction with the Blue. Beautiful country this. Good building stone in abundance for several miles we passed to day. Day fine, wind south west. A light sprinkling of rain before day.

Monday June 7, 1858. Drove about 17 miles. Crossed several small streams, branches of the Black Vermillion and the main stream twice, the last time the bank high and very steep. In all the streams has gravil or rock bottom. Day cloudy and cool. Wind north. Evening pleasant. Wind east.

Tuesday June 8, 1858. Terable thunder and lightning with a little rain before day. Morning fine. Drove 2 miles to the last crossing of the Vermillion. The great freshet a few days ago worked the bank so that it was rather difficult geting into the stream. In geting up the bank Millers waggon got a little off the tract and struck a stump and broke an axel tree, an iron one. Difficult to get it repaired here. Then we camped and washed. Miller swaped wagons. Got an old one. We think it may go through. Gave 2 dollars [to] boot when he ought to have had ten, but so it is when a man is in a tight place.

Terable thunder and lightning with heavy rain during the night. Splendid country, the land good with abundance of lime stone in quarries for all the buildings that will ever be wanted and a great deal of fence.

A freshet was a sudden rise in the stream or flooding caused by heavy rains.

Wednesday June 9, 1858. Morning hot with appearance of rain. We waited a while for the road to dry a little [because] the hills were so slippery. Miller split his great toe with an ax, which rendered him unable to drive his team. Edmund drove for him. When we got about two miles on our way over a hilley rough sidleing road, Edmond drove into a gulley by the side of the road and upset the waggon turning it upside down with Mrs Miller and child in it, but all escaped with but little injury besides breaking the bows and tearing the cover. Then we came to a halt and the rain poured down for a while. When we got Millers waggon fixt, the rain came on again for to make out the day.

Here the Vermillion empties into the Big Blue about 25 miles from Manhaten (Freight line) on the Kansas, more than thirty by the road.

A sidling road sloped horizontally toward the road edge. On a muddy hillside, it probably did not take much of a gully to overturn the wagon.

Thursday June 10, 1858. Rain early in the morning. The wind rose with the sun from the north. Blew hard.

The road was so wet and slipery that we laid by. Fixt our waggon tongue that was broken. It cleared off in the afternoon.

Friday June 11, 1858. Day cloudy and cool. We drove 11 miles. Road cracked and a great many creeks to cross, some very steep places. Came to where the Blue backed up into the small creeks and made it impassable, so we camped and explored a passage up a ravine to the high prarie. The bluffs are three or four hundred feet high, only here and there a place where a team can get up. Report sais that it is 22 miles to Manhaten.

Washington's reference to a report revealed that he had a written guide of distances.

Saturday June 12, 1858. Morning clear and cold, almost a frost. Made our way up a ravine to the high prarie. Kept the ridge until afternoon. We came to a road which we supposed to be right. Took it and at night found ourselves three or four miles out of the way at Pleasant Creek. Drove about seventeen miles. Found that we had 12 miles more to Manhaten. In the morning it was 25. Day fine. Found an ox yoke broken. Commenced to make one.

Sunday June 15 [13—date written in error in Journal]. Rain in the night. Finished our yoke and made two pair of ox bows. Drove 8 miles to the Blue where we expected a ferry boat, but it had vammosed. Then instead of 4, we had 8 miles. Took the road into the bluffs. Found the old road fenced up and the new one into every bad place that we could see, and after driving 5 miles found that we had six more ahead. When we were about 1-½ miles from Manhaten, we had to go of[f] to get round a bend in the river. Upset one wagon. Afternoon fine.

In 1876 editor E. N. Morrill wrote, "The year 1858 will be remembered by the early settlers as a very wet one. The months of April and July were especially noted for the heavy rainfalls; the streams overflowed their banks rendering it impossible to cross them for days in succession."[4] Undoubtedly, the heavy rains contributed to the inaccuracy of Washington's road guide.

Monday June 14, 1858. Crossed the two ferreys, the Blue and Kansas at Manhaten. A very pritty site for a town. Some good buildings. Appears to be a place of considerable business. It is the largest town that we have seen since we crossed the Missouri. Swaped a cow and heiffer in calf for one of each that would come in after we got through. Day pleasant, rather warm.

Tuesday June 15, 1858. The wind rose in the night and blew a stiff breeze from the south. Drove from our camp 8-½ miles from the ferry about two miles up the river, then up a revine and assended the bluffs. We found them much higher than we expected. We think it a 1000 feet above the river. Then took a divide. Expected to find Moss Spring at 11 miles. Drove 20 but no spring. Camped in a hollow, plenty of water and a little wood. Was on an Indian trail for 8 or 9 miles which we intend to follow to Counsil Grove. We were told that it was 11 miles to the spring and 25 to the grove. If it is more than 20, what is 25? Afternoon very hot. We [had] to unyoke several oxan. One we think is seriously injured.

Wednesday June 16, 1858. Laid by and washed. Overhalled our loads and fixed things in general. Day fine but hot wind south.

Thursday June 17, 1858. Started in good time. In two miles we came to Moss Spring. Here a road came in from Fort Riley. Drove 20 miles.

[4] Morrill, *History and Statistics of Brown County, Kansas*, 30–40.

The road kept on a divide but bore two [too] much to the east. We had some fears that we might be [w]rong but are sure that we have followed our directions. Day fine. Stiff breeze from the South East.

The ox that we thought hurt day before yesterday stood it well.

As the Pecks struggled to find their way through the prairies, they seem completely isolated from the rest of civilization, but an event that occurred that day in the United States would impact their lives three years later. After delivering his famous "House Divided" speech, Lincoln was unanimously declared the Republican candidate to run against Douglas for the senate seat from Illinois.[5] This led to the Lincoln-Douglas debates that editor Harold Holzer proclaimed "galvanized public attention north as well as south." The *New York Evening Post* declared, "The Prairies are on fire."[6] The Civil War was one step closer.

Friday June 18, 1858. Drove about 12 miles and met a man who told us that we were going wrong, that we had lost about 45 miles, so we left the road and took our course south for the Santa Fee road about 10 or 12 miles. Drove about 3 and camped on a beautiful prarie by a small creek. Strong breeze from the south west. Appearance of rain. A light sprinkling of rain at night.

Saturday June 19, 1858. A little rain before day. We got ready to start when it commenced to rain so we unyoked and waited until after noon, then drove about 9 miles to the Santa Fee road. Camped on Elm Creek, 20 miles from Council Grove. We have lost 3 days travil by being directed wrong.

George swaped cows. Made a good trade. Three mule teams camped by us going to Walnut Creek with goods.

Sunday June 20, 1858. Drove 16-½ miles. Passed two creeks. Camped at Rock Creek. Here is a good farm with a large two story stone house. Road good, only two bad mud holes. Day beautiful. Wind South.

Monday June 21, 1858. Passed Council Grove, quite a village. 2 stores and a blacksmith shop. Drove to Elm Creek and camped. Made 15 miles.

Saw two Mexicans. Their is a company of them a head going to Santa Fee loaded with merchant goods, 8 waggons in all.

Day hot, a pleasant breeze blowing from the south.

---

[5] Davis, *Don't Know Much about History*, 159–61.

[6] Holzer, *Lincoln–Douglas Debates*, 1–2, 375.

William B. Parsons, a member of the gold-seeking Lawrence Party, traveled this same route in 1858, about a month ahead of the Pecks. In Parsons' guidebook, published in 1859, he described Council Grove as the "outpost of civilization."[7] He advised that although a few houses would be found beyond, it was the last good place to stock up, especially on hardwood timber, necessary for axletrees and ox bows.

Tuesday June 22, 1858. Drove 7 miles to Diamond Spring and then found 15 miles to Lost Spring. No good water intervening. Continued on to the Spring but did not find it. Drove off the road in the next hollow to water and camped. Day warm but a strong breeze made it pleasant. The road was over a beautiful gently roling prarie without timber and but little water.

Diamond Spring was the site of a mail stage station. And Lost Spring truly was difficult to find, according to Parsons' guidebook.[8]

Wednesday June 23, 1858. Drove 14 miles to Cottonwood Creek. Very dusty. Strong wind. Appearance of rain. Country same as yesterday. Here was two companies of Mexicans going to Santa Fee. One of these wants us to go in company with them.

Unlike the Pecks' previous trip on the Oregon Trail where most traffic was headed west, the Santa Fe Trail was heavily traveled in both directions by military detachments and freight caravans who provided up-to-date information to emigrant wagon trains.

Thursday June 24, 1858. Laid by and washed etc. Afternoon a party of 8 men with two waggons came up going to Arizona New Mexico. Also a company of five packers returning from California. Reports Buffaloes plenty and grass good to Santa Fee.

Near night came a shower of rain with hard wind and at night another with heavy thunder and lightning which continued most of the night.

Martin refused to do his part of camp duty. We advised him to leave and he done so.

New Mexico Territory included Arizona at that time. Parsons commented on guard duty: "Every person . . . should be compelled to per-

[7] Hafen, *Pike's Peak Gold Rush Guidebooks of 1859* (Parsons Guidebook), 173.

[8] Taylor, *First Mail West*, 35; and Hafen, *Pike's Peak Gold Rush Guidebooks of 1859* (Parsons Guidebook), 174.

form guard duty, and no one should see to excuse himself on any ground except absolute inability from sickness."[9]

Friday June 25, 1858. Morning rainy so that we did not start as early as common. Found the road very slipery and soft. We intended to go 15 miles but did not find water until we had gone 22. Camped on a small creek, ¾ of a mile from the main Turkey Creek. The land is becoming more sandy and level. We met some men that had been out hunting Buffaloes. They had some jerked meat that they gave us a taste. It would have been first rate if it had been salted a little.

Saw a hare. Tom took after it full run not knowing what it was, vainly expecting to ketch it.

Saturday June 26, 1858. Drove to a creek with water in holes. The heat was oppressive so we turned out and waited awhile. When a breeze sprung up, then we drove on to Red Creek eleven miles and camped.

Passed t[w]o Buffaloe carcases and saw several horns.

In the evening the mosquitoes was Terible so that their was no rest for man or animal. The night was excessively hot until just before day. The wind started up and blew hard and cool with thunder and lightning but no rain.

The Pecks were passing from the tall grass prairie to the short grass prairie, the home of vast buffalo herds.[10] At this place a few weeks earlier, on May 14, 1858, John Udell reported that there were immense numbers of buffalo: "Our young men shot them down for sport, and left them for the buzzards and wolves."[11] This is the same John Udell whose 1850 trip to the California gold fields paralleled the Pecks' trip.

Sunday June 27, 1858. We started early. Expected to reach Little Arkansas in 7 miles, but we found 17 miles well laid on. Cool breeze all day. When we reached the creek, we found the company of 8 going to New Mexico.

We are now fairly in the Buffalo country. Passed quite a number of dead ones. Some appeared to have been killed and the meat cut off. Others appears to have died from some cause or other, but we have not seen any yet that is alive and kicking.

---

[9] Hafen, *Pike's Peak Gold Rush Guidebooks of 1859* (Parsons Guidebook) 173.

[10] Duffus, *Santa Fe Trail,* 150.

[11] Udell, *Journal of John Udell,* 7, May 14.

A very high cottonwood on the Little Arkansas River acted as a marker on the trail because it was visible from far out on the plains.[12]

Monday June 28, 1858. Drove 12 miles to Jarvis Creek. The road was more hilley the later part of the way than we have had for some time. Passed some vilages of prarie dogs. Day hot. Fine breeze from the south which made it quite comfortable.

The Jarvis Creek crossing is approximately five miles east of today's Lyons, Kansas.[13]

Tuesday June 29, 1858. Passed Little Cow Creek. Here we were met by a party of Indians. They followed us to our camp on Big Bow Creek 3 miles to trade. We bought a little Buffalo meat and then they left without beging. Day fine. Stiff breeze from the south. Made eleven miles.

The stage carr[y]ing the mail Passed in the afternoon. Three six mule teams, three men mounted and 8 large animals.

At the beginning of 1858, Hockaday and Hall held the U.S. Mail contract, which required that semimonthly trips from Independence to Santa Fe, a distance of 840 miles, be completed in twenty-five days. Beginning July 1 a new contract was awarded to Hall alone that required weekly mail service within twenty days, with stages leaving from each end at 8 A.M. every Monday. The mail was carried in six-mule coaches with three-man teams. While one man drove, another rode alongside the team to keep the animals moving at a fast pace by cracking his long whip, and the third looked after the extra animals. The teams were exchanged every four to six hours. By running at night also, they covered fifty to seventy miles a day.[14]

Wednesday June 30, 1858. Soon after we started we saw a lot of Buffaloe to the left of the road. George, Edmond and Wood went in pursuit while we drove on and then near Plumb Butes we saw them in every direction among the hills, but when we got to the ridge at the butes we had an extensive view with thousands of Buffaloes scatered over the plain as far as the eye could reach. All the afternoon they continued to dash across our road ahead of us. Just as we were going to camp, George*

[12] Simmons, *Following the Santa Fe Trail*, 92.

[13] Simmons, *On the Santa Fe Trail*, 68n6. Franzwa map 35.

[14] Taylor, *First Mail West*, 29, 45–48.

pursued one and I followed as soon as we camped. He had wounded it so that it had stoped, but our amunition was gone. Some Indians came up and killed it and gave us some meat.

*Here Washington ran out of ink, so he continued his diary in pencil.

Although Plum Buttes were only a hundred feet high, they were visible from Cow Creek, ten miles away. In 1867 Captain Charles Christy described the buttes as "a collection of low sand hills, surrounded by dense plum thickets."[15]

It was difficult to bring down a buffalo. That great shaggy mane on the forehead became so thickly matted with sand and dirt that it formed an impenetrable protective shield in addition to the animal's very thick skull bone.[16]

Thursday July 1, 1858. Drove 5 miles to Walnut Creek and stoped to wash about a mile from the ford. Hard wind from the south. Evening a slight sprinkling of rain.

Washington did not mention passing the trading post and stage depot at Walnut Creek, which Bill Allison and Frances Booth had started in 1855.[17] Fort Zarah was later established there at the eastern boundary of today's town of Great Bend.

Friday July 2, 1858. Went on to Pawnee Rock. Found water a mile from the road to the south. Wind North west, the first time that it has been out of a southerly course for 18 days past. Drove 15 miles.

Pawnee Rock was a landmark to travelers crossing the Great Plains and was not far beyond the Great Bend of the Arkansas River. Although not particularly high, from the top travelers could see the rolling plains in all directions.[18] Arthur King Peters, author of *Seven Trails West*, reported that in 1867 Colonel Richard Irving Dodge stood atop Pawnee Rock and "watched the last great bison herd on the Arkansas River: twenty-six miles wide and fifty miles long, the shaggy mass took five days to pass a given point. Twenty years later, in 1887, only 261 lonely bison were left wandering on the range."[19]

[15] Simmons, *On the Santa Fe Trail*, 108; Simmons, *Following the Santa Fe Trail*, 96.

[16] Mattes, *Great Platte River Road*, 259.

[17] Simmons, *On the Santa Fe Trail*, 57; and Simmons, *Following the Santa Fe Trail*, 96.

[18] Adams, *Sunlight and Storm*, 208.

[19] Peters, *Seven Trails West*, 46.

Saturday July 3, 1858. Drove about ten miles to the mouth of Pawnee Fork. Their we struck an old road that followed up the River. Drove about six miles off the road.

A few Rapijos [Arapaho] Indians came to us. We gave the chief a little Coffee and Sugar and he left, much to our satisfaction.

From this point there was no firewood for 200 to 300 miles. The travelers had to burn buffalo chips.[20]

Sunday July 4, 1858. Morning fiered [fired] a pistol. Thought Uncle Sam [the United States] was [the] same. Breakfasted and drove on. Passed about 5000 Indians incamped each side of the road, composed of the Commanches, Chiannas [Cheyennes], Rapahoes, Kioways, and a few Apaches. The Kaws having got afraid of their friends and left a few days before. They have assembled to receive their presents from Government. After passing the village, an Indian asked for a hiefer and we refused him. He shot an arro into it and kiled it. We drew our revolvers and every one got his gun and we threatened him and sent for the chief, which frightened him and he felt they all appeared to disapprove of the act. We drove ten miles and doubled our guard.

James H. Pierce, who had passed by a month earlier, also mentioned the large number of Indians camped in this area: "There were about two thousand Cheyennes and Arapahos camped at that place, but they were entirely friendly."[21] By the time the Pecks arrived, a substantially larger number of Indians appear to have gathered. Author A. B. Adams reported that in 1853 "the government had negotiated a treaty with the Comanches, Kiowas, and Kiowa-Apaches at Fort Atkinson," Kansas. In return for allowing the United States "to build posts and roads in their territory," the Indians were to receive $18,000 in gifts per tribe annually for ten years.[22]

Monday July 5, 1858. Drove 15 miles. Saw no Indians. Road levil. Rather sandy in places. Camped by the side of the river. Day very pleasant.

Tuesday July 6, 1858. Drove ten miles and camped to alow our cattle rest. Saw a Buffalo. Two small parties of Commanches came to us on their way to join their tribe below. We gave them a little provisions and

---

[20] Udell, *Journal of John Udell*, 7, May 19th.

[21] Pierce, "With the Russell Green Party" (May) 6.

[22] Adams, *Sunlight and Storm*, 284.

they went on, much to our satisfaction. Stiff breeze from the south west. Evening cool.

Wednesday July 7, 1858. At daylight a Buffalo appeared on the oposite side of the river. Soon crossed a little below. George & Edmond took after it and killed it, a fine cow but not fat. Laid by and dried meat. Several Indians called. We treated them all to buffalo meat. Wind blew hard from the South.

Thursday July 8, 1858. In the morning as we were geting ready to yoke, a company of Indians came up, moveing up the river to the Apaches, but few of them stoped. They went faster than we did and soon left us. Drove about 15 miles and camped close to the river. Grass good. Day very hot.

Friday July 9, 1858. The wind sprung up in the night. Cool and pleasant. Drove 15 miles. Passed the other road that comes in from Pawnee Fork. Camped about a mile from the road by the river. Afternoon appearance of rain. A light shower at dusk. Camped by a pile of bones. 11 skulls of horses or mules were arainged in a row; and two holes shaped like graves, but appear not to have been filled up, at a little distance. Passed an old Fort. 15 miles.

Is this rather odd arrangement of skulls symbolic of something? In April of 1859 Kellogg described finding a large circle of eighty-five horse skulls near Fort Kearney and speculated that they might commemorate the site of an Indian Massacre.[23]

The old fort was Fort Atkinson, which had been the site of the 1853 treaty negotiations that led to the massing of the Indians seen earlier. It had been abandoned in September of 1853, reoccupied temporarily in June of 1854, and then permanently abandoned in October of 1854. Fort Dodge (and later Dodge City) would be established nearby.[24]

The Pecks were taking the Mountain Branch of the trail, avoiding the Cimarron and Aubry cut-offs.

Saturday July 10, 1858. Just as breakfast was ready, the rain poured down and we rushed into our wagon and took our grub in a huddle. It

[23] Kellogg, "Across the Plains in 1858," *Trail* 5:no. 8 (January 1913):12.

[24] Hafen, *Pike's Peak Gold Rush Guidebooks of 1859* (Parsons Guidebook), 177; and Simmons, *Following the Santa Fe Trail*, 114.

held up about ten oclock. We started at noon. Drove about five miles when it come on to rain again and we camped. Roads slipery.

Sunday July 11, 1858. We were met by a few Indians of the Cheyenna tribe. The main body were encamped a few miles above the crossing. We camped near them. A throng gathered round of all ages and sex. The boys run horses, shot at marks with bows and arrows. We traded some with them for moccasins. 2 capitans and 2 others stoped all night. They all conducted themselves well. We distributed a little bread and Buffalo meat among them and they appeared satisfied. Near night a train crossed the river. Made 15 miles.

When the Lawrence Party, fifty men strong, came through three weeks earlier, they were warned by the men on the mail run to keep the women in their party out of sight of the Indians. When the Indians did see one of the women, they offered to trade two squaws for her.[25] A similar story has been handed down in the oral history of the Peck family. An Indian chief, who was intrigued with Emma's red hair, offered two ponies for her. After Washington refused, the chief kidnapped her, but the Pecks recovered her unharmed. The story cannot be confirmed, but Washington omitted many details in his often-brief daily entries and he never mentioned the women during the seven months they were on the road.

Monday July 12, 1858. Started early. Found it 8 miles to the Indian village. When we got in sight, their was a stream of Squaws and pappooses runing to the road to see the Eliphant. Altho surrounded by hundreds, they behaved with decorum. We got a poney for which we gave a pair of blankets and $8.50 in money. A great number followed us to where we watered our stock and took our dinner when we thought they were going back, but two capitans & a dozen others continued on til we camped. After they got a bit to eat, they all left but the Capitans, one squaw, and three papooses. They staid all night. Appeared to be afraid, whether of us or other Indians, we knew not. Made 20 miles.

The phrase "seeing the elephant," made popular during the California gold rush, meant seeing an exotic sight, something unusual, or to have an adventure. Kellogg described a similar scene in October of 1858 at an Arapaho village where they saw "dozens of naked children mounted on

[25] Holmes, *Covered Wagon Women, 1854–1860*, Vol. 7 (Julia Anna Archibald Holmes), 201.

ponies, sometimes two or three to a pony; the children rode alongside our wagon train showing the same interest in us as white boys . . . would show in a circus coming to town."[26]

Tuesday July 13, 1858. Our Indian friends left us. We parted in great friendship. Met one wagon and four men returning from gold hunting on the South Platt. Drove 25 miles. Road splendid. Camped close to the river, a little below where the river comes in near the bluffs. Some wood on the islands opposite. Grass first rate.

The Colorado gold rush of 1859 resulted in quick disappointment for the gold seekers who arrived in 1858. They expected to pick up handfuls of nuggets, expectations similar to early California gold rushers. The earliest 1858 prospectors in Colorado spent less than a week prospecting before they headed home.[27]

Wednesday July 14, 1858. Stoped and washed in the forenoon, then drove ten miles and camped where the road comes to the river after leaveing it several miles back and geting up on the high lands on bluffs. We counted 51 Buffalo heads without leaving the road. Grass good. A little rain in the evening with thunder and lightning. A heavy shower went to the South.

Reverend Edward Parrish, who crossed the plains in 1844, was appalled at the wasteful destruction of buffalo he witnessed when his party killed enough buffalo for 40,000 pounds of meat, but left most for the birds, "God forgive us for such waste and save us from such ignorance."[28]

Thursday July 15, 1858. Drove 15 miles and camped rite where the road goes up over the bluffs where the river runs in against the bank. Grass good. We passed more timber than we have seen for some time, a number of trees on the right among the hills. A slight shower of rain in the evening.

The Pecks were entering Big Timbers, a forty-five-mile-long grove of cottonwoods that extended along the Arkansas River Valley. It was the first significant stand of timber west of Council Grove and a popular campground for Plains Indians.[29]

---

[26] Kellogg, "Across the Plains in 1858," *Trail* 5:no. 7 (December 1912):12.

[27] West, *Contested Plains*, 104.

[28] Faragher, *Women and Men on the Overland Trail*, 85.

[29] Simmons, *Following the Santa Fe Trail*, 123.

Friday July 16, 1858. Drove 18 miles. We found as we advanced that it had rained heavy the night before. In the afternoon it rained a little. We drove off the road to the river and camped a little below a grove of timber, the largest that we have seen on this stream. Several showers in the night.

Saturday July 17, 1858. Morning rainey which detained us some time. Roads muddy in the forenoon. Drove 18 miles. Camped a mile from the road and about five above the Big Timber. Prarie very rough between the road and river. Met a company of Cherikee Indians returning from a gold hunting expedititon. They report that the gold is in two [too] small quantities to pay. Also met a company of Mexican traiders packing. Slight shower of rain at night.

These Cherokee gold seekers had been part of the Green Russell Party. William Green Russell and Cherokee John Beck were old friends from Lumpkin County, Georgia, who had met in the gold fields of California. Green Russell, who was now living in Kansas and married to a Cherokee, had kept in touch with John Beck following his removal to Cherokee Country (Oklahoma). During the winter of 1858 they decided to prospect for gold in the Rocky Mountains. Each organized a group of men to leave in the spring. They met here at Big Bend on the Arkansas (near Pawnee Rock). Under the command of Cherokee George Hicks, the party of 104 arrived at Bent's Fort on June 12 and proceeded to Ralston's Creek where they began prospecting on June 26.[30]

The Cherokees wanted to take time to build a fort. Civilized and educated, they told prospector James Pierce that were afraid of attack from "wild" (Western) Indians.[31] Most of the miners felt that it would be a waste of time because they had not seen any Indians since leaving Pawnee Rock.[32] They were there to find gold. The Cherokees knew better because they had encountered hostile Indians while prospecting in the area the previous summer.[33]

The finds were so meager that the men quickly became disheartened. They scattered in different directions to prospect, but by the evening of

[30] Spencer, *Green Russell and Gold*, 49.

[31] Pierce, "First Prospecting of Colorado," 7.

[32] Pierce, "With the Russell Green Party," 6.

[33] Hafen, *Pike's Peak Gold Rush Guidebooks of 1859*, 48–50.

July 3 all had returned to camp where they held a meeting. Philander Simmons was just back from near the Cache Le Poudre River where he had met some packers that reported a thousand lodges of hostile Cheyennes nearby.[34] That was enough for the Cherokees. By ten o'clock the next morning, they had started for home.[35]

Sunday July 18, 1858. Heavy showers of rain in the night. Drove 16 miles. Road muddy in the forepart of the day. The green flies was very bad at noon. Camped near the road. No thunder or lightning. It is a long time since we had a night without.

Monday July 19, 1858. Drove 15 miles and camped about two miles below Bents Fort. We expected to pass it, but it was farther than we expected. More sandy roads than we had any day previous. Sprinkling of rain in the evening.

Bent's Fort was one of the most famous landmarks on the trail. This was the new fort that had been completed by William Bent in 1853. The sixteen-foot-high stone walls had twelve rooms with ten-foot-high ceilings built around an inner courtyard.[36]

Tuesday July 20, 1858. Drove 17 miles. Passed Bents Fort in the morning. Did not stop because their was quite a number of Indians camped by a high stone wall. After passing the Fort, the bluffs came in so that the river bottom is narrow. The road kept on the bluffs most of the day. Good wheeling, but hard on cattles feet. We have several lame. Sprinkling of rain in the evening.

Apparently the Pecks were afraid to stop at this major trading post because of the Indians near the Fort. William Bent was in Kansas City at the time, but in 1858 he reported that the Arapahos and Cheyennes were "very uneasy and restless about their country" because of the large number of whites settling there.[37]

Wednesday July 21, 1858. Laid by. Washed and attended to our lame cattle. Two Mexicans passed going to the Fort and returned in the evening.

---

[34] Ibid. (Cherokee Expedition of 1858), 304.

[35] Spencer, *Green Russell and Gold*, 52.

[36] Lavender, *Bent's Fort*, 347, 444 n. 7.

[37] Ibid., 358–59; and Marks, *In a Barren Land*, 145.

Thursday July 22, 1858. Drove 20 miles. Road good, hard on cattles feet in places. Our lame cattle are better. Camped 1-½ miles below Bents old Fort.

The Pecks were approaching the ruins of Bent's Old Fort, which had been built by Cerain Saint Vrain and the four Bent brothers in 1833 with solid adobe walls thirty inches thick and fourteen feet high, plus two round towers eighteen feet tall. The large courtyard opened into twenty-five rooms.[38]

Friday July 23, 1858. We expected to ford the river at the ruins, but found it too deep. Had been told that the ford was 5 miles above, so we drove on 8 miles and found no ford. Camped. Three boys went up and two down to prospect. Those from above reported a place where the river could be forded 1-½ miles above.

In the morning when we were yokeing, an ox came up and very politely asked to accompany us (as plainly as an ox can speak). We answered in the affirmative and he came on.

Saturday July 24, 1858. Went up to try the ford. Found it good. We took one wagon at a time. Got all over safe and dry. Drove 4 miles down to the Timpas, then struck out south to the road which soon crossed the creek where we found water in holes & camped, being about 13 miles from the Old Fort and 580 miles from the Missouri river. Day very hot and calm.

Sunday July 25, 1858. Sixteen miles over a levil beautiful road brought us to the Timpas. Good camping a mile from the road. Water brackish. Shower of rain at night.

Monday July 26, 1858. We expected to find water in the Timpas wherever we came to it. At noon we stoped to water. Found the creek dry. Then drove to the Willows. 19 miles in all. Here we were sure of water but were disappointed. Some showers of rain fell which relieved our cattle of thirst. Kept on for Hole in the Rock, 9 miles farther. At dark we found some pools of water in the bed of a creek from the rain to day. Turned our cattle loose, picketed the horses, took a drink of milk, and went to bed, Guard excepted. Night cool.

Tuesday July 27, 1858. Started a little after sun rise. Two miles we found water among rocks. Did not know whether it is Hole in the Rock

[38] Peters, *Seven Trails West*, 68.

or not, but we halted, cooked breakfast, and spent the day in rest and hunting. Hole in the Rock is one mile farther on the left of the road. Plenty of wood and water but little grass.

Hole-in-the-Rock was the headwaters of the Timpas Creek. It was a deep hole that held water even when the creek was dry.[39]

Wednesday July 28, 1858. Laid by to rest and recruit our lame cattle. Edmond & Wood each killed a hare & Hunted antilopes but got none.

Thursday July 29, 1858. Drove 16 miles over a splendid road to Hole in the Prarie. Found plenty of water and grass but no wood. When we were about starting, a wild horse came up near, but was very shy and soon left. Our lame cattle are all better. All the boys went a hunting, returned with two antilopes.

Friday July 30, 1858. Drove to Purgatory 11-½ miles. Grass poor. The boys killed two turkeys.

This is the Purgatoire River.

Saturday July 31, 1858. Went on to where the road leaves the creek and camped. The boys went out to hunt. All returned as they went except Edmond. He brought in six turkeys. Afterwards he and Wood killed another.

Near night six men came up. They had been gold hunting near Pikes Peak. Now they are going to Arizona or California.

Here we wedged our wagon wheels preparitory to going through the Raton Pass.

Hot in the middle of the day. Evenings and morning cool.

The six men may have split off from the Cherokee party or were some of those who had left camp on July 25. Writing of his experience in 1876, Philander Simmons named the twelve white people in the Cherokee party as: Mr. Kirk, wife and family, Mr. Brown, George McDougal, Mr. Tubbs, Levi Braumbaugh, Johns, Taylor, Mr. Kelly, and himself.[40]

Although the mountain route over the Raton Pass had the advantages of more water and fewer Indian attacks than the Cimarron Cut-off, it was a formidable obstacle which few immigrant wagons attempted to cross

[39] Simmons, *Following the Santa Fe Trail*, 132.

[40] Hafen, *Pike's Peak Gold Rush Guidebooks of 1859* (Cherokee Expedition of 1858), 301.

until Dick Wooten built an improved toll road through the area a few years later. The summit rose to over 7,800 feet.[41]

Sunday August 1, 1858. Commenced the ascent of the Raton. After driving 11 miles, we camped. Good grass & water. In the night our horses took fright and broke loose and stampeeded the cattle. We found the cattle scatered on the mountain sides and two horses. The six men spoken of yesterday camped by us and their horses went with the rest.

Monday August 2, 1858. Got safe over the pass and camped a little before the road reaches the valley of the Cannadian. Drove 10 miles. We found a few very bad places in the road, but upon the whole the road was better than we expected.

Found all our horses after a search of two hours, which detained us til late in the morning.

While hunting the horses, Wood killed a deer. Also Brown of the other company killed one.

In comparison to the relatively easy crossing by the Pecks, historian Arthur King Peters described Raton Pass as "almost impassable for wagons."[42] And diarist Susan Magoffin reported that in 1846 their party never made more than half a mile an hour. One day they made only six hundred to eight hundred yards. It took them five days to cross with the wagons being hauled over by hand.[43]

Tuesday August 3, 1858. Drove to the Canadian, crossed, and followed the stream to where the road turnes to the Bluffs and camped. Good grass and water.

Brown killed an antelope and gave it to us.

Wednesday August 4, 1858. While at breakfast McDowel, an old mountaineer, picked a quarel with Brown, the chief man of the company, and chalanged Him to fight with rifles. Brown declined when McDowel used very abusive language which but few men would bear. At night Brown told him that he must leave in the morning as we were at the settlement, which he refused to do and made some threats.

Drove 18 miles to the Vermijo. We expected water at ten miles but found none.

---

[41] Simmons, *Following the Santa Fe Trail,* 116; and Duffus, *Santa Fe Trail,* 250.

[42] Peters, *Seven Trails West,* 56.

[43] Duffus, *Santa Fe Trail,* 153.

Thursday August 5, 1858. Before sunrise before all was up, McDowel took his rifle and stood before the tent and asked Brown if he intended to stick to what he said last night. He said yes when Mc instantly fired, the ball taking effect in the right side. As Brown fell, He sprung on him and took his revolver, warned all not to follow him and walked off.

Poor Brown survived four hours and a half when he bid adue to all earthly things. In the afternoon we intered his remains in as becoming a manner as circumstances would admit about 150 yards from the crossing of the Vermajo on the west side and 20 feet south of the road with a stone at the head and feet.

In the evening 3 sanyards [Spaniards] came and camped by us. 12 pack animals.

Washington likely had met George McDougal, but either misspelled or misunderstood his name due to accent. McDougal's history includes an accusation of his being run out of California by a Vigilance Committee for killing two men. On October 24, 1858, McDougal was reported living in a cabin near the ruins of the old Pueblo (now Pueblo, Colorado) with his Mexican wife.[44] A further report of McDougal and three other men going to a tent, pointing their guns at the occupants, and demanding an apology has a familiar ring to it. On another occasion, McDougal insulted a member of the Kellogg party, trying to entice him into a duel, which they wisely avoided because McDougal was "known to be a dead shot with either rifle or revolver."[45]

One possible identity of Mr. Brown is John Lowery Brown,[46] who was an experienced Cherokee gold miner. In documents filed forty years later, in 1909, his daughter reported that he died in 1859 and gives her birth date as December 1859,[47] but there's room for speculation considering

[44] Kellogg, "Across the Plains in 1858," *Trail* 5:no. 7 (December 1912):10.

[45] Ibid., Jan. 1913, 9–10.

[46] Wright, "The Journal of John Lowery Brown of the Cherokee Nation en Route to California in 1850," *Chronicles of Oklahoma* 12:2 (June 1834):177–213. Brown had returned to Tahlequah, Oklahoma, where his sons David (1856) and Martin (Feb. 1858) were born, leaving open the possibility that Mollie could have been born in December of 1858. (Birth years are included in Mollie's application no. 3148, see note 106, below.) Unfortunately, the *Cherokee Advocate* in Tahlequah, Oklahoma, did not publish from 1853 to 1870, thus there are no newspaper accounts of the return of the Cherokee party from Colorado. Washington's description of Brown as leader is in keeping with Brown's experience, but Washington does not identify him as a Cherokee. Was this detail unimportant to Washington, or was it not obvious?

[47] NARA M1104, Roll 34:7, *Eastern Cherokee Roll of 1909 (Guion Miller Roll)*, Application no. 3148, Mollie K. Trent, nee Brown.

that she was told she was born the year he died, and that year in actuality may have been 1858.

Although the identification of Mr. Brown remains a mystery, his gravesite does not. He was buried near the Santa Fe Trail crossing of the Vermijo River. Today there is a Santa Fe Trail marker located a few hundred feet north of this crossing on the road off Highway US64 that leads to the abandoned coal-mining town of Dawson.[48]

Friday August 6, 1858. Drove to the Cimeron ten miles, very short ones. Stoped and washed. Here is a Rancho up the creek near the mountain. Great many cattle and sheep.

Saturday August 7, 1858. Drove 15 miles to a pass in the mountains. Good place to camp. Passed Maxwells rancho on the Rio Riyore. The buildings were in sight and some wheat and corn, unfenced. Saw a great many cattle and sheep. Rain at night.

Lucien Maxwell began the small community of Rayado in 1848 where he built an adobe house in the 1850s. He later moved north to Cimarron where he built a large mansion on the plaza in 1864 and eventually possessed a land grant of 1.7 million acres.[49]

Sunday August 8, 1858. Drove 17 miles to the Ocate, crossed the stream, and camped. Soon after it commenced to rain from a small cloud overhead, and in a few minuits it poured down torrents of rain and hail until the hail and water covered the ground to the depth of two or three inches. Slacked a little two or three times and then poured down again and continued until after dark. It beat through our wagon covers and tents until wet our beding and almost every thing we had. We divided our bread so that each one got a piece and some dried meat, then went to bed cold and wet.

Monday August 9, 1858. Laid by to dry our things. The hail did not all melt til near night.

Tuesday August 10, 1858. Drove to Fort Union 18 miles. Road first rate. We camped a mile and a half above the Fort. Grass poor.

Wednesday August 11, 1858. Visited the Fort. Swaped our Bull for a

---

[48] Simmons, *Following the Santa Fe Trail*, 138.
[49] Ibid., 138–43.

cow & calf. Also traded our Indian pony for a mare. To all appearances as good as the pony, and got first rate saddle and bridle to boot.

George sold his muly [one horn or hornless] hieffer for $8.

Afternoon drove past the Fort about three miles and camped by a salt pond, but we found a spring of fresh water near by. Grass good.

This was the first Fort Union, a series of small log buildings that was built in 1851 against a side hill where it was sheltered from the ever-blowing winds. Fort Union was the major supply depot for goods received from the East for distribution to the isolated small forts sprinkled throughout the vast District of New Mexico, which stretched all the way to California.

The salt pond, with cattle grazing in the surrounding fields, is still visible on the road to the fort along with deep wagon ruts that cut across the grasslands surrounding the fort.

Thursday August 12, 1858. Drove over an excelent road 22 miles to the creek, about two miles from Las Vegus. Grass very short, being nipt off by the stock that runs here and the great numbers that camp here. No wood.

The Raton (or Mountain) and Cimarron branches of the Santa Fe Trail had converged a short distance above this location, which accounted for the great numbers camping here.

Friday August 13, 1858. Morning we missed 9 head of our oxen. We hunted all day and found them not. We fear that they are stolen. Afternoon offered a reward of 10 dollars. Several Mexicans went out to hunt for them but did not bring them in.

Saturday August 14, 1858. Still we are waiting in hopes of geting our cattle. Afternoon we offered $20. In the evening it commenced to rain. Our cattle got scatered and the rain continued to pour down in torrents the most of the night.

In the evening Tom went for the horses to picket for the night and by mistake got a wild one in place of the poney that we got at Fort Union. When he discovered his mistake it was so dark that we could not find it, so after a fruitless search we gave it up.

Sunday August 15, 1858. We found our cattle and poney. The little creek by our camp was swolen to that degree that it was not fordable. We offered $5 per head for our lost cattle.

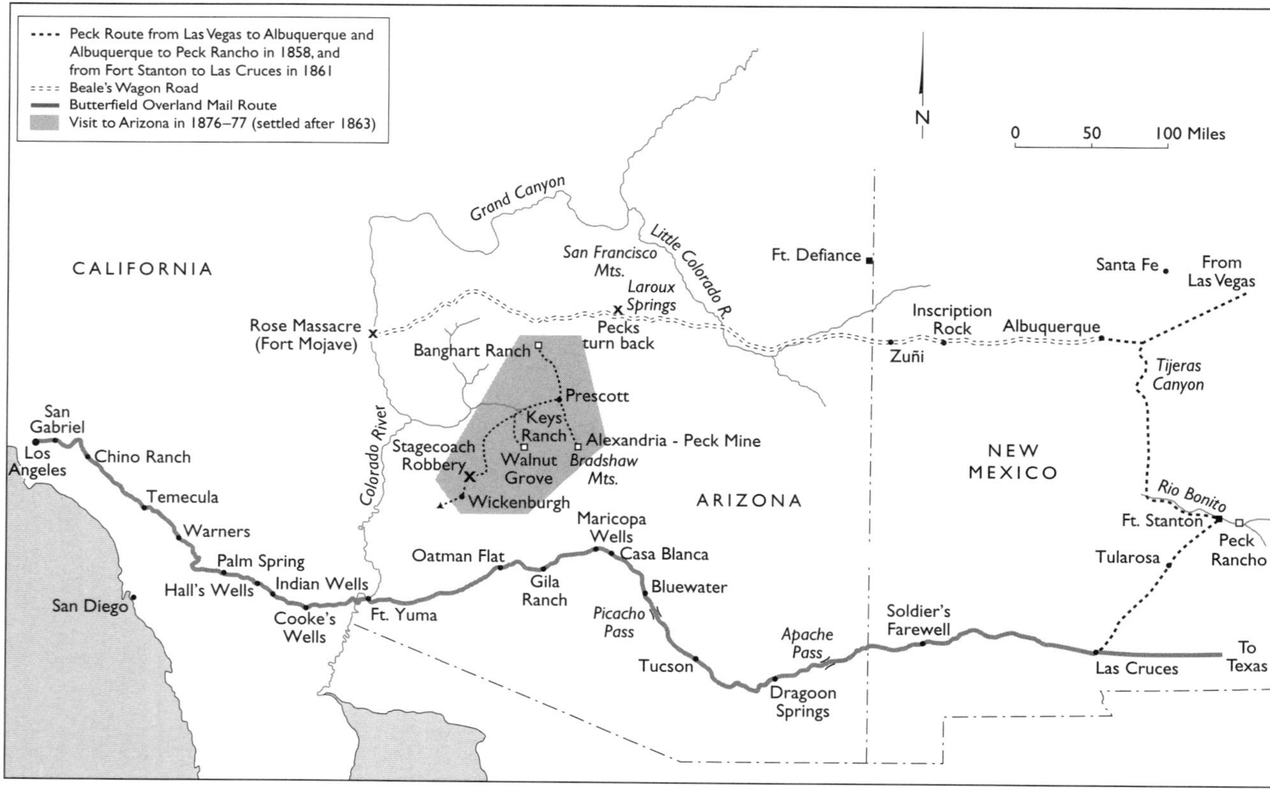

From Albuquerque the Pecks traveled over Beale's Road as far as Laroux Spring, just west of today's Flagstaff. There they met the Rose Party who had been attacked by Indians at the Colorado River. They returned to Albuquerque and then moved to the Rio Bonito Valley near Fort Stanton. Just prior to the outbreak of the Civil War, deteriorating conditions forced them to leave. In the spring of 1861 they went south to pick up the Butterfield Overland Mail Route to San Gabriel, California. In 1876 Washington and Mercy visited their family in the Prescott area, which had developed after 1863 when the Territory of Arizona was created. They were held up in a stage robbery in 1877 on their way to Oakland, California.

Washington had learned on his previous wagon crossing that missing cattle did not always wander off by accident. When William Napton traveled the trail in 1857, he reported problems with some Indians and white men who stampeded cattle at night, hid them, and then came around to find out if a reward was offered for their return. After making a deal for so much a head, the men then "found" them.[50]

A daytime stampede had a different purpose. Napton wrote: "Suddenly, two of the young bucks raised up a loud whoop and started their horses at full speed. Taking a corner of their blankets in each hand and holding them above their heads so that they made a flapping sound in the air, they went sweeping along right against the cattle, almost instantly creating a stampede." This stampede was not for stealing cattle, but for the Indians' amusement; some of them even helped stop the stampede they had started. Needless to say, the teamsters herding the cattle were not amused.[51]

Monday August 16, 1858. Drove on about 5 miles past Las Vegus. Found good grass. After passing a can[y]on, we left the Santa Fee road, turned to the left on the road to Albiquerque following the course of the mountain on the left.

The Pecks left the Santa Fe Trail at this point to go south toward Albuquerque, thereby missing Santa Fe, which was about forty miles slightly northwest of their location.

Tuesday August 17, 1858. Continued our course along the foot of the mountain to near its termination and camped near a small creek and rancho. Road good, the land sandy with a great deal of pine and cedar timber, some of considerable size. The creek we camped in is called Apachee Spring.

This morning we were joined by 4 young men. We hawl their stuff. They appear decient fellows. Two of the yong men that were with us left to go to Santa Fee to get what letters is in the office for the company.

Wednesday August 18, 1858. Crossed the Rio Pecos. Here is a small Mexican town, Antono Chico [Anton Chico]. The river is crowded between high hills. The narrow bottom lands is about all under cultiva-

---

[50] Napton, *On the Santa Fe Trail in 1857*, 13.

[51] Ibid., 22.

tion. Soon after leaving the town we came into the Sante Fe road and crossed a high ridge, rockey most of the way to the sumit. Camped near water on the left in holes in the bed of a creek. Good grass. Here we were overtaken by a young man with a letter from a man in Las Vegas offering 4 yoke of oxon and two mules for Georges mares and our claim on the cattle we lost. We wrote that we would take it and are going to wait a day for them.

Thursday August 19, 1858. Laid by waiting for Mr Dall to come with the mules and oxon. Washed and rested. Evening came but no Dall.

The Dahl Brothers Trading Post and Warehouse was located in Cimarron. They owned two hundred teams of oxen and mules and made two trips a year back to Westport, Missouri.[52]

Friday August 20, 1858. We started with the ox teams while George waited until noon, but he did not come. Then George left and overtook us. We camped near the mouth of Canon Blanco by a small lake or pond. Our road lay through a rough mountain country, yet the road was good, rather sandy near our camp. Grass good.

Saturday August 21, 1858. Passed through Canon Blanco with mountains almost perpendicular on each side for 10 or 12 miles. The road smoth and almost livil, rather sandy the first part. When we left the canon, we ascended gradualy to the top of the mountain which was an extensive plain of gentle rolling prarie with patches of cedar timber. Camped by the Lagunas. We drove a little two far in passing a train in camp and found the grass very short while the rain poured down, so we had to stop. Drove 20 or 22 miles.

Sunday August 22, 1858. Drove about 8 miles when it came on to rain. Their was a little mudy water in holes, so we camped and spent the remainder of the day with plenty of wood and grass. Levy and Frank returned from Santa Fee and brought a lot of letters.

The two young men were probably Levi Braumbaugh, one of the white members of the Cherokee party, and Frank B. Howell.

Monday August 23, 1858. Drove about 12 miles over a beautiful prarie covered with gramma grass and camped by some holes of water, and

[52] Simmons, *Following the Santa Fe Trail*, 140–41.

soon the rain poured down in torrents until the ground was flooded. After ditching a little we raised a mound of earth and made a fire on it with some wood that we brought with us and cooking commenced, but proceeded very tardily, however we got a kind of a supper, felt thankful, and went to bed. A drizling rain continued the most of the night.

Black grama and buffalo grass grew in this area. Buffalo grass was described by agriculturist Raymond Pool as "being notoriously nutritious both in fresh and dry state, and therefore good forage year round."[53]

Tuesday August 24, 1858. Morning the clouds heavy and lowering. While we were takeing breakfast, it commenced to rain and in a little time it poured down, which continued until afternoon.

Wednesday August 25, 1858. Drove 15 miles. Road good, but rather soft. In the night some thieves came and stole, while the guard was out tending to the horses, a rifle, a pair of holster pistols, brass kettle, and a pair of boots. In the morning we searched the wagons of a train that camped near us with Mexican drivers but found nothing. This is the first day . . .

Washington's last sentence is unfinished. Perhaps he was interrupted by the shot fired by the guard in the next entry.

Thursday August 26, 1858. Drove about 18 miles through a narrow pass among high mountains to the valley of the Rio Grande. Camped on high table land near a creek. Grass very short. In the night one of the guard saw something crawling up to a horse. He leviled a musket loded with a ball and 3 buck shot and fired when up jumped a man and run. In a few minuits a Mexican cart that camped near us hitched up and left.

Friday August 27, 1858. Drove to Albiquerqui. Camped near the river. Grass very poor. Concluded to wait a few days until a dispatch is received from Fort Defiance. Then we will know whether it is safe to go Beals route. George gave his mares and $10 for four mules.

A Mexican was taken and whiped for stealing. In the morning he was found hung at the Court House. It was said that he hung himself. It may be that he did and it is posible that he was assisted in the performance of so important an act, which rid the world of a thief.

---

[53] Pool, *Marching with the Grasses*, 136–37.

Washington had been talking to the people in Albuquerque who were promoting Beale's Wagon Road, which ran along the northern part of the territory. His original intent was to go south and travel along the southern border of the territory.

Saturday August 28, 1858. Moved down about four miles to better grass. Day hot. Edmond killed a wild goose.

Sunday August 29, 1858. Day hot. Sprinkling of rain near night.

Monday August 30, 1858. Continues hot.

Tuesday August 31, 1858. No dispatch from Fort Defiance. Hot and dry.

Beale's Wagon Road

By the time the Pecks arrived in Albuquerque, three large wagon trains had taken Beale's Wagon Road. The first left on June 30.[54] Cautious and used to making his own decisions, Washington weighed the information and waited for word from Fort Defiance, which was the farthest western outpost along Beale's Road. It was located just west of the current New Mexico-Arizona border and a little north of Beale's Road.

In 1857, the year before, Lieutenant Edward F. Beale had been appointed to find the best route from Zuni to the Colorado River along the thirty-fifth parallel. Historian Bertha Dodge wrote, "Steep slopes were to be cut down and graded with pick and shovel, holes to be filled in," and campsites located with nearby fuel, water, and grass to accommodate ongoing migration to California. In addition, Beale was at long last getting a chance to test his belief that camels could fill a need in the southwest desert for an animal "that few Indians would covet, but that could pack heavy loads, walk endless miles, feed upon the unappetizing plants native to desert regions, and survive days, if need be, without fresh water." The camels soon proved their worth. Not so the guide he had hired, Savedra, who had been there before. He should have been able to lead them to good camping places with plenty of water and around the deep impassable canyons, some thirty to forty miles long. Beale wrote,

[54] Udell, *Journal of John Udell*, June 30, 14.

"We unfortunately have no guide, the wretch I employed at the urgent request and advice of everyone in Albuquerque, at enormous expense, being the most ignorant and irresolute ass extant."[55]

Wednesday September 1, 1858. Went to town and took in supplies and started for the Rio Puerco, 18 m, to wait for news from Navajos. Drove until dark to find grass and camped without water. Edmond and Mr. [____] stoped in town and did not overtake us. Very heavy sand most of the way from the river. Forded the river without difficulty by doubling teams.

After five days of waiting, the Pecks were anxious to get on their way. Albuquerque was on the east bank of the Rio Grande, which they had to ford. En route to the Rio Puerco River, they would meet any soldiers coming from Fort Defiance with a dispatch while they put a few miles behind them.

Thursday September 2, 1858. Got up before day, got breakfast, and started just after sunrise and reached the Puerco half past nine o'clock. Grass tolerable. Road heavy a great part of the way.

Friday September 3, 1858. Still waiting. Day hot.

Saturday September 4, 1858. Washed and fixed up a little.

Sunday September 5, 1858. Concluded to start tomorrow. Wedged our wagon wheels. No express yet.

Monday September 6, 1858. A small company of soldiers overtook us going to Defiance. We drove 20 miles. Camped near the Rio Rito Road. Good but rather sandy. A train passed returning from Fort Defiance. The news they bring is rather favorable. 20 [miles].

The Pecks were deceived. The situation with the Navajo at Fort Defiance had been tumultuous for three months. The problems had begun when Navajo cattle wandered into the Fort's hayfields to graze. When they were not removed as requested, sixty were shot. Chief Manuelito was furious. On July 11 a Navaho shot an arrow into the back of a young black boy, who died. He was a slave belonging the post commander, Brevet Major William Brooks. On July 21 Brooks demanded that the Navajo turn the

[55] Dodge, *Road West*, 92–93, 120–21.

murderer over to them within twenty days, but he had little belief that they would do so. Thus he had requested permission from headquarters to begin a campaign against the Navajo. Major Brooks had reported this information to headquarters on August 1, more than a month earlier.[56]

On August 29 a small skirmish took place at Bear Spring on the road from Albuquerque to Fort Defiance.[57] The men coming from Fort Defiance would have known of the ongoing problems, so it is hard to understand why they left the Pecks with the impression that it was safe to proceed. The Pecks' route passed a few miles south of Bear Spring.[58]

Soldier William Woods Averell, who was serving at Fort Defiance, reported that the Navajo War began in earnest on September 9 when Lieutenant Colonel Miles led an expedition of 310 men to punish the Navajo in Canyon de Chelly. Although Canyon de Chelly is north of Fort Defiance, the Navajo nation included parts of New Mexico, Arizona, Utah, and Colorado. There were from 17,000 to 20,000 Navajos, whom Averell described as "the most powerful nation then known and [they] could assemble from 2,000 to 4,000" warriors in two days.[59]

Tuesday September 7, 1858. Drove 15 miles. Passed the Lagunas, a Town of Pueblo Indians, and camped near Cevero [Cubero]. Grass first rate from Rito to Lagunas. The most of way is heavy sand. Up the valley from the latter to camp hard and good. A little rain in the fore part of the night.

Bought a sheep for a dollar. Good mutton, but small. 15.

Washington had obtained a copy of an illustrated Congressional Report as evidenced by his diary entries noting that he expected to find water holes, rivers, and other landmarks at specific distances. The mileage recorded by Washington and Udell, who was ahead of the Pecks, was similar. They seemed to be using the same road report with the major difference being that Washington used Spanish names while Udell used English translations.

Wednesday September 8, 1858. Passed Cevero [Cubero], a small Mexican Town. Drove to near the forks of the road, the left hand going

[56] Eckert, *Ten Years in the Saddle*, 149–51; U.S. Congress, 1867, *Condition of the Indian Tribes*, 331.

[57] Eckert, *Ten Years in the Saddle*, 168.

[58] Giese, *Forts of New Mexico*, 1.

[59] Eckert, *Ten Years in the Saddle*, 154, 170.

to California via Zuni, the other to Fort Defiance. Made 17 miles. Road good, being in a valley all the way. On a mountain to the right it snowed in the night until the sumit was covered with snow. 16.

Thursday September 9, 1858. Soon after we started we had to cross a bit of pumis stone 3 miles wide. Very hard on cattles feet. The[n] followed a beautiful valley to the left round a point of mountain and entered the pass of the Rockey Mountains. Found the road good except rockey in places. No hill of any account but a gradual assent which elevated us several hundred feet. We found the 21 to be 27 miles instead of 21 as expected. Reached Aqua Frio after dark hunguary, thirsty, and weary. Camped in a grove of tall pines. Good grass. 27.

The lava flow they crossed is now part of El Malpais National Monument. In contrast to Washington's concern for his cattle's feet, John Udell noted only that the pumice stone was hard on the wagons. Udell described Cold Spring (Aqua Frio): "Around this spring is an open forest of large, fine pine timber, plenty of grass and good soil."[60]

Friday September 10, 1858. Started at noon. Drove 13 miles. At about 3 miles after leaveing camp we crossed the back bone of North America. The last ridge was steep and very rockey in the decent. We soon came out in a beautiful valley. Road good. Camped without water. We did not expect it for 27 miles. 13.

The Continental Divide passed through the Zuni Mountains. On July 7, John Udell wrote: "This morning we came over the dividing ridge between the Atlantic and Pacific waters. It was formerly hard to ascend but Mr. Beale has since improved it and made it easy."[61]

Saturday September 11, 1858. Started at sun rise. Drove to Moro or Inscription Rock, 7 miles. Found water in a hole. The cattle ran into it and stirred it up and would not drink it, so we drove on to Ojo Piscado, 13 miles. Found excelent water and grass. Road rockey and lose sand in places, but upon the whole it is a good road. No hills of any note. Made 112 miles in six days. From Albiquerque 132 miles.

I have not rated the distance in some places as high as the most of the company thought it, but I prefer to follow my own judgement.

---

[60] Udell, *Journal of John Udell*, Sept. 9, 15.

[61] Ibid., July 7, 16.

Travelers had been carving their names and pictographs on El Morro or Inscription Rock since the 1600s.[62] Udell described it as two hundred feet high, which extended back half a mile, and then sloped off gradually so that it could be climbed easily up the slope, and "it has the ruins of an ancient fortress on top." L. J. Rose and John Udell inscribed their names on the rock on July 7, and the John Bradford Cave wagon train, which followed them, camped there for three days from July 28 to 30.[63]

In the six weeks of summer heat since the Rose and Cave wagon trains had stopped, the water level likely had dropped. Washington was more concerned with finding water for his cattle than stopping to write on the rock.

Sunday September 12, 1858. Laid in camp. Washed and wedged our wagon wheels etc.

Monday September 13, 1858. Passed Zuni, situate[d] in a large valley, town on a Rock. Pop 1200, about 14 miles from Pescado Spring. We expected it was 18 miles to the next water. Passed the town about 8 miles and camped without water. A number of Puebloes came and spent the night and traded for blankets and deer skins. Made 24 miles.

Udell stated that the Pueblo Indians were civilized, spoke Spanish and Indian languages, and raised wheat, corn, beans, pumpkins, melons, and stock, with enough surplus to sell to the army. Fearful of the Navajo around them, they kept a sentinel on top of the mountain and were assisting the army in the war against the Navajo. Fort Defiance was fifty miles north, close enough to be somewhat of a protection for them.[64]

Tuesday September 14, 1858. We might have got water about 3 m from camp and 2 from the road, but we expected it was not more than 10 to water, so we drove on, but instead after it proved to be 27 which made it very hard on our cattle. Reached Ojo Ridondo at sun set, which is a hole in a levil plain of about 200 ft deep, 30 rods [500 feet] in diameter at the top with a deep pond of water 80 ft in diameter at the bottom. Clear but a little brackish.

At night 3 of the company came up with nine ponies that they had

---

[62] Young, *Kokopelli, Casanova of the Cliff Dwellers*, viii.

[63] Udell, *Journal of John Udell*, Sept. 7, 16; Dodge, *Road West*, 139, 148; and Baley, *Disaster at the Colorado*, 78.

[64] Udell, *Journal of John Udell*, July 10, 17.

stolen from the Indians. George and self was carrying their provisions etc. So we put their stuff out of our wagons and told them that we would not travil any longer with them. After super they left, leaving their stuff with Tubs. Made 27 miles.

Disgusted at the boys' behavior, Washington could not let the foolish young men endanger his small wagon train of mostly women and children in the middle of Indian country.

Ojo Redondo was also called Jacob's Well. Udell wrote that it was difficult for stock to get down to the water because they had to get down a sand bank. He did not care for the taste of the brackish water, but the cattle loved it and drank so much that they could hardly get out of the well.

The Pecks were passing from New Mexico to present-day Arizona.

Wednesday September 15, 1858. Laid by to rest. About 9 o'clock 7 Indians came up in persuit of the horses taken yesterday. We put them on the trail and the[y] went in persuit. At night Levi, one of the 3, returned. Came off the road. Saw no Indians.

We find that we passed El Monte yesterday without seeing it, so we made two drives in one. The water was Ojo Redondo or Round Spring.

Washington's help to the Indians was the only sensible response that could distance them from the boys' thievery and help safeguard his family.

El Monte had been described by Udell as "a curious rock, standing alone, on the left of the road; it resembles an extremely large monument, eighty or one hundred feet high."[65]

Thursday September 16, 1858. Soon after we started, we met two Indians returning from persuing the thieves. They reported that they found the two asleep, took the horses and left them. We passed the Ojo Navajo at 7 miles, a great number springs, some very mirey. Drove on to the Aroyer de Carriso 7 miles. Found good grass and water in holes. Made 14 miles.

In the night the two boys came up. They say that the Indians came on them while asleep before sun set & got the 9 horses and 3 belonging to the boys and then made a rush on them with a yell. They awoke and ran, leaving everything but their arms. Laurence escaped with shirt, pants and shoes. Barker saved all his clothes but his shoes.

[65] Ibid., July 10, 16–17.

Udell described Navajo Springs, also called Mud Springs, as being tinctured with sulphur and surrounded with concealed mire-holes. "The ground will appear perfectly hard where a person or animal is walking, and in an instant they will drop through, and it takes hard labor to get either out."[66]

Friday September 17, 1858. Drove 22 miles to the bed of a creek with a little dirty water in holes. Grass very poor. We found it 20 miles to where the road leaves Aroyer de Juan Chavis and 12 miles to this place. Road good, rather sandy in places. Made 22 miles.

Levi was waiting here when we came. He tells a great yarn about being chased by Navijoes and how he killed two, but it sounds very fishey. I told Tubs that as those horse thieves was with him that I would not travil with them, and from that time we were two companies.

Tubs and co camped near us.

Saturday September 18, 1858. Our road followed the bed of the creek most of the fournoon and deep and heavy wheeling. Near noon a cow calved and we had to wait. Tubs and co went on. We went on near night. Stoped without water. Grass in bunches. Country very levil with here and their a chunck of a hill that has not washed down yet. Made 16 miles.

Brought Forward	*132 miles*
Made this week	*103*
	235 Total

Udell noted that finding water for the next fifty miles was uncertain. They expected to cross seven creeks between here and the Little Colorado, which would have dry sand on the surface, but by digging from one to three feet deep, they could find water.[67]

Sunday September 19, 1858. Morning found water in holes in the bed of a creek near camp. Our camp was ½ a mile from some rockey hills that shut in on the river. In passing we will have to drive in the bed of the river, now dry. Continued down the river road. Good. Turned off the road to camp. Grass good. About 18 miles down we after came to the dry bed of the river. A stream of runing water came in from the south East with a strip of cotton wood and brush along its margin. Made 20 miles.

---

[66] Dodge, *Road West*, 173; Udell, *Journal of John Udell*, July 12, 17–18.

[67] Ibid., July 14, 18.

Udell reported finding some muddy white water running in one creek. Although unsure of its content, they used the water and "were not poisoned."[68]

Monday September 20, 1858. Continued down the river 19 miles and crossed ford. Good. Here we leave the river on our right. Bunch grass the most of the way along the river road. Very good the most of the way. In some places it is washed in gullies, which makes it rough and slow getting along.

We passed Tubs etc about 4 miles. Their team appears to be geting tired. Made 19 miles.

Tuesday September 21, 1858. We thought this morning that we left the Colorado Chiquito, but a drive of 18 miles brought us to it again. Road rather soft. Our course was NW. Made 18 miles.

The river meanders back and forth along their route. Because of the quicksand bottom, it could be forded in only a few places.[69]

Wednesday September 22, 1858. This morning we bid adue to the Colorado Chiquito. But a drive of 10 miles brought us back to it again. 4 miles farther after passing three red butes, we left it and its brackish water for certain and steered for the mountains. Drove 8 miles from the river and camped without water. Made 24 miles.

From the Colorado Chiquito to Tenejas Negras	*75 m*
To Cuerna de los Covinos [Coconino Caves]	*9 m*
To Ojo de Laroux	*20 m*

Thursday September 23, 1858. Drove to the Tenejas Negras, 7 miles, where we expected water. Found very little and that among the rocks where our cattle could not get at it, so we kept on to the next water, 9 miles. Water good and plenty, but we had to camp a mile from it in a valley. The water is a hole in the bed of the creek a little to the left of the road. Tubs & co came up and camped. Made 16 miles. Here we found wild grapes and walnuts.

At this location Udell mentioned that a number of people became quite sick. They blamed it on the water, but he thought it was from eating green fruit because some who drank the water were fine.[70]

[68] Ibid., July 15, 18.

[69] Ibid., July 16, 18.

[70] Ibid., July 25, 20.

Friday September 24, 1858. Started at noon. Drove 13 miles. Road good. Camped without water. Good grass all the way. We killed two turkeys. Tubs and co passed us in the night. Made 13 miles. We are now in the San Francisco Mountains near the Sumit road. Good except rockey. No bad hills to ascend or decend.

The rocks on this road were very large, at least twelve to fourteen inches in diameter. They formed a difficult uneven trail surface for the oxen and wagons as they worked their way between the pine trees. The rocks can be seen on the west side of the Arizona Historical Society Pioneer Museum in Flagstaff.

Saturday September 25, 1858. Started at sunrise and drove to Ojo de Laroux, 7 miles. Road exceeding bad, being a bed of rocks the most of the way. The spring is to the left about 40 rods and the same distance from a little water that crosses the road. Grass plenty. Laid by the rest of the day to wash and rest our cattle. Made 7 miles.

Made this week	*117*
Brought forward	*235*
	352 Total

Sunday September 26, 1858. Drove about 5 miles when we met 21 [men] of the first trains that went this road. They report that Roses train that was ahead lost half his cattle, 200 head, between this and the Colorado for want of water and grass. That in one place they were 2 days going 2-¼ miles over a mountain. They had to pack the stuff up and down and let the wagons down by ropes and they had to fight the Indians for several days, and when at the river, their cattle, many of them, were killed and run off by the Indians and then they attacked them in force. Killed one man and wounded the most of the balance and killed a family of 7. Then they all returned and all that are on the road are coming in a very destitute condition.

The L. J. Rose train had about a hundred people, twenty wagons, four hundred Red Durham cattle, and thirty-seven horses.[71] Merchants in Albuquerque, who wanted the town to become a supply center similar to Santa Fe, had persuaded them to be the first emigrant train to try Beale's Wagon Road. After being told there would be more forage for their large

[71] Rose, *L. J. Rose of Sunny Slope*, 4–5.

herd, they agreed, but then they were either advised, or ordered, by the military to hire a guide.[72] They felt fortunate in being able to hire Savedra, who had guided Beale the previous year. Unfortunately, Beale was back East and unable to tell them that Savedra was worthless as a guide.[73]

The Indians began harassing the Rose Train about ninety miles from the Colorado River, stealing and wounding many of their cattle. The last few miles of road to the river turned out to be almost impassable. Rose wrote that they "toiled two nights and two days incessantly." The animals were unhitched so the wagons could be let down with block and tackle. The men and animals were suffering greatly due to lack of water and temperatures that reached 130 degrees.[74] Savedra, their highly recommended guide, lacked the one essential skill that guides require—a sense of direction. He could not remember where water holes were from one trip to the next. As they neared the river, the Baley family wagons made camp and sent their worn-out animals to the river with Rose to be recruited.

After resting for a day, the men begin building a raft to ferry the wagons and cattle across the river. Some Mojaves came into camp and talked with them, then left. They seemed friendly enough but questioned the emigrants again and again about their intention to stay. Rose repeatedly told them they were not staying.

Various reasons have been given for what happened next—the attack on the wagon train. Although Lieutenant Beale had found the Mojaves friendly the year before, this was the very place he had pointed out as a dangerous crossing for emigrants. He recommended that a military post be established there.[75] Lieutenant Joseph C. Ives' "Report on the Colorado River of the West, Explored in 1857 and 1858" included information that in the spring of 1858 Mormon scouts were stirring up problems by telling the Mojaves that immigrants intended to settle on their lands.[76] Historian Charles Baley discovered an old Mojave's reminiscence of the attack that blamed it on "five young firebrands," who persuaded the elders that the white man would destroy their way of life and take over their lands.[77] But perhaps the attack was precipitated by the decision of

[72] Ibid., 13.

[73] Dodge, *Road West*, 91.

[74] Rose, *L. J. Rose of Sunny Slope*, 14–15, 29; and Cleland, *Cattle on a Thousand Hills*, 267.

[75] Dodge, *Road West*, 145.

[76] Smith, *John Udell*, 33–35; and Dodge, *Road West*, 217.

[77] Baley, *Disaster at the Colorado*, 132–33. Mr. Baley's book covers the incident in detail.

the emigrants to cut down the cottonwoods to build rafts. In her history of the Mojaves, *Bitterness Road*, Lorraine Sherer explained that the Mojaves considered the cottonwoods their trees. They provided shade for their desert oasis, poles for their houses (which they cut sparingly), and clothing, which was woven from the soft inner bark. Furthermore, Sherer wrote, "Their hundreds of animals were trampling over the places along the river where . . . Mojave farmers planted their crops."[78]

On the morning of August 30, the party counted about 250 Indians crossing the river toward their side. In the afternoon, while climbing on a wagon wheel, twelve-year-old Sallie Fox spotted the Indians who had surrounded them and shouted, "The Indians are coming and they will kill us all!"[79] The Indians fired a continuous barrage of arrows into the wagons for two hours while running most of the cattle across the river. When the attack ended, Alpha Brown, Sallie's stepfather, was dead, and eleven were wounded, including Sallie Fox, who was shot in the torso with an arrow. Only seventeen cattle and a few horses remained.[80]

The seven-member Bentner family had been caught while traveling between the two trains and all were killed. The Rose party survivors struggled back to the Baley camp, but they had to abandon all the wagons because they had no oxen. Ninety people, half of them women and children, carrying what little they could, began the long walk back to Albuquerque, over five hundred miles.

As they retraced their steps over the steep mountainous road, they met the Cave train from Iowa.[81] They too had been harassed by the Indians and were considering turning back. They helped the Rose party as much as they could, but now their provisions for sixty had to be stretched to feed a hundred and fifty. Two weeks later they met the Smith train, which had a herd of five hundred cattle. Now all were returning.[82]

The hard flinty road destroyed the shoes of most of the women and children, who were now walking on blistered, bleeding feet, and Rose's few remaining cattle soon died. They often traveled at night. One of the children, Julia Brown, wrote, "When for five minutes, there was a halt allowed, the weary oxen, women and children dropped upon the sand

[78] Scherer, *Bitterness Road*, 85.

[79] Rose, *L. J. Rose of Sunny Slope*, 24.

[80] Cleland, *Cattle on a Thousand Hills*, 271.

[81] Dodge, *Road West*, 211.

[82] Udell, *Journal of John Udell*, Sept. 16, 32.

and slept."[83] They held onto the wagon wheels to feel its first motion for fear they would be left behind, which did happen to one of the little girls, who was quickly found.

By the time the Pecks met the Rose Party, the group had been walking across the desert for four weeks.

Monday September 27, 1858. Staid in camp. Let those that are returning have 376 lb of flour. Some of them are intirely out of everything of provisions. They are killing 2 head of cattle per day. Rose had 409 head of cattle. He has lost all and several others are left with nothing but their clothes. Howel killed a hare.

Sixty-three-year-old John Udell learned from Rose that a "small train had come as far as [Leroux] Spring" and that Rose had bought as much flour as they could spare. Udell asked for a small amount. Rose refused.

> Thinking that my wife must die unless she had some soon, I . . . made all speed ahead to overtake the little train . . . and overtook them encamped at a stream of water. Mr. Washington Peck, who was the proprietor of the train, said that, on hearing of our sufferings, he had sold to Messrs. Rose and Mr. Cave's men all he could spare; he had spared so much that he would be short before he could get back where he could get any; he sold it to them at five and seven cents per pound—the price he paid for it—upon the faithful promise that it should be equally divided among the sufferers—most of whom did not receive one mouthful of it, although the Messrs. Smith and others who had money said they would willingly have paid one dollar per pound for the four hundred pounds, and divided it out among the starving women and children. Mr. Peck's train were from Missouri. Their ladies did have compassion upon us aged persons, and made them up among them fifteen or twenty pounds. I immediately started back to my wife, to share with her the previous boon bestowed upon us by those generous-hearted people.[84]

Tuesday September 28, 1858. We are retracing our steps. Drove to the next water and camped.

The Pecks' decision to retrace their steps took into account that the water holes were drying up, and with their diminished supply of flour, any further delays would put them in a precarious situation.

---

[83] Heath [Julia Brown], "A Child's Journey through Arizona and New Mexico," 16.

[84] Udell, *Journal of John Udell*, Sept. 26 and 27, 34–35.

Wednesday September 29, 1858. Started for Colorado Chiquito. About noon we got out of the timber and mountains and entered the great plain again. Dry camp at night. Note: There is a great deal of excelent Pine timber in those mountains, some large & straight, with abundance of grass.

The dairy herd provided milk to drink at their dry camp. In addition, descendant Bob Butterworth related that the Pecks sometimes washed with milk, especially when they came upon harsh alkaline water that burned the skin.[85]

Thursday September 30, 1858. Drove to the river in the morning. Watered and baited our stock, then went on to some ponds of water and camped.

Friday October 1, 1858. Reached our camp of the 21st. Wedged our wheels again. It seams as if our wheels will never get done s[h]rinking. Wood killed two small ducks.

Saturday October 2, 1858. Camped near the crossing. A slight sprinkling of rain, the first since the 7th ult [ultimo, last month].

Sunday October 3, 1858. Made a short drive. Day cool with a brisk wind from the SW. Eight years ago to day we left Great Salt Lake City for California.

Monday October 4, 1858. Made about 16 miles. Camped on a large flat. Grass in bunches. Day very pleasant and warm. Light breeze from the south.

Tuesday October 5, 1858. Reached the point where the road leaves the river. Strong wind from the SW. Day pleasantly cool.

Wednesday October 6, 1858. Drove 10 or 11 miles. Found water and camped. We expect no more for 36 miles. Day clear. Wind light from the N.

Thursday October 7, 1858. Drove 20 miles to a dry creek where we expected to get water by diging for our horses but were disappointed. The cattle got scaterd in the night. Called all hands and when we found them, we concluded to yoke up. Saw hot black clouds in the north near night. Appearance of rain.

[85] Family oral history from Robert (Bob) Butterworth.

They have decided to travel through the night to reach water.

Friday October 8, 1858. Started a little after twelve Oclock [midnight]. Reached the water the sun an hour high in the morning. Afternoon drove to Ojo Redondo, which some have designated Jacobs Well. Cloudy with now and then a few drops of rain. A little rain in the evening.

Saturday October 9, 1858. Morning rainey. Late breakfast. Two men met us from Zuni that had been in for supplies for the back trains. They report that the Navajoes are at war with Americans and hardly safe for small companies to proceed. So we concluded to wait for those companies to come up as we are rather out of their range here. Killed an ox for beef as we are out and have to remain for several days.
Cleared off. Cool in the afternoon.

The "Navajo War of 1858," as William Woods Averell called it, was finally becoming known. After being sent to Fort Defiance specifically because of the Navajo War, he was incensed when he heard about the Rose party. "How this helpless emigrant train could have been permitted . . . to undertake a journey . . . with no guard nor guide excepting an illustrated Congressional Report, is beyond comprehension. . . . It was the highest criminal negligence to permit them to attempt to pass through a country adjacent to that in which we were carrying on a destructive war and which should have been regarded . . . as within the theatre of hostilities."[86] A letter to the *Santa Fe Gazette* dated Sept. 29, 1858, from officer William B. Lane further drew attention to the war in its headline: "Seat of the Navajo War, Fort Defiance."[87]

Sunday October 10, 1858. Morning cold. Hard frost. Laid in camp all day. At night 11 men came up in a starving condition. They are a part of Smiths Com[pany] that undertook to pack across to the Pimo vilages but had to turn back for want of water. They have suffered everything but death. We got them some supper, the first full meal they have had for a long time (Poor Fellows).

On September 20, twenty to twenty-five of the young men among the returnees decided to try to get to California. They headed south across

[86] Eckert, *Ten Years in the Saddle*, 153, 209–10.
[87] *Santa Fe Gazette*, Nov. 13, 1858.

the desert toward the Butterfield Overland Mail Route that ran along the southern boundary of the territory. The party had split up to look for water, which three men found, but when those men returned, the rest of the group was gone, having left a trail of abandoned guns, ammunition, and food. On September 30, the three returned to the main party believing that the rest had died. The others staggered into camp on October 3 and left again, heading for Albuquerque the next day.[88]

One of the young men was Ed Akey, who had been hired by Rose to help herd cattle. In later years he told his story, which began when Smith killed an ox to provision them and salted it to speed drying. At noon the men set out with little water because they expected to reach water by evening. When they found the waterhole, it was dry. Exceedingly thirsty from the salted beef, they pushed on through the night but found no water, nor on the following day or night. By then they were staggering and able to travel only short distances before resting. Akey wrote, "On the morning of the second day, they came to a waterhole that was so foul they smelled it before they got to it. . . . It was alive with 'a kind of white worm, an inch or so long' but at least it was wet," so they strained it through their handkerchiefs and drank it anyway.[89]

Monday October 11, 1858. After breakfast we gave the men that came last night a small piece of beef and a few biscuits and they went on their way rejoicing.

Tuesday October 12, 1858. Dr Abell [Udell] and 20 men came up almost starved. They had lived on a little dried beef and the last few days they had nothing but about a spoonful of flour per head and horseflesh (they had killed a horse that was too poor to travil). The Dr has left his family in Smiths train in the San Francisco Mountains and is on his way to the Settlement to obtain provisions. They are living on poor beef. We gave them breakfast and 2 lb of flour each and started on in the afternoon. Drove until after dark and camped without water.

This group had left Smith's Company on October 7 to go on ahead, thus reducing the demand for food on the train. The Smiths decided to

[88] Udell, *Journal of John Udell*, Sept. 20, Sept. 30, Oct. 3–4, 33–34.

[89] Cheney, "The Story of an Emigrant Train," (Ed Akey's story), *Keosauqua* (Iowa) *Republican*, Apr. 29, 1915.

stay at Leroux Springs for two to three weeks to recruit what was left of their large herd, but they had supplied Udell and a number of others with teams and enough food to get to Zuni.[90]

Wednesday October 13, 1858. Started at day break. Found the creek dry. So we had to drive to Zuni, which we reached before night. Found provisions plenty but very little for sale and that at exorbitant prices. Here a war party started to the Navajoes country consisting of about 200 men. We suppose to run off stock belonging to the Navajoes. No grass for our cattle. We brought a few corn stalks for our horses.
We lost our Coffy pot. Suppose the Indians stole it.

On August 19, Major Brooks had gone to Zuni to seek their help in the campaign against the Navajo, promising them arms and a share in the booty—Navajo horses and sheep. He now sent word for them to come. "On the 15th [October] the greatest show ever seen in the Navajo country arrived. It was made up of 160 Zunis the most of them mounted and all armed and equipped in the most amazing costumes, masks of animal faces and horns and feathers on their heads and hideous shields in their hands."[91]

Thursday October 14, 1858. The company that left us on Monday returned the provisions that we let them have. We bought 2 sheep at $2 per head and drove 5 miles up the creek and camped. Grass tolerable. Wood killed 7 plovers. Morning cold. Very warm in the middle of the day. Wind west. In overhauling several little things are missed, conclusion Stolen by the Indians or worse charicters.
I Bought a poney for $25
George & Howel Do Do [ditto] $20

The mention of Howell revealed that Tubbs and the four boys were still traveling with the Pecks. Recent life and death events had overshadowed mention of Tubbs and company.[92]

[90] Udell, *Journal of John Udell*, Oct. 7, 34. At this point some discrepancies appear in Udell's journal, but they are understandable considering the condition that he was in and his worry about his wife.

[91] Eckert, *Ten Years in the Saddle*, 160–62, 206.

[92] Some of the young men who left Colorado in 1858 may have returned when the big strikes were discovered in 1859. Avery B. Tubbs and Philander Simmons Barker are among those who joined the Colorado Volunteers during the Civil War. Whether or not they are the same Tubbs and Barker is unknown.

Friday October 15, 1858. Morning cold, wind East. Somewhat cloudy. Wind soon changed to the west. Blew fresh all day.

At night Mr. McCoy & family came up. They report that Caves train will not be up 2 or 3 days. So we concluded to go on in the morning.

Saturday October 16, 1858. Before day the wind blew very hard and continued all day. We drove to Fish Sp[r]ing.

Heard that Caves train had arrived at Zuni. At night they came up.

Washington previously called this spring by its Spanish name, Ojo Pescado.

Sunday October 17, 1858. Laid by all day. Cold and chilley.

Monday October 18, 1858. Soon after we started we met a company of 80 Soldiers going to Fort Defiance. The Capt promised to send relief to Smiths company that is still behind. Passed El Moro. No water. Drove on. Camped without water. Night very cold.

Tuesday October 19, 1858. Before we reached the sumit we were met by a wagon with an escort of 10 men containing provisions for Caves company.

600 lb flour
400 " Bacon
200 " Sugar
100 " Coffey

which was [carefully] divided, the company numbering 100.

Crossed the sumit and camped at Aqua Frio.

Wednesday October 20, 1858. Drove to Ojo del Gyo. The Soldiers camped with us again. Turned two Dutch men out of the company for refusing to stand guard.

Thursday October 21, 1858. Passed Cevero about a mile and overtook the Soldiers and camped together. Edmond swaped his rifle for a horse.

Mr Rose's Morgan horse took Sick. Also one of Georges mules.

At Fort Defiance, Averell became concerned when Captain Whipple did not return when expected. He spent three anxious days fearing an attack by the Navajo. Whipple arrived October 21 with the first report of the Rose train disaster and explained that his delayed return was due to his having gone to the aid of some who had become "scattered and lost, and some were crazed with suffering and fright." He rescued all he could find, bringing six with him to the fort and sending others on to Albuquerque.[93]

Friday October 22, 1858. Wood traded his rifle for a poney. Passed the Lagune. Afternoon cloudy and cold.

There was a spectacular event happening in the night sky at this time that Washington did not mention, but others did—Donati's Comet had appeared. It was a brilliant fireball with one long tail and two smaller tails on either side. In Colorado, on September 26, diarist David Kellogg wrote: "The comet has been very brilliant for the last two evenings; it stretches clear across the Western sky." And on October 11: "All the Indians met lately predict a hard winter on account of the comet."[94] Averell at Fort Defiance recalled, "There was a comet of surpassing splendor visible about this time which we were told filled the Indians with fearful forebodings of war and disaster."[95] But most frightened of all was seven-year old Julia Brown of the Rose party survivors. She later wrote, "Often we traveled in the night to escape the heat of the day, and then I kept always in the wake of my mother's skirts, for fear of that comet."[96]

Saturday October 23, 1858. A little rain early in the morning. Made a long drive. Dry camp. Cold with high wind.
Mr Roses horse died.

Rose had a considerable investment in three Morgan horses that he planned to use to start a stable of trotting horses. He paid $2,500 for Black Morrill and $350 each for two fillies.[97] He took extra precautions to prevent the stallion from being stolen by fastening a heavy chain around his neck and through a ring on the halter, which was padlocked. In camp the stallion was usually secured to the feed box at the rear of a wagon. The day of the attack, because of the excessive heat, the stallion had been chained in the shade under a mesquite tree. When the Indians could not release the horse, they cut his throat and left him hanging in the halter.[98] The horse that died was one of the Morgan fillies.

---

[93] Eckert, *Ten Years in the Saddle*, 209.

[94] Simmons, *On the Santa Fe Trail* (David Kellogg's Diary, 1858), Sept. 26, 55 and Oct. 11, 59.

[95] Eckert, *Ten Years in the Saddle*, 168.

[96] Heath, "A Child's Journey through Arizona and New Mexico," 16.

[97] Dodge, *The Road West*, 212.

[98] Rose, *L. J. Rose of Sunny Slope*, 25–26.

Sunday October 24, 1858. Got up at two oclock and started before day. Had to drive 17 miles to the river. Reached the river in good time. Camped oposite to Albiquerque. Grass poor. We have now got to where we were the first of Sept, haveing traviled 700 miles for nothing.

After arriving back in Albuquerque, most of those from the Rose train spent some months recovering, not only physically, but also financially. Many found work to earn enough to outfit themselves for another try at California, but some, like Ed Akey, had "seen the elephant" and returned east. With a loan from his brother-in-law, L. J. Rose went to Santa Fe where he purchased La Fonda, a well-known inn marking the end of the Santa Fe Trail, and quickly recouped his financial losses.[99] Mary Brown and her four daughters, including Sallie Fox, who had recovered from her arrow wound, went to California in the spring of 1859 under the protection of E. O. Smith.[100]

In March of 1859 when Beale returned to Albuquerque and set out to improve the road further, he felt such a great sympathy for the Udells that he took them along with his expedition. Continuing problems at the Colorado crossing resulted in the establishment of Fort Mojave in the spring of 1859.[101]

Monday October 25, 1858. Went into Town. Tried to sell or trade our cattle for mules intending to fit out and go Cooks route by Tuson to California. Found no sale for cattle, only at a great sacrifice, so that we gave it up and concluded to go to Rio Bonito near Fort Staunton. We have the offer of a house and corral free from rent for the winter. The place is highly recommended for good land and grass, the land but little of it taken up. Afternoon a heavy squall of wind. A little rain in the night.

Washington intended to continue the trip via Cooke's Road, the southern route that he had intended to take in the first place. Not willing to sell off their animals at a loss, the family decided to stay through the

---

[99] Ibid., 34.

[100] Ibid., 32. On the way to California, Sallie picked up some walnuts that she put into her apron pocket with her two-inch India rubber doll. She planted the walnuts on her uncle Josiah Allison's ranch, one of which grew into the large walnut tree that stood for years in the Nut Tree Restaurant Complex near Vacaville, California. Sallie's apron, with the arrow hole, is kept at the Vacaville Museum along with her tiny India rubber doll. The items are displayed annually on Sallie Fox Day.

[101] Utely, *Frontiersmen in Blue*, 165.

winter after meeting Mr. Carley, who supplied food for the soldiers at Fort Stanton and to the Indian agency.[102]

South to Fort Stanton

Tuesday October 26, 1858. Crossed the river in the morning and started for the Fort. Cold, the mountains white with snow. Camped in the canon 14 miles from Albiquerque.

The road went a few miles east, on today's I-40, then south into the Tijeras Canon on SR327.

Wednesday October 27, 1858. Persued our course up the canon, which was narrow crooked and rockey. The road very good for such a place. Passed the sumit and camped after sun set by a spring. Grass short. Night very cold. We were overtaken by one of Rose's men which told us that Uncle or Mr Horner, which was sick 3 or 4 days before he reached Albiquerque, died yesterday.

State Route 327 is designated as a scenic highway and is still narrow and crooked.

Mr. Horner remains unidentified. The final number who died from starvation, heat prostration, and dehydration is not known, but Mrs. Brown's baby, Owen, is one who died and was buried by the wayside. One of Mrs. Brown's children wrote, "We had grown stoical with starvation and danger . . . but, as my mother turned . . . to look her last upon the lonely hillside, she cried, 'Oh, my boy, my boy! How can I leave him there?'"[103] Ed Akey recalled that to keep from going crazy, Mrs. Brown unravelled a sock and knit it over and over again.[104]

Thursday October 28, 1858. Morning the two Smith cows calved which detained us until noon. Drove past Chilleli about 3 miles. Dry camp. At the town we missed one cow which we supposed had gone back to look for her calf. Edmond & Howel went back but could not find it. Good grass.

---

[102] Letter from Major Charles F. Ruff to Michael Steck, May 31, 1859. Michael Steck Papers, MSS 134 BC, Box 2, Folder 8.

[103] Heath, "A Child's Journey through Arizona and New Mexico," 15. Kate Heath was a pseudonym for one of Mrs. Brown's children, likely Julia Brown.

[104] Cheney, "The Story of an Emigrant Train," (Ed Akey's story), *Keosauqua* (Iowa) *Republican*, Apr. 29, 1915.

Chilili was a small Spanish land grant, which today is a private land reserve held by family descendants. A current highway sign states that no one is allowed to take pictures.

Friday October 29, 1858. Morning one of George's poneys was missing. Offered a Mexican five dollars to find it. He brought up just as we were camping. Hadley and Edmond went back to look for the cow. Passed two Small villages, the first called Taquique [Tajique], the other Torione [Torreon] and camped at rancho Guerbo. Good grass. Some corn stocks.

Milton S. Hadley, age twenty-eight, was another young man who joined the Pecks from one of the returning wagon trains.[105]

Saturday October 30, 1858. The boys overtook us with the cow. Got to Mansano before noon. Miller got a situation and stoped. We got a table of distances, drove 6 miles and camped. Grass good. Night cold.

Manzano was the last village before the road dropped down off the mesa to the desert floor.

Sunday October 31, 1858. Watered the horses. The cattle we thought would not drink So early and only 15 miles to water. So we drove on, but when we came to where the water should have been, it was dry and appeard to have been so for a month or 6 weeks. We fear that Charley has deceived us. We expect no water for 28 miles further. If that is a failure, we shall have 80 miles with out water. (Gloomey prospect). Hitched up at dark and drove 11 miles. Night very cold.

The desert stretched ahead of them to the horizon. It is unclear whether Washington's reference to Charley meant Charles Beach, who had married into a Hispanic family in Manzano, or Mr. Carley at Fort Stanton.

Monday November 1, 1858. Started early. Drove to the point where water was expected. Found a little so that 3 or 4 horses got a little. We rested until sun down, then drove on until about 12 oclock. One ox gave out and we had to leave him. Road very good, on the levil. Had to cross a high ridge of the Gallina Mt. Rockey and steep assent and decent. Edmond and Hadley took the horse that could be spared and kegs and went on to the water intending to bring the kegs full back to meet us. Edmonds poney came up missing.

---

[105] *Prescott Arizona Miner*, Apr. 24, 1869, 3:1.

Tuesday November 2, 1858. Started at day light. Drove til 11 Oclock, then laid by to rest until 4. When we hitched up, our cattle appeared very tired and looked bad. One was sick, so we yoked another in his place and started for the water. Distance about 14 M, which we reached before 12 Oclock. Edmond met us 8 miles from the water with 8 Gal of water, which we distributed among those that appeared most in need after which they came on first rate to the water. The whole distance we think is 85 miles, a long distance to drive without water. But the weather was cool this day. Cloudy. Turned our stock loos and went to bed after eating a biscuit and takeing a drink of water each.

This was the first time that the Pecks suffered a severe water deprivation for their animals or themselves in two trips across the country.

Wednesday November 3, 1858. Morning the ground covered with snow. Cold wind with a little fine snow falling. Found our stock all rite. Washed our faces and hands and combed our hair which we have not done since Sunday morning. Breakfasted on turkeys killed by Hadley yesterday. Collected a lot of dry wood. Made a good fire. Had a glorious time in general and a very interesting time in particular. In the middle of the day it misted and froze. Covered the bushes with ice. Evening snow again. Several of the boys went hunting and returned without any game. Reported Bear sign plenty.

Thursday November 4, 1858. Morning very cold with four inches of snow. Clear and calm. The boys went a hunting. Hadley returned with three turkeys, the others with Plumb nothing.

Friday November 5, 1858. Drove a few miles. The snow all went off in the valleys. Wood killed a turkey. Night pleasant.

Saturday November 6, 1858. Drove to the Rio Bonito. Found the grass for 8 miles all eaten up by the prarie dogs except on a few of the hills. The Fort is in a pritty place, but the whole valley is over run with squirrels or prarie dogs. The stream enters a narrow canon some three miles before the Fort.

The entrance to the Rio Bonito Valley has returned to a beautiful grassy plain, long since recovered from the prairie dog colony. The prairie dogs not only fed on the grasses, but they cleared stalks surrounding their burrow openings in order to see approaching predators, which left the ground looking barren.[106]

Sunday November 7, 1858. Started in high hopes of finding a beautiful and excelent location, but after going several miles down the canon, we met some men that lived there. They told us that the country was the same as far as settled. Below that the canon widens out so that it may be called a valley, but it is destitute of timber.

The Rio Bonito Valley is very narrow, running east between steep mountain ranges on both sides. From the valley floor, elevation about 5,200 feet, El Capitan rises to 10,230 feet on the north and Sierra Blanca has an elevation of 12,003 feet on the south.

Monday November 8, 1858. After going a mile or two, the mountain on each side became more sloping with grass on their sides and the valley somewhat wider. When we arrived at Charley Rancho, Mr Carley received us very kindly. He has raised a great quantity of corn and some fine potatoes and other vegetables. Here is a good and extensive range for stock among the mountains with the best of water at the creek. They are moveing into the new house and we are to have the old one. Edmond, Wood, Howel and Lawrence went to work for Mr. Reese. George Seirs got work here. Only Hadley and Tom is with us now.

B. L. Reese supplied corn and beef to the Indian Agency and sometimes helped with distribution to the Apaches.

The Pecks were trailing a whole herd of young men along with their cattle: B. F. Howell (thirty-two), Lawrence Dersh, George Sears (twenty-three), George Wood, and Tom Flowers, the latter two having come with them from Missouri.

Tuesday November 9, 1858. Cut and drawed stuff for to enlarge the coral. Brisk wind from the west. All the snow has disappeared from the mountains. Evening warmer than for some time past.

After six months on the trail, the exhausted families had to build a corral to secure the cattle and horses that they had taken such effort to bring through safely, including the Banghats' pet cow. Then they began

[106] Koford, "Prairie Dogs, Whitefaces, and Blue Grama," *Wildlife Monograph No. 3*, 6.

to look around for a place to buy and sent letters home to let the family know where they were.

In mid-November a couple of the boys went to Beckwith's farm to help him dig potatoes in return for a share. Hugh Beckwith was a supplier to Fort Stanton who was known for his activities during the Civil War as a Confederate sympathizer when he stirred up problems for neighbors and former friends. Later he became involved in the Lincoln County War.[107]

On November 18 Washington found "a better place than we expected. Plenty of land to cultivate and an extensive range for stock."

Wednesday November 24, 1858. Killed our ox. Very little fat on it. Quite disappointed. Warm and pleasant.

Concluded to take up a ranch and make a home.

Washington's Rancho lay at the confluence of the Rio Bonito and Rio Ruidoso Rivers. George Banghart bought adjoining land to the east. It was a major intersection within the valley. The road from Fort Stanton ran past the rancho easterly through and out of the Hondo Valley to the Llano Estacado (Staked Plains). Another road ran south through the mountains.

The deed describing the Peck Rancho is one of the few surviving deeds from Socorro County from that time. The property boundaries are described as adjoining H. W. Beckwith's property on the west, along the base of the mountain on the north, adjoining George Banghart's on the east and along the Rio Bonito River on the south.[108] Although the mountain and river boundaries were fixed, the extent of the property and total acreage from Beckwith's to Banghart's is unknown.

They spent the rest of the year building stone houses because timber was not readily available. A number of days that December, it was so cold that they could not work the whole day and had to quit early.

---

[107] For further information about Beckwith's later activities, see John Wilson's *Merchants, Guns and Money*, and Dudley Cramer, *The Pecos Ranchers in the Lincoln County War.*

[108] New Mexico, Socorro County Records 1851–1885, Roll 1, Book A, 151–52.

6

The Final Years

Fort Stanton, New Mexico, 1858

The Pecks had arrived in a place markedly different from the southwest desert that surrounded the Rio Bonito Valley. It was an oasis of grass and water and rich farmland. A mere handful of white and Hispanic families had settled along both sides of the Rio Bonito River that divided the narrow valley, which ran from Fort Stanton eastward for twenty miles to the confluence of the Ruidoso and Rio Bonito rivers. A young army wife, Lydia Spencer Lane, who arrived at Fort Stanton the day after the Pecks, described Fort Stanton as "a beautiful post . . . but it was like being buried alive to stay there. Nothing ever passed that way."[1]

In the spring of 1859 the Pecks' daughters Jane and Emma married. Jane married Calvin Keys, from Fayette County, Texas, and Emma married George W. Rector, origins unknown, on April 19, 1859.[2] The two young couples shared a stone house built for them on the family property.[3]

By June of 1859 a drought had begun that would last for two years. Lack of forage led the Pecks to burn the thorns off prickly pear cactus to make cattle feed.[4]

George Wright and his family arrived in 1859 and settled east of the Pecks along the Hondo River.[5] His eighteen-year-old daughter, Lucy Mima Wright ("Mima"), kept a diary that recorded many of the Peck family activities during the following two years.[6] She provided the only record of how Mercy and her young married daughters spent their days, as she joined them often. Mercy took care of a flock of Shanghai (Cochin)

[1] Lane, *I Married a Soldier*, 64–65.

[2] Washington State Archives, U.S. District Court of the 2nd Judicial District for Thursday, Nov. 16, 1865.

[3] *Lucy Mima Wright Diary*, Dec. 17, 1860.

[4] *Tarkio* (Mo.) *Avalanche*, Mar. 18, 1965, 10:1.

[5] Ward, *George Wright, 1815–1905; An American Pioneer*, 13–14.

[6] *Lucy Mima Wright Diary*, hereinafter referred to as *Wright Diary*. From this point forward references to the Peck family activities and trip to California come from this diary.

Jane S. Peck Keys and Calvin Keys, circa 1859, from a tintype. *From author's collection.*

chickens while her daughters each took care of a new baby, and they all helped take care of Mary Ann's three little girls. They sewed nightcaps, read *Carter's Ladies Book,* and discussed religion. Mima learned that the Pecks had become interested in the spiritualism movement that was sweeping the country.

Living at the junction provided the Pecks with ample opportunity to keep in touch with neighbors and visitors passing by and to watch the soldiers coming and going from the fort, but it also provided horse thieves with numerous opportunities to make off with their animals. At the beginning of 1860 some of the Pecks' horses were stolen. Mima's father suspected that the Mexicans working on the Wright ranch had helped steal them. Edmond Peck, then twenty-five, joined Captain Claiborne's weeklong attempt to recover them, which began in a snowstorm. The terrain covered during the scout was brutal—running along mountain trails, over rocky ridges, and through steep canyons. Five of the Pecks' horses escaped from the Indians and returned on their own, but the others were never recovered.[7]

[7] Report of Captain Thomas Claiborne, Jan. 31, 1860. M1120, Roll 11, Item C1.

Emma Ester Peck Rector and George Washington Rector (seated), circa 1859, from a tintype. Unknown couple behind. *From author's collection.*

In mid-December Mima wrote of another Indian raid on the Peck horses. This time the men returned on foot "and nearly starved, having been without food two and a half days and two nights." Instead of finding their horses, their mounts had been stolen. The only animal they recovered was one of the Banghearts' mules, which came home later on its own.

Mima described warm evenings by the fireside and days spent sewing nightcaps, but her cozy picture of life on the Rio Bonito was far from reality. The nation was on the brink of war. Lincoln's November 1860 election had triggered South Carolina's secession from the Union. By the end of 1860 rumblings of the Civil War were reverberating through the posts in New Mexico where officers and enlisted men were embroiled in arguments and discussions over slavery and a state's right to secede. The result of this preoccupation was that the army did little to attempt to control the Indians.[8]

[8] Keleher, *Turmoil in New Mexico,* 143.

When the military offered to provide safe escort to those who wished to leave, Washington began arranging his affairs. After a stay of just over two years, the Pecks were migrating again. On January 8, 1861, he quitclaimed his property to Avery M. Clenny and began getting their wagons ready to travel.[9] They needed enough supplies to last for a three-month trip across the desert.

Five more states seceded from the union before mid-February and joined South Carolina to form the Confederate States of America. The Texans followed, officially seceding on March 2. Then rumors began to circulate that the Texans would invade New Mexico.

Historian Lee Myers wrote that by March the threat of a Confederate invasion from Texas left the Indians "free to maraud the settlers, miners and immigrants of the territory. Times were bad in New Mexico."[10] As early as February of 1861, the Mescalero Apaches joined forces with the Mimbres band to attack settlers.[11] George Banghart lost a hundred head of cattle during a series of raids on his livestock, but fortunately not the family pet cow.[12]

The Wrights decided to go with the Pecks. While the Wrights were busy husking and shelling corn to take with them, they learned that wagon trains were being robbed a few miles south on the route they would be taking to California. They hurried to finish the corn and moved in with the Pecks for a day, but the situation was worsening so rapidly that by the following day, they were advised to move into Fort Stanton until ready to go. During the following days, the men left the safety of the fort just long enough to return to their farms and finish loading the wagons.

Mima wrote, "Finally, Capt Clayborn [*sic*] told them they could not stay at the fort any longer. Thirty soldiers had their discharge papers and were going east and they would have to go east with them." When the Pecks and Wrights insisted on going to California, in spite of his warning that they would never make it, Claiborne's chilling response was, "I wash my skirts of your blood." Just as they were ready to go, Claiborne relented and said that in return for a place to ride and for food, he would

[9] N.Mex. Socorro County Records, 1851–1885, Roll 1, Book A, 151–55.

[10] Myers, *Fort Stanton, New Mexico*, 11.

[11] Ryan, *Fort Stanton and Its Community*, 41.

[12] *Prescott Arizona Miner*, June 1, 1867.

send an escort of eight soldiers who would get their discharge papers in California.[13]

Butterfield Overland Mail Route to California, 1861

On March 14, 1861, the wagons rolled out. It was none too soon. New Mexico would soon be in shambles. After a two-and-a-half-year delay, the Pecks were again on their way to California. The Peck family was fifteen members strong: Washington and Mercy, Edmond, the three young couples and their six children, plus an untold number of animals that included the Bangharts' dairy herd and their pet cow, who had walked as many miles of trail as the Pecks since they left Canada.

The settlers staying behind hated to see them go. A brave group of them rode eight miles out to the first wagon train camp to spend one last evening together. They brought a fiddle and carried on most of the night, not heading back until after sunrise.

The wagon train traveled south to Las Cruces, then turned west to follow the Butterfield Overland Mail Route begun in September 1858. John Butterfield had received a mail contract to provide twice-weekly service from St. Louis and Memphis to San Francisco within twenty-five days. He had established a string of stage stations, which the wagon train followed and found it business as usual at the Cow Spring station.[14]

The travelers were headed directly into another Indian War, which had been precipitated on February 19, 1861, when Lieutenant George Bascom had hung six Apaches, including Cochise's brother. Bascom had wrongly accusing Cochise of kidnapping a young boy from a rancher. Cochise was so furious he began a war that lasted for ten years.[15] Historian Frank Lockwood wrote that Cochise's "scouts would scan the valleys and mesas for small parties of careless travelers or unguarded wagon trains, and then . . . would ambush them—slay, burn, and loot, with little loss on their part."[16]

The wagon train spent three weeks traveling through the heart of the hostilities during a two-month period that saw one hundred and fifty whites

[13] *Biographical History of Nodaway and Atchison Counties*, "E. E. Peck," 375; and Ward, *George Wright, 1815–1905; An American Pioneer*, 16.

[14] Wright and Bynum, *Butterfield Overland Mail*, xi–xii.

[15] Utley, *Clash of Cultures*, 20–23.

[16] Lockwood, *Apache Indians*, 107.

killed.[17] On April 1 the wagon train passed the skull of a recently killed man and on April 17 they arrived at Apache Pass, site of the hanging.

Was the wagon train warned to keep together? It does not seem so because from Apache Pass forward the wagon train did not travel as a single unit. A number of small groups existed within the wagon train. The day they left the pass, the Pecks half-watered their cattle, and while the Wrights continued to water, the Pecks went on ahead, then drove a mile off the road to make camp by themselves and rejoined the rest of the train the following day. Although the wagons stayed close, they leap-frogged each other, maybe because they had too many cattle to water at the same time in the small springs or maybe to spread out because of the dust.

On April 12, 1861, the day the Civil War began, the wagons reached Stein's Peak at sundown and found the station deserted. On March 2 Congress had passed a bill to discontinue the mail line fearing that it would fall into the hands of the Confederates.[18] By May 1 the wagon train had made it west of Tucson, where they found all the Butterfield stage stations deserted. On May 3 the wagon train met eight men with Southern Confederacy mail, who gave them the news that South Carolina had taken Fort Sumter and that the war had begun.

The Pecks camped at the deserted stage station at Oatman Flat where the Oatman family was buried. Yavapai Indians had killed six members of the family in March of 1851. The Pecks knew about the Oatman tragedy but were unaware that they could have suffered a similar fate. After this stop, the wagons stayed closer together. They often traveled at night to avoid the intense daytime desert heat.

One death occurred on the trip. On May 17 Martha Wright gave birth to a baby girl, who lived only three days. The Wrights sadly took apart the family cradle to make it into a coffin.

From those they passed, they continued to hear news about the Civil War. On May 22 they learned that President Lincoln had ordered Union forces against Texas, Fort Stanton was deserted, and the Indian attacks were getting worse in the desert behind them.

On May 25 they reached Arizona City (Yuma) on the Colorado River. They ferried across to California and started north. A few days later they passed a burning Butterfield Overland Mail station near Cook's Wells, a

[17] Thrapp, *Conquest of Apacheria*, 18.

[18] Taylor, *First Mail West*, 86.

sign of the confederate support in southern California. They continued north along the abandoned stage route to El Monte where they arrived on June 14 and heard the bells of San Gabriel Mission. The crossing had taken almost three months.

Back in New Mexico, the situation had deteriorated rapidly. On August 1, Lieutenant Colonel Baylor established the Confederate Territory of Arizona in southern New Mexico Territory, which included Fort Stanton and extended east to the California border.[19] On August 2, 1861, Fort Stanton was set afire and abandoned by retreating Union forces in the face of the Confederates, who stormed up from Texas, but after one month the Confederates moved on, leaving the Apaches in control of the surrounding area. Within a few days most of the remaining settlers had fled.[20] When a group of twenty to twenty-five men went down from Manzano at the end of September to harvest the abandoned crops, the Apaches murdered them all.[21]

San Gabriel, California, 1861

The Pecks arrived in beautiful San Gabriel Valley in June of 1861. Recent visitor Judge Benjamin Hayes wrote, "The plains in front of them, and all the hills [were] covered with . . . cattle, and horses, and sheep" under a bright California sun.[22] It seemed like paradise.

Significant changes had taken place in the ten years since Washington and Mercy spent New Year's in 1851 on the San Gabriel Mission grounds, then in ruins. The once-neglected mission orchards and vineyards were being coaxed back to life by a handful of settlers, and a small village was growing up around the Mission, but the Mission lands granted by the Land Commission had shrunk from thousands and thousands of acres to a mere hundred and ninety.[23] The town and valley combined were home to about five hundred people.[24]

There in the valley the Pecks found their old friends, Amanda and L. J. Rose, who had arrived from Santa Fe a few months earlier. They had sold

[19] Carmony, *Civil War in Apacheland*, 2.

[20] Ryan, *Fort Stanton and Its Community*, 43–46.

[21] Wilson, *Merchants, Guns and Money*, 15–16.

[22] Wolcott, *Pioneer Notes*, 217.

[23] Robinson, *Land in California*, 31.

[24] 1860 Federal Census, Los Angeles County, San Gabriel.

their inn in Santa Fe, La Fonda, and bought 1,300 acres of the Santa Anita Rancho.[25] They were renting an adobe house until they had time to build. They still had Old Bob, the only horse to survive the massacre.[26]

Michael White, one of the earliest settlers in the valley, lived next door to the Roses. After his marriage to Maria Rosaria de Guillen, he received a small land grant of seventy-eight acres of former Mission lands in 1845, which he named Rancho San Ysidro.[27] He built a wonderful adobe home where the chickens and dogs ran in and out along with his many children.[28] On the north side of the property was a big swamp that was a plus, not a minus, because it was fed from underground springs that White dammed to provide water to irrigate his vineyard and orchard.[29]

Washington bought two hundred square varas—about twelve acres—from Michael White, and he negotiated one very important item—water rights for irrigation.[30] He received two-sevenths of the water from White's dam, in return for which he paid two-sevenths of the repairs. Washington took his water from the ditch from sundown Saturday night to sundown Monday. His place was about two miles from San Gabriel village.

The Bangharts bought forty acres that included the original Francisco Sales Rancho, plus two adjoining small properties.[31] Their rancho was about a mile from the San Gabriel Mission.

In November of 1861 fall rains began, which lasted two weeks; on December 24 they began again and continued nonstop for four more weeks, resulting in a flood of catastrophic proportions, possibly the worst in California history. Historian Robert Glass Cleland wrote, "Scores of adobe buildings became saturated and collapsed." Vineyards were swept away, fruit trees destroyed, cattle drowned by the thousands, and the San Joaquin Valley, to the north of San Gabriel over the Transverse Range, turned into an inland sea described by Cleland as "250 to 300

[25] Los Angeles County Deeds Book 6:391, Mar. 8, 1861; and Scheid, *Pasadena: Crown of the Valley*, 20.

[26] Rose, *L. J. Rose of Sunny Slope*, 52, 58.

[27] Kielbasa, *Historic Adobes of Los Angeles County*, 211.

[28] Wolcott, *Pioneer Notes* (letter by Emily Hayes, Mar. 13, 1852), 89.

[29] White and Savage, *California All the Way Back to 1828*, unnumbered map. The Michael White Adobe is one of the few surviving adobes in southern California and is under the care of the San Marino Historical Society.

[30] Los Angeles County Deeds, Book 5:344, July 11, 1861.

[31] Ibid., Book 6:188, July 5, 1861.

miles long and from 20 to 60 miles wide" that flooded three and a half million acres.[32]

Conditions improved more rapidly in the San Gabriel Valley, so that by late March the roads had dried out enough for the Bangharts to go into Los Angeles, a distance of about ten miles.[33] There they met Mima Wright and her mother, whom they had not seen for nine months. The Wrights had settled a few miles south of Los Angeles. The Bangharts invited Mima to come home with them for a week. After a night at the Bangharts, she stayed with the Pecks. Mercy was happy to have a young girl in the house again, and she filled Mima's days with a busy social schedule, introducing her to friends and neighbors, such as the Roses next door. Twenty-year-old Mima was keeping her eyes open for a suitable husband, so she was delighted to meet a good looking young man at the Roses, where she was "rather energetic in denunciation of secessionists, [then] learned afterward he was one."[34]

The Civil War had followed the Pecks to California where a call for troops was underway. Twenty-three hundred young men (mostly from northern California) joined the California Column, which was California's contribution to the Union Army. Sparsely settled southern California was filled with Confederate supporters.[35] In fact, before the outbreak of the Civil War, five counties in southern California had voted to secede from the state and form the Territory of Colorado.[36] Feelings between the two factions were so bitter that no Fourth of July celebrations were held in Los Angeles in 1863 or 1864.[37]

During her visit Mima discovered that the Pecks were still interested in spiritualism when they spent the evening in a game of table tipping to try to contact the spirits. As they joined hands and rested them on a three-legged table, someone spoke the letters of the alphabet and the spirits caused the table to tilt and knock on the floor.[38] For two and a half hours the group sat around the table, which Mima said "trembled and

---

[32] Cleland, *Cattle on a Thousand Hills*, 127–30; and Farquhar, *Up and Down California in 1860–64*, 242–44.

[33] Farquhar, *Up and Down California in 1860–64*, 13; and *Wright Diary*, 12, June 21, 1861.

[34] *Wright Diary*, 16, Mar. 23–31, 1862.

[35] Carmony, *Civil War in Apacheland*, 6–7, 32–35; and Utley, *Frontiersmen in Blue*, 252.

[36] Cleland, *Cattle on a Thousand Hills*, 124–25.

[37] Newmark, *Sixty Years in Southern California 1853–1913*, 321, 330.

[38] Goldsmith, *Other Powers*, 31, 35.

rocked, but the chain was broken so much that [they] couldn't expect much" because one of the young men kept them all laughing. It is difficult to determine whether the Pecks' interest in spiritualism was merely a parlor game for entertainment or a serious desire to contact the dearly departed. In any event, they were not alone. By 1863, the number of people interested in spiritualism was estimated at seven million.[39] Mima enjoyed her week at the Pecks and left with regret.

In the fall of 1862, a fearsome epidemic struck. Cleland reported that "a virulent outbreak of smallpox swept over southern California and took an appalling toll of life on the ranchos, as well as in the towns." It grew steadily worse through the winter with fifteen to twenty deaths a day in Los Angeles.[40] Two of the Peck grandchildren—Rudy Banghart and Elizabeth Rector—are not listed on any family records from that time forward, perhaps victims of the epidemic.

Then came the drought—two long years—a drought so devastating that it ended the cattle industry in southern California forever. Starving cattle were slaughtered for the value of their hides and horns. Cleland noted that "to make matters worse, the late spring [of 1863] brought a succession of hard, scorching winds from the desert; and millions of grasshoppers swept across the country like a devastating fire." As the summer turned into fall, then winter, Cleland continued, "The cattle died by the thousands on sun-baked ranges and beside waterless streams."[41] Only four of the Bangharts' forty-eight cows survived the drought, one being their dear pet, but she went blind from lack of water.[42] The value of Washington's water right was self-evident.

By the second winter of drought, Washington had had enough. His California dream was over. He and Mercy moved north to Washington Territory even before he sold his land. Their youngest daughter, Emma Rector, and her family went with them. In January of 1864 the Pecks signed the sale deed in Thurston County.[43]

One additional concern may have influenced Washington's decision to sell. The ongoing process of assessing the early Spanish and Mexican

[39] Ibid., 78.
[40] Cleland, *Cattle on a Thousand Hills*, 80, 132.
[41] Ibid., 130–37.
[42] Thrapp, *Conquest of Apacheria*, 62.
[43] W. Peck to Gustavos L. Mix, Jan. 5, 1864, Los Angeles County Deeds Book 6:363.

land grants that had started in 1852 was far from finished. The United States Land Claims Commission was deciding who, amongst conflicting claimants, was entitled to possession, and once they decided, a patent was issued to the successful claimant. But with over eight hundred cases before the courts, it took an average of seventeen years to complete the process.[44] Washington was taking no chances that some unhappy long-lost relative of the original grant might appear to claim his land.

The two remaining Peck daughters and their families (the Bangharts and Keys) stayed two years longer. On Christmas Day of 1865 the Bangharts sold their rancho but stayed until after their son Georgie was born in early 1866. Then they packed up their five children, their faithful old cow, who had recovered her eyesight and was still providing milk for the family,[45] and moved to Prescott, Arizona, probably encouraged by Mary Ann's brother Edmond Peck, who had settled there.[46] The Keys joined Washington and Mercy in Washington Territory where they bought a half section adjoining the Pecks' farm.[47]

The Roses stayed and became one of the most prominent families in the area, with their Sunny Slope Ranch becoming famous. From the vineyards that Rose began planting in the first year, he produced his first wine in 1864.[48] He continued to buy property for many years, and in fulfillment of the dream he had had when he left Iowa in 1858, he developed a stable of beautiful trotting racehorses.

The Wright family became permanent residents of southern California, later settling in Azuza, but sadly, Mima Wright never found her young man. She and her mother died in a measles epidemic in 1869.[49]

Grand Mound, Washington Territory, 1864

Everything was so green—the prairie grasses, the evergreen shrubs, and the dark dense forests. Washington and Mercy settled on the prairie near Grand Mound in Thurston County where settlers had been taking

[44] Robinson, *Land in California*, 106.
[45] Thrapp, *Conquest of Apacheria*, 62.
[46] Los Angeles County Deeds Book 7:479, Dec. 25, 1865; and Thrapp, *Conquest of Apacheria*, 62.
[47] Henry J. and Jane Hale to Calvin Keys, Mar. 20, 1867, Thurston County Deed Book 5:453.
[48] Rose, *L. J. Rose of Sunny Slope*, 53, 59.
[49] *Glendoran*, "Pioneer Wright Family," Nov./Dec. 1998, 63.

up Donation Land Claims from the early 1850s. Grand Mound was the hub of the settlers' activities—celebrations, elections, and church services.[50] By the end of 1864 the Pecks had purchased a 320-acre farm a mile west of abandoned Fort Henness, which had been built by the settlers during the 1855–56 Indian War as a refuge. The Indian War had not amounted to much in this area because the local Chehalis Indians were friends with the settlers and the fort never came under attack.[51]

Emma and George began having marital problems soon after they arrived. George left Emma, who delivered twin sons in May of 1864. After hearing nothing from George for over a year, Emma was granted a divorce, charging him with abandonment and lack of support, but George then reappeared and abducted his son Frank.[52] The sheriff rescued the child and arrested George, who was fined ten dollars and ordered not to molest Emma or the children.[53] With that, George W. Rector disappeared as mysteriously as he had arrived in New Mexico in 1859.

As always, Washington and Mercy continued to be outgoing and gregarious. They made new friends, took an interest in the community, and socialized with their neighbors. They soon met Ignatius Colvin, who made more trips to the land office than the Pecks. Family history describes how he took one look at Emma and "that was it." They were married on October 26, 1866, in Grand Mound.[54]

In the summer of 1869 Washington was persuaded to run as the Republican candidate for the House of Representatives in the Territorial Legislature. The partisan *Olympia Territorial Republican* described him as "an honest intelligent farmer, and a true representative of the 'bone and sinew' of the country. . . . Vote for an honest farmer to represent you in the Legislature, Washington Peck."[55]

Washington took a leadership roll from the start. He made the first motion of the new session by nominating the Speaker *pro tem*. Two mem-

---

[50] Smith, *Centralia, The First Fifty Years*, 18.

[51] Thomas and Elizabeth Harper to Mercy M. Peck, Nov. 12, 1864, Thurston County Deed Book 5:113; and GLO BLM Serial WAOAA 093132 and 093133 (80 acres each), Dec. 9, 1864.

[52] Washington State Archives, U.S. District Court of the 2nd Judicial District for Thursday, Nov. 16, 1865.

[53] Family oral history from Lester Rector; and Washington State Archives, U.S. District Court of the 2nd Judicial District for Feb. 5, 1866.

[54] Indian War Pension Claim of Widow for Service Pension, filed by Emma Colvin, Sept. 22, 1902.

[55] *Olympia Territorial Republican*, June 7, 1869.

Washington and Mercy Peck, circa 1870. Yantis & Gray's photographer, Olympia, Washington Territory. *Courtesy of John Wells Heap.*

bers formally escorted the Speaker to the front of the House, indicating a respect for the job they had been elected to do and an understanding of protocol.[56] With his knowledge of law apparent to his colleagues, Washington, a Justice of the Peace, was appointed to three committees—Judiciary, Roads and Highways, and Agriculture, of which he was appropriately named Chairman.[57] The House passed ninety-four acts during the session, including some whose effects can still be seen. They requested funds to build lighthouses in Puget Sound at Point Defiance, Alki Point, and Point No Point,[58] and they approved the purchase of Fort Steilacoom—abandoned by the military in 1868—for use as an insane asylum (today Western State Hospital).[59]

[56] Territory of Wash., *Journal of the House of Representatives, 1869*, 4, 8.

[57] Seattle Genealogical Society, *Washington Territory Donation Land Claims*, 116, 281; and *Olympia Territorial Republican*, Oct. 16, 1869.

[58] Territory of Wash., *Statutes of the Territory of Washington, 1869*, 543.

[59] *Olympia Commercial Age*, Jan. 1, 1870; and Territory of Wash., *Statutes of the Territory of Washington, 1869*, 543.

Washington's honesty prevented his re-election. He spoke out against his own party when they attempted to pass a resolution without a quorum. The *Washington Standard* recalled that the action "called forth from Mr. Peck an indignant protest against the proceeding as illegal and unfair. For this manifestation of honesty . . . he was 'laid on the shelf,' although possessing more brains than any who have succeeded him."[60]

In 1870 Mercy helped organize the suffragettes. Three years earlier, the legislature had passed an act giving all white American citizens over twenty-one the right to vote. Suffragette Mary Olney Brown interpreted this to mean women as well as men, not exactly what the men had in mind, and urged women to vote in the next election. Although she was turned away in 1869, "my going to the polls was noised abroad, and set men as well as women thinking. They examined the law for themselves, and found that women had a right to vote." In May her sister, Charlotte Olney French, who lived in Grand Mound, "began talking the matter up; and . . . soon had the whole neighborhood interested. With the assistance of an old lady, Mrs. Peck, she planned a regular campaign." On Election Day, June 6, 1870, they headed off to the schoolhouse, where Washington was the Election Inspector, and fixed the men a picnic lunch. "Directly after, while the officers of the election were in good humor (wives will understand the philosophy of this)" seven of the women, including Mercy, "handed in their ballots as if they had always been accustomed to voting, and everything passed off pleasantly." In the fall of 1871 Susan B. Anthony addressed the Territorial Legislature on women's right to vote, but the men passed another law overruling it. The Legislature twice more passed women's suffrage, but the courts overturned them. Women finally won the right to vote in Washington State in 1910, ten years before the 19th Amendment was passed.[61] On April 21, 2005, a plaque honoring the first fifteen women, including Mercy Peck, to vote in a Washington Territorial election was dedicated in Grand Mound.

With Mercy's interest in Spiritualism, it is not surprising to find that she was a suffragette. Historian Barbara Goldsmith explained that Spiritualism "became a major—if not *the* major—vehicle for the spread of

[60] *Olympia Washington Standard*, Nov. 18, 1871, 2:1.

[61] Stanton and Anthony, *History of Women Suffrage*, 3:781, 784; *Olympia Transcript*, May 6, 1870, and June 11, 1870; and Angie Leventis, "Thurston County honors trailblazing Washington suffragettes," *Tacoma News Tribune*, Apr. 26, 2005.

woman's rights ideas." Spiritualism brought comfort to women who had lost so many babies and young children. Mercy had lost three children, and all but one of the Peck family women had lost babies by that time. By the end of the Civil War, the movement had attracted ten million believers. Goldsmith wrote, "The unbearable death of a generation of young men . . . encouraged the belief that these souls had simply 'passed over.' They were reachable in a land just beyond the living."[62]

After four years in western Washington, Jane and Calvin Keys decided to move to Klickitat County on the Columbia River.[63] Its arid climate was more familiar to Calvin, who had spent his boyhood in Texas. Mercy bought the Keys farm to give Jane and Calvin the capital to go into the stock raising business. They bought a quarter section near the blockhouse that had housed United States Calvary troops during the Yakima Indian War. After the troops pulled out in 1860, the dry rolling hills surrounding the blockhouse became grazing land for cattle and horses.[64]

In 1870 the Northern Pacific Railroad began building northward from Kalama on the Columbia River to Puget Sound. By then Washington and Mercy owned almost a thousand acres in Grand Mound. As they watched a land boom develop along the rail line, they anticipated that Olympia would be next, so they bought four lots in town.[65] When the line reached Grand Mound in November, 1871, they determined that it was the opportune time to sell, so they sold their farm and moved into town.[66]

Olympia, Washington Territory, 1871

Early historian John C. Rathbun wrote that Olympia "was to be the New York, the New Orleans, the Chicago, the San Francisco of the Northwest. Urged on by mad speculation, purchasers offered fabulous prices for real estate."[67]

---

[62] Chandler, "In the Van," *California History* (Fall 1995), 189; and Goldsmith, *Other Powers*, 35, 48, 139.

[63] Federal Census, 1870, Wash., Klickitat County, 141, June 28–29; and BLM GLO Certificate 1726, issued Mar. 13, 1875, and filed in Klickitat County Deeds Book 4:214 on Sept. 12, 1885.

[64] Coon, "Klickitat County," *Washington Historical Quarterly* 15:4 (Oct. 1923):248–61.

[65] Charles and Margaret Williams to W. Peck, Apr. 19, 1871, Thurston County Deed Book 7:368; and J. M. Brewer to W. Peck, Oct. 7, 1871, Deed Book 8:236.

[66] W. Peck to Francis Marion Rhodes, Mar. 29, 1872, Thurston County Deed Book 8:385; and W. Peck to F. M. Rhodes and wife, Mortgage Book A:148.

[67] Rathbun, *History of Thurston Co., Washington*, 56–59.

By October of 1872 the rail line was completed to Tenino, which became the end of the line for eight months while the railroad went through some financial difficulties.[68] This was just long enough to spark the growth of Tenino. When the railroad resumed building, they changed course toward Tacoma, bypassing Olympia. Land prices plummeted.[69]

By this time Washington's ever-present dark beard had become streaked with white. Fifteen years had passed since the Pecks left Missouri. One of Egerton Peck's daughters, Anna Eliza Peck, became the family letter writer. She was the child Hannah had been expecting when the Pecks started along the Santa Fe Trail in 1858. Washington wrote to her regularly.

Olympia Oct. 6, 1874

Dear Eliza,

I received yours of the 14th ult. Were glad to hear that you were all well. . . .

The season here has been first rate, all kinds of crops are abundant. I am glad that you sent some of the seeds to Susie Whiffen [her cousin]. I have not written to them for a long time as they never answered my letters.

Inclosed is a few seeds of the satten fower [satin flower, Lunaria, or Silver Dollar plant] & a specimen of the same. . . . Plant early in the spring. They are hardy. Also a few seeds of the candy top . . . and some of the quilled China aster. . . . There is a very great veriety [sic] of beautiful flowers here and extensively cultivated. . . .

The fall is very warm. No frost yet Oct 18th. This is the latest that we have known beens [sic] and tomatoes to be grown.

If my health would admit, I would gladly except your kind invitation to make you a vuisit. I should injoy it very much to see you all. Also to see the Eastern country once more would afford me great pleasure. But my race is almost run. I feel as if there is but a step between me and the spirit world. But I thank God that I have no dred, no fear to take that step.

I look upon death as a friend, not an enemy to the human family when we have lived until the system is worn out and life become a burden. Then death removes us from our infirmities and places us in a better world. . . .

---

[68] Dwelley, *Tenino: The First Hundred Years*, 6.

[69] Rathbun, *History of Thurston Co., Washington*, 61.

Anna Eliza Peck Ware, daughter of Egerton Ezra Peck, who corresponded with her grandfather, Washington Peck, circa 1880. *Courtesy of Carolyn Dodds Schaeffer.*

Our love to all. I remain your affectionate Grand Father,
Washington Peck

According to your request, we send you our picture.

The fine seed is snapdragons. They will seed themselves. At least they do here.

Washington was one of many pioneers who helped spread plant specimens across the continent by mailing seeds to his granddaughters in Missouri and Ontario.

Washington was beginning to feel his age, though he would live another fifteen years. By December, the Pecks were fortunate to find a buyer for two of their four Olympia lots, so they moved to Tenino, where real estate prices had also fallen.[70]

[70] W. Peck to John C. Murray, Dec. 23, 1874, Thurston County Deed Book 10:701; and Dwelley, *Tenino, The First Hundred Years*, 6.

Tenino, Washington Territory, 1874

When the Pecks got settled in Tenino, Washington wrote to Eliza again and filled her in on their move.[71]

Tenino Feby 27 1875

Dear Eliza

We received yours of Dec 19, a long time ago, and we would have answered it sooner, but we had sold out in Olympia and was in the bussle of moving. The weather extremely cold, the coldest ever known by white folks here, it being eight below zero.

We stoped at Colvins some time and then it took quite a while to get things fixed up in any kind of order, which has delayed our writing until now. This place Tenino is 16 miles from Olympia on what is called the Northern Pacific Rail Road, which road connects the Columbia River with Pugets Sound. This place is 40 miles from Tacoma, the terminus on the sound, and 61 miles from Kalama on the Columbia River, which is about 50 miles from Portland, Oregon.

Two years ago last fall the Road was finished to this place from the River and the people went crazy over it. A town was laid out and lots sold from $100 down to $40 each and quite a number of buildings was erected and money plenty, but when the Road was extended on to Tacoma, a reaction took place. No more building and about one year after, more than half the buildings were empty. One store remains, which is doing a good buisiness and two taverns doing fair. Three saloones is closed and empty except a family living in one. One man bought two lots at $100 each, erected two saloons. One is 40 × 20 ft. The other not quite so wide, and a stable about 18 by 40 ft and other out houses. It is said that the improvements cost him $1000. He is now offering the whole for $250. I think of buying it. One is rented for $3.00 per month. It and stable will rent for about $40.00 a year. The other will make a good house by partitioning off into rooms. The Rail Road has killed Olympia by leaveing it out in the cold. I sold for $500.00, about one third of cost. We thought it better to take that than get less and perhaps nothing.

We can settle ourselves here just as comfortable as we were in Olympia for less than we sold for there and save about 25 dollars municipal tax, and fire wood costs only about half as much here as their. If this is

[71] Philip Hiltz to W. Peck, Mar 4, 1875, Thurston Co. Deed Book 10:745.

a small place, it is not dull as the train stops at 9 o-clock in the morning and 3 in the afternoon, Sundays excepted. Some think that the place will come up and become quite a village. I think it doubtful but can never get any lower than it is. It is a pleasant location on a small prarie, the station house close by a wood. The place that we think of buying is only 60 ft from the station house, the best location for any business in the place. We are three miles from Emmas.

I am sorry that I cannot comply with your request to send you our pictures, but you will have to wait until we get more taken. When that will be, if ever, is very uncertain. I promised to inclose a specimen of the satten [satin] plant and forgot to do. I now inclose it.

My health has been rather better than usual this winter.

Calvin Keys, Janes husband, and family started to come over the mountains late last fall, went . . . 100 miles north to a pass in the mountains, found the snow so deep they went back about 40 miles to a settlement to winter. He wrote Dec 17, said the snow was a foot deep. Since then we have not heard from them. The snow is deep and cold intense. Cattle is dying in that country and we expect that they will loose [lose] what stock they had.

Pleas to give our love to your father and Mother and all the family. . . . Please to write often. From your affectionate Grandfather

W Peck

Pleas give our best respects to all inquireing friends. We would be very glad to see you all again, but never expect to until we meet in the summoned land.

WP

The extremely cold weather that trapped the Keys in the Cascade Mountains lasted for weeks. The lower Columbia River froze over, cutting off Portland. Historian David Wilma wrote that the "overland mail service from Portland . . . to Puget Sound stopped, and when ocean steamers couldn't dock at Seattle and Tacoma, communication by sea also ceased."[72]

Washington's next letter to Eliza revealed that Washington and Mercy had made a gradual shift in their spiritual beliefs during the past four years.

[72] Wilma, "*Cold weather freezes wharves and rivers in Washington in January 1875.*"

Tenino, Oct 29th, 1875

Dear Eliza,

Yours of the 14th inst was duly received and we were glad to hear from you once more. We began to fear that you had forgotten us. . . . We assure you that you have a warm place in our affections. And although we may never meet in this world, I do fully believe that we shall meet in the spirit world. . . . I feel that I have got almost there, that I am standing on the brink liable to pass over any moment. . . . I feel that I am not going to that gloomey hereafter described [in the hymn "And Am I Born To Die?" by Methodist Charles Wesley] as:

> *A land of deepest shade,*
> *Unpierced by human thought,*
> *The dreary regions of the dead,*
> *Where all things are forgot.*[73]

I believe that I am going to join my dear friends that have gone before. I do know that their spirits are around me to encourage and strengthen. The spirit of your Grand Mother . . . [Sophia, Washington's first wife] is with me a large portion of the time. Their has not been a day for more than four years but I have felt her hands laid caressingly on my head as palpable as though she were in the body. I feel them now while penning these lines and a great many other ways has she made me feel her presence as well as to spell out a number of communications by the alphabet [on a Ouija Board], but it does not take away my strength as heretofore.

We were members of the Methodist church for about 25 years, but we never experienced the happiness that we have since we became spiritualists. We have renounced all creeds. Our trust for future happiness is in God alone, not in consequence of a belief in any creed or dogma. If we make the golden rule the rule of our lives here, we will be happy here and be prepaired to enter on a state [of] happiness in the spirit land.

We do hope, dear Eliza, that you will strive to be useful to your fellow creatures more than to be fashionable that when you enter upon the great hereafter, you may be welcomed with well done, good and faithful servant.

We have had a pleasant fall. This morning was the first frost. The beens [beans], pumpkin vines, and tomatoes still look green and fresh. Crops has been good. We have raised abundance of vegetables in our little garden for our own use.

---

[73] This hymn was sung in the movie *Cold Mountain*, released in 2003.

We are about as well as when we last wrote. I have spells of feeling very bad, but it does not take away my strength as heretofore.

Your uncle Edmond has struck a big thing in Arrizonia. We suppose you have seen in the papers some account of the Peck or Silver Prince mine that was discovered by him. There is 5 in the company working it. He wrote to us before it got in the papers. If it is one quarter as rich as represented, it is a big thing. . . .

Mother joines me in our love to you and Josiah [her brother] and all the folks at home.

I remain your ever affectionate Grand Father,

Washington Peck

The spiritualism that the Pecks became interested in as early as 1860 in New Mexico was no longer a parlor game to Washington. He was sounding a little strange and he had been ready to pass over for a year. Was he suffering some physical ailment or was he depressed? It must have been disconcerting for Mercy to have the spirit of his first wife, Sophia, hovering around all the time.

But the big news was about Edmond. Edmond Peck had indeed made a big silver strike. He had shared his excitement with Washington and Mercy before the story broke in the *Arizona Weekly Miner* on July 2, 1875, and within two weeks mining claims had been filed for two miles in all directions from the discovery.[74]

Edmond offered his sister Jane and husband Calvin Keys a place to live. With a fresh outbreak of Northwest Indian problems arising from the Government's decision to reopen the Nez Perce reservation in the beautiful Wallowa Valley to white settlers and the disastrous winter snows that killed most of their livestock, the Keys gladly accepted his offer. As they left, Annie Keys, then eight, looked down into the valley from the ridge of a hill where they had stopped their wagons to rest and saw smoke rising from their home and those of their neighbors. They had been set afire by Indians.[75]

Edmond may have invited Washington and Mercy to come share his wealth, or he may have needed guidance with developing legal problems. Suddenly Washington seemed to feel better, and he sold the Tenino place and the last lots in Olympia. By late May, he and Mercy were on

[74] *Prescott Weekly Arizona Miner*, July 2, 1875, 5:3; and *Tucson Arizona Citizen*, July 3, 1875, 2:2.

[75] Oral History from John A. (Jack) Taylor, grandson of Annie Jane Keys Rousseau.

Washington and Mercy Peck, circa 1875. *Courtesy of Sharlot Hall Museum.* *(opposite, left)* Ellen/Ella Serena Alexander Peck, circa 1870s. *Courtesy of Sharlot Hall Museum.* *(opposite, right)* Edmond George Peck, circa 1870s. *Courtesy of Sharlot Hall Museum.*

the move once again, this time to Arizona.[76] It had been twelve years since they left California, the longest stretch of time they had stayed in one territory since they had left Ontario thirty-five years earlier, and they were about to find that life still had some adventures in store for them.

Arizona Territory, 1876

Washington and Mercy rolled into Prescott on the Arizona and New Mexico Express Company stage on Tuesday morning, June 6, 1876.[77] When the stage stopped and the dust settled, undoubtedly, some of their large, growing family were there to meet them. Edmond had married

[76] W. and Mercy Peck to Sarah Tilley, Apr. 8, 1876, Thurston County Deed Book 11:299; and W. Peck to George Forbes, May 6, 1876, Book 11:317.

[77] *Prescott Weekly Arizona Miner*, June 10, 1876.

Ellen Serena Alexander, daughter of one of his mining partners, and they had a baby girl, Minnie. Jane and Calvin Keys had arrived in January, then settled their eight children on a ranch at Walnut Grove as baby Grace arrived.[78] Mary Ann and George Banghart had three children living at home, but their oldest three daughters had married prominent young men in Prescott and had borne several great-grandchildren for the Pecks to meet.

Prescott was booming. Miners flooded into town and filled the saloons on Whiskey Row, along with "fancy girls" and gamblers. This was the Wild West depicted in cowboy movies, the post–Civil War era that spawned gunfighters and lawmen like the Earps. In fact, a wagon train led by Nicholas Earp arrived in Prescott during the Pecks' stay.[79]

Washington and Mercy made the rounds visiting their children and grandchildren. The Bangharts lived on a ranch north of Prescott in the Chino Valley. They had a herd of a hundred and twenty-five cattle, of

[78] Ibid., Jan. 14, 1876, 3:2 and Feb. 25, 1876, 2:2.

[79] Chaput, *Virgil Earp: Western Peace Officer*, 25.

which fifty were milk cows, and they were making excellent cheese in addition to the milk and butter that they sold in town.[80]

But the Bangharts' faithful old pet cow was not in the herd. After fourteen years, she had survived 4,500 miles on the trail, torturous desert treks, numerous Indian raids, droughts, and blindness only to be driven off with some other stock in an Indian raid in May of 1867, a year after the Bangharts arrived in Arizona. For fourteen years she had given ten to twenty quarts of milk a day and had a new calf every year. The story in the *Prescott Arizona Miner*, "A Traveled Cow," reported that "the loss of so faithful and valuable an animal and one so identified with the movements of his family is keenly regretted by Mr. Banghart, and if she could be recovered, he would willingly lose the remainder of his stock." Unfortunately, they never found her.[81]

At the Keys' in Walnut Grove, south of Prescott, Jane's husband Calvin was platting out a town site to be built on his ranch acreage.[82]

At the Peck Mine, Edmond had built a new house for his wife Ella, while he and his partners—T. M. Alexander, C. C. Bean, and William Cole—spent a busy year getting the mine into operation. Washington and Mercy were there to witness the boom of the Peck Mine, which began to produce fabulous riches when veins of almost pure silver were discovered. In November the mine was incorporated and the company issued 100,000 shares of stock at $10 per share for a value of a million dollars. The men laid out a new town, Alexandra, to serve the miners, which author Bruce Wilson described as having "two stores, three boarding houses, four saloons, two livery stables, six houses, one butcher shop, and a blacksmith shop. . . . The Peck had spawned a boom town."[83]

In August, Edmond went to San Francisco to set up the Peck Mining Company of California in order to raise additional investment capital. Among the California partners was William Tecumseh Sherman. The company issued 100,000 shares of stock at $100 each, which raised $10 million in capital.[84]

---

[80] *Prescott Weekly Arizona Miner*, Dec. 31, 1875 and Feb. 4, 1876, 1:4.

[81] *Prescott Arizona Miner*, June 1, 1867.

[82] Plat of the Town of Walnut Grove, Oct. 1876, Walnut Grove file, Sharlot Hall Museum, Prescott, Arizona.

[83] *Prescott Arizona Citizen*, Nov. 25, 1876, 3:3; and Wilson, *Crown King*, 34.

[84] Henderson, "The Peck Mine," *Arizona and the West* 3:1:235; and Yavapai County Articles of Incorporation Ledger, 3–16.

Edmond decided to take Ella to Oakland where the weather was milder. Washington and Mercy decided to move to Oakland with them. Ed would help get them settled, but he would be running back and forth attending to mining business. Ella may have been suffering from early symptoms of consumption (tuberculosis), which were often vague and could develop slowly over many years. The disease was not yet known to be contagious.[85]

Charles Beach, an old acquaintance from New Mexico, was at the stage the morning they left. Publisher of the *Prescott Weekly Arizona Miner*, Beach wrote, "We met the old gentleman and lady this morning, for the first time in eighteen years. . . . They are still well preserved. . . . They are very intelligent people and have lived sensible lives."[86] Washington's health was decidedly better than a couple years earlier when he thought he was about to pass over.

Calvin Keys abandoned his idea of building a town site on the ranch and decided to take Jane and the kids to Arkansas, where he had family. They left the same day as the Pecks—September 27, 1877—and started east.[87] This was another goodbye for Washington and Mercy, who apparently never saw Jane and Calvin again. Eventually the Keys settled in No Man's Land, the panhandle of Oklahoma, where they raised cattle on a large ranch near Kenton that has remained in the family.

Edmond loaded two large bars of silver bullion, worth $3,000 to $4,000 each, into the Wells Fargo Express box and climbed into the California and Arizona stage with the rest of the family. A rash of robberies had taken place that year. The stages were robbed so often that Wells Fargo ran a standard $300 reward notice alongside news of the latest robbery.[88]

Late in the afternoon a few miles outside of Wickenburg, a robber, masked in black gauze, stepped out of the bushes with a double-barreled shotgun and stopped the stage. After ordering the men to break open the express box, he packed up $600 in Post Office cash, $2,000 in gold dust and small bars, and registered letters with money and checks, but, as Edmond had hoped, the silver bars were too heavy to pack off. The stage continued on to Wickenburg, where the station agent telegraphed news

[85] Rothman, *Living in the Shadow of Death*, 15–17, 179.

[86] *Prescott Weekly Arizona Miner*, Sept. 21, 1877, 3:1.

[87] Ibid., Sept. 28, 1877, 3:2–3.

[88] Ibid.; and Theobald, *Wells Fargo in Arizona Territory*, 58.

Jane/Jennie S. Peck Keys and Calvin Keys, circa 1900. Note on back: Jennie burned down the local saloon—three times. She and Calvin apparently had some problems. *Courtesy of Ruby Labrier.*

of the robbery to Prescott. Although a posse set out in pursuit, it was almost a year and many robberies later before a sheriff's posse near Tucson killed William Brazelton after a tip from an informant.[89] Migration by stagecoach had proven to be no less dangerous than by wagon train.

Alameda, California, 1877

The Pecks had left the Wild West and arrived in a bustling cosmopolitan city. The San Francisco area had a population of almost 200,000. The Pecks rented a house in Oakland for the winter, and Edmond commuted by ferry to the Peck Mining Office at 318 Pine Street in the financial district of San Francisco.[90]

[89] *Prescott Arizona Citizen*, Oct. 6, 1877; Lauer, *Tales of Arizona Territory*, 7–9; and *Prescott Arizona Enterprise*, Aug. 21, 1878, 3:3.

[90] Bishop, *Bishop's Oakland Directory*, 374; and Langley, *The San Francisco Directory*, 695.

The following spring, in 1878, Washington and Edmond bought houses on Alameda peninsula (now island) on Alameda Avenue.[91] Half a block away, a new narrow gage railway ran along Encinal Avenue to the ferryboat landing at Alameda Point, where the ferries took businessmen to work and sightseers to ride the new *California Street Cable Railroad* that began running on April 10, 1878. A huge crowd of 6,000 had witnessed the first two-car trolley travel up the hill.[92]

The return ferries brought flocks of summer visitors to the resort bathhouses that crowded Alameda beach. Visitors learned to swim in the sunshine, away from the San Francisco fog. The *Alameda Directory* proclaimed that the resort area had "establishments as extensive and elegant as those of any Atlantic City."[93]

The Pecks stayed for two years before deciding to return to Washington Territory where Emma's sons were having problems.

Grand Mound, Washington Territory, 1879

After an absence of three-and-a-half years, the Pecks moved back to Washington Territory at the end of 1879.[94] In March of 1880 they bought a farm on Grand Mound Prairie, not far from their previous place. At seventy-eight years old, Washington did not plan to farm. He and Mercy registered the deed in trust for Emma's three sons until the boys turned twenty-one.[95] Apparently they did not get along with their gruff stepfather, Ignatius Colvin.

The Bangharts came to visit at the end of March 1880. Mary Ann was in poor health and hoped the change in climate would help her recover.[96] The Bangharts had been through a disastrous year that started when their ranch house burned. Their grandson, Eddie Marion, died a few days later.[97] Then, in July their fifteen-year-old son, Georgie Banghart, was struck by lightning in the hills west of the ranch where he'd gone to get the dairy cows. He was found two days later beside his dead horse

[91] Alameda County Deed Book 155:388, Mar. 8, 1878; and Deed Book 158:175–76, Mar. 26, 1878.
[92] Hilton, *Cable Car in America*, 193.
[93] Bishop, *Bishop's Oakland Directory for 1879–80*, 563.
[94] *Chehalis* (Wash.) *Bee Nugget*, Aug. 4, 1899.
[95] Thurston County Deed Book 12:530, Mar. 25, 1880.
[96] *Prescott Weekly Arizona Democrat*, Mar. 26, 1880, 6:1.
[97] *Prescott Weekly Arizona Miner*, Dec. 13, 1878, 1:7; and *Prescott Arizona Enterprise*, Dec. 28, 1878, 1:5.

(*left*) Emma Peck Rector Colvin, circa 1880. *From author's collection.*
(*right*) Ignatius Colvin, circa 1880. *Courtesy of Doris Colvin.*

and was buried on the ranch.[98] They stayed for six weeks, but Mary Ann didn't improve. It was the Pecks last visit with the Bangharts. Mary Ann remained ill with a kidney affliction for the next year and died May 13, 1881, not quite forty-nine years old.[99] For the rest of his life George remained on the ranch in the Chino Valley, which eventually became a stage stop, then a railroad station.

Chehalis, Washington Territory, 1886

After Washington disposed of the Grand Mound farm, he and Mercy moved twelve miles south to Chehalis in Lewis County in April of 1886, where they built a new house.[100] The newspaper reported: "Mr. Peck is

[98] *Prescott Weekly Arizona Miner,* Aug. 1, 1879, 1:6.
[99] Ibid., Apr. 30, 1880, 3:1; and May 7, 1880, 3:2; and *Prescott* Arizona Democrat, May 13, 1881, 5:3.
[100] Lewis County Deed Book L:454, Apr. 3, 1886; and Book M:609, Oct. 27, 1887.

Peck family on the porch of the Colvin home, March 1880. From left: Mary Ann Peck Banghart, Nellie Banghart, Sadie Colvin (child), Emma Colvin (seated), Flora E. Banghart Marion (?), George W. Banghart, and Washington Peck. In 1877, while Washington and Mercy were in Arizona, Ignatius and Emma built this new house, which is now listed on the National Register of Historic Places. *From author's collection.*

a new comer."[101] He was an eighty-four-year-old newcomer with a snowy white beard.

History is silent on the Pecks' travels during their latter years. They lived close enough to the railroad to step out the door and onto the train, but whether they periodically visited Ella Peck in Alameda, where they still owned a house, is not known. Ella died of consumption (tuberculosis) in October of 1887 at age thirty-two and left three small children. Over the next few years the three children also died from consumption. Edmond returned to Arizona where he spent the remainder of his life. Plagued with legal wrangles from the very beginning, eventually Edmond lost the Peck Mine through some shady dealing by his trusted California

[101] *Chehalis* (Wash.) *Nugget*, Apr. 16, 1886, 3:2.

(*left*) Mary Ann Peck Banghart, circa 1880. *Courtesy of John Wells Heap.*
(*right*) George Washington Banghart, circa 1880. *Courtesy of John Wells Heap.*

partners. After losing the Peck Mine, he returned to prospecting. Washington and Mercy sold their Alameda house the following June.[102]

Centralia, Washington Territory, 1888

Washington and Mercy moved one last time, five miles north to Centralia where they built their final home.[103] The following year, a boom hit. Herndon Smith's compilation of Centralia history noted that "the population grew from 700 to 3,200. Plans were made for Centralia to be the radiation point of five railroads." Coal mines, lumber mills, and

[102] Sharlot Hall Museum, Obituary Book; and Alameda County Deed Book 351:245–47, June 18, 1888.

[103] Lewis County Deed Book O:177, Oct. 2, 1887, and 409, Oct. 28, 1888.

Washington Peck's gravestone is located in the Pioneer section of Mountain View Cemetery, Centralia, Washington. *From author's collection.*

shingle mills swung into operation. "A hundred buildings were under construction at the same time."[104]

Washington's life was winding down. He lived to see the Territory become a state on November 11, 1889, then put his affairs in order. On December 7 he transferred a deed to Mercy that he marked with an *X*—too weak to sign his name.[105] He died on December 27, 1889, at eighty-eight years and five months of age.

The *Washington Standard* of Olympia carried a brief obituary noting that he had been a resident of Washington for over twenty-five years, and the *Chehalis Nugget* carried the following obituary:[106]

> Washington Peck, an old pioneer of this country, died at his home in Centralia on Friday, 27th, after a protracted illness, at the ripe age of 88 years. He was highly esteemed and respected by all who knew him. He leaves a loving wife and several children to mourn his loss.

[104] Smith, *Centralia, The First Fifty Years*, 19.

[105] Lewis County Deed Book V:170, Dec. 7, 1889.

[106] *Olympia Washington Standard*, Jan. 3, 1890, 3:3, and *Chehalis (Wash.) Nugget*, Jan. 3, 1890, 3:3.

Mercy's final land purchase was Washington's burial plot in Butterworth's Cemetery, now Mountain View Cemetery, in Centralia, Washington.[107] His white marble gravestone is carved with two hands meeting, that of a man and a woman.

Washington's lifelong obsession to own land led him to hold onto at least one piece of land each time he moved. True to that pattern, he still owned the Chehalis town lots when he died.[108]

Mercy remained in Centralia where she witnessed the boom of 1889 become the crash of 1893. Smith wrote, "People left the city as quickly as they had come. For more than six years the town was as if dead. Lots . . . sold for a dollar."[109]

One small story has survived from Mercy's final years. Granddaughter Annie Jane (Keys) Rousseau brought her son Lovell, age six, to visit in 1898, on their way to the Klondike gold rush. Lovell was fascinated with watches at the time. He wanted a watch and fob, so great-grandmother Mercy, used to a lifetime of "making do," made a hole in a silver dollar and presented it to Lovell as his very own "watch," which he treasured throughout his life.[110]

On July 28, 1899, Mercy died. The *Chehalis Bee-Nugget* wrote that she had died "very suddenly at the home of her daughter, Mrs. [Emma] Colvin, at Centralia, Friday at 2:30, aged 93. . . . Mrs. Peck was loved by all who knew her." Funeral services were held at the Methodist Church.[111] If Mercy had stopped attending church during her fling with spiritualism, apparently she had returned. When the Fox sisters had revealed that their spirit rappings were a fraud, author Barbara Goldsmith wrote, "It dealt a 'death blow' to Spiritualism" in 1888.[112] Presumably, Mercy is buried beside Washington, but there is no marker for her.

Washington and Mercy's lifespan corresponds to the opening of the West. In 1801, when Washington was born, the Northwest referred to the area that became Illinois, Wisconsin, Ohio, Indiana, and Michigan. The United States was only twenty-five years old and Lewis and

[107] Lewis County Deed Book 10:1, June 14, 1890.
[108] Estate Peck, April 25, 1894, Superior Court of Lewis County, Case No. 143.
[109] Smith, *Centralia, The First Fifty Years*, 20.
[110] Oral history from JoAnne Rousseau, Lovell's daughter.
[111] *Chehalis (Wash.) Bee-Nugget*, Aug. 4, 1899.
[112] Goldsmith, *Other Powers*, 426.

Clark had not yet gone west. By the time Washington died, the United States had grown from sixteen states along the eastern seaboard to forty-two states that spanned the continent. Likewise, the Confederation of Canada, formed in 1867, spanned the continent after British Columbia became a province in 1871. Railroads crisscrossed both countries and digging had begun on the Panama Canal.

Washington Peck possessed an adventurous spirit fueled by a great curiosity. He was knowledgeable and sociable, staying well informed on local and world affairs. He made up his own mind after weighing information carefully. He was fair, honest, and compassionate, and he knew and respected the law. He accepted troubles as they came, resolved whatever problems he could, and moved on, all without complaint.

Mercy Mary was dynamic, energetic, and fun loving—always at the center of things—surrounded by family and friends, especially the children. She read about fashion, delivered babies, nursed the sick, bought and sold property, and worked as a suffragette. And she lived right alongside Washington as they traveled thousands and thousands of miles.

The Pecks were eyewitnesses to the making of the nation. Indeed, they helped to make it. They bought and sold enough property in their lifetime to make up a small state, and they left more than 50 grandchildren and 125 great-grandchildren when they died. Washington and Mercy lived longer lives than any of their children, a testament to their hardy constitutions and certainly some good luck. They dodged more than one bullet, but a lifetime of hard work and traveling had made them stronger, and perhaps their undying curiosity had made their tomorrows too exciting to miss.

Bibliography

Manuscripts and Collections

Armour, Philip D. Biographical Information File. California History Room. California State Library. *Grizzly Bear*, Nov. 1907, 57–63.

Bruff, Joseph Goldsborough. *Diaries, Journals and Notebooks, 1849–1850*. Yale Collection of Western Americana, Beinecke Rare Book and Manuscript Library, WA MSS 50.

Diary of Washington Peck, 1850–1851: held by the Burton Historical Collection, Detroit Public Library, Washington Peck Collection.

Diary of Washington Peck, 1858: in the possession of the author.

Johnson, Janet Cox, unpublished family history: shared with the author.

Lester, Paul Arnold. "Michael Steck and New Mexico Indian Affairs, 1852–1865." PhD diss., University of Oklahoma, 1986.

Lucy Mima Wright Diary, 1860–1862: in the possession of the author.

Macy Centennial, 1850–1950. A Record of the centennial meetings, sponsored by Mary E. Foy and Ella Foy O'Gorman and held by the descendants of Dr. Obed Macy and wife, Lucinda Polk Macy, in Los Angeles, Calif., April 1950. F860 M299, Bancroft Library.

Michael Steck Collection, 1818–1883. MSS 134 BC, Papers, 1841–1880. Center for Southwest Research. University of New Mexico.

Plat of Town of Walnut Grove, Walnut Grove file, Sharlot Hall Museum, Prescott, Ariz.

Sharlot Hall Obituary Book, Sharlot Hall Museum, Prescott, Ariz.

Smith, David A. "The Military Participation in the Discovery and Development of Yosemite National Park, Calif." Master's thesis, 1984, on file at Yosemite Research Library, Yosemite National Park, Calif. Excerpt, "The Mariposa War," on file at the California State Military Museum.

Stine, Henry Atkinson. Copy of the Letters and Journal of Henry Atkinson Stine on His Overland Trip to California from St. Louis to Sacramento, May 4, 1850 to October 25, 1850. Call #B S85. California History Room, California State Library, Sacramento.

Tyrrell, Mrs. Wm. to her son H. G. Tyrrell, 1 TLS (typed letter signed) May 20, 1891, Weston, Ontario. William Tyrrell Papers. Thomas Fisher Rare Book Library, University of Toronto.

Ward, Lorne G. *George Wright, 1815–1905: An American Pioneer from Sea to Shining Sea.* Undated biography (before 1879) about his grandfather, on file at the Lincoln County Historical Society, Carrizozo, N.Mex.

Washington Peck's Letters to Eliza, 1875–1876: in the possession of Carolyn Dodds Schaeffer.

Washington Territory Donation Land Claims: abstract of information in the land claim papers of persons who settled in Washington Territory before 1856. Seattle Genealogical Society, 1980.

Woodbridge Mackenzie Site (AkGv-2). Report prepared for the Town of Vaughan by Meryl Oliver, March 1983, requesting designation as a Heritage Site under the Ontario Heritage Act.

Government Documents

Canada—National Records

• Archives of Ontario

District Marriage Registers: Huron, Johnstown, London, Newcastle, and Ottawa Districts, MS248, Reel 3.

Ontario Death Records, MS937, Deaths 1869–1924, Reel 8.

Records of the Registers General, Marriages in the Home District 1823–1845, MS248, Reel 1—Index #59.

Township Papers, Militia Land Grants, MS658, Reel 61, Page 268.

Upper Canada Land, C103, Book K.

• National Archives of Canada

Census 1851, Roll C-11738, Delaware and Westminster Townships.

Census 1851, Roll C-11759, Vaughan Township.

• United Church Archives of Canada

Wesleyan Methodist Baptismal Registers, 1825–1910, Reel 1.

Canada—Provincial Records

• Ontario County Land Registry Offices

Lambton County LRO—Deeds of Sarnia and Sarnia Township.

Middlesex County LRO—Deeds of Caradoc, Delaware and Lobo Townships.

Old York Registry, Toronto LRO—Deeds of Etobicoke and Vaughan Townships.

United States—National, State, and County Records

⬩ United States Congress

Condition of the Indian Tribes. Report of the Joint Special Committee, Appointed under Joint Resolution of March 3, 1865. With an Appendix. Washington: Government Printing Office, 1867.

⬩ United States National Archives and Record Administration

Federal Census: 1850 Wis., Sheboygan County.

Federal Census: 1860 Calif., Los Angeles County, San Gabriel.

Federal Census: 1860 N.Mex., Santa Fe County, Santa Fe.

Federal Census: 1860 N.Mex., Socorro County, Rio Bonito.

Federal Census: 1870 Wash., Klickitat County.

Federal Census: 1870 Wash., Thurston County, Grand Mound Precinct.

Federal Census: 1880 Colo., Las Animas County, Trinidad.

Indian Wars Muster Rolls Military Record ARB2-1-12-1332 Indian War Pension Claim of Widow for Service Pension for Ignatius Colvin service in Washington Territory Indian War.

M1072, Letters Sent by 9th Military Dept., The Dept. of New Mexico, and the District of New Mexico, 1849–1890.

M1120, Letters Received and Letters Received by Headquarters, Dept. of New Mexico, 1854–1865.

RG75, Records of the Bureau of Indian Affairs, Guion Miller Report and Exhibits, Eastern Cherokee Applications, Application #3148, M1104, Roll 34, 7.

⬩ United States State and County Records

Alameda County (Calif.) Deed Books 155, 158, and 351.

Atchison County (Mo.) Deed Book 4.

Green Bay (Wis.) BLM GLO (Bureau of Land Management General Land Office).

Kendall County (Ill.) Deed Books A, B, D and E.

Kendall County (Ill.) Marriage Book A1.

Klickitat County (Wash.) Deed Book 4.

Lewis County (Wash.) Deed Book L, M, O, V, and X.

Los Angeles (Calf.) Deed Books 4–6.

Sheboygan County (Wis.) Deed Books C and F.

Socorro County (N.Mex.) Records 1851–1885, Roll 1, Book A.

Superior Court of Lewis County.

Territory of Washington. *Journal of the House of Representatives of the Territory of Washington.* Olympia, Wash.: James Rodgers, 1869.

———. *Journal of the Proceedings of the Council of the Territory of Washington.* Olympia, Wash.: James Rodgers, 1869.

———. *Statutes of the Territory of Washington*. Olympia, Wash.: James Rodgers, 1869.

Thurston County (Wash.) Deed Books 5, 7, 8, 10, 11, 12, 15.

Thurston County (Wash.) Mortgage Books A and B.

Washington State Archives, U.S. District Court of the 2nd Judicial District, 1865.

Yavapai County (Ariz.) Articles of Incorporation Ledger.

Yavapai County (Ariz.) Deed Book 5.

Books and Articles

Adams, Alexander B. *Sunlight and Storm: The Great American Plains*. New York: G. P. Putnam's Sons, 1977.

Allen, Eleanor. *Canvas Caravans*. (Based on the 1852 Journal of Esther Belle McMillan Hannah.) Portland, Oreg.: Binford, Mort, 1946.

Arnold, James R. and Roberta Wiener. *The American West: Living the Frontier Dream*. London: Blandford Press, 1996.

Atwood, Margaret. *Days of the Rebels 1814/1840*. Toronto: Natural Science of Canada, 1977.

Bagley, Will. *Blood of the Prophets: Brigham Young and the Massacre at Mountain Meadows*. Norman: University of Oklahoma Press, 2004.

Baley, Charles W. *Disaster at the Colorado: Beale's Wagon Road and the First Emigrant Party*. Logan: Utah State University Press, 2002.

Bancroft, Hubert Howe. *History of California. 7 vols*. San Francisco: The History Company, 1884–1890.

———. *History of Utah, 1540–1886*. San Francisco: The History Company, 1889.

———. *History of Washington, Idaho, and Montana, 1845–1889*. San Francisco: The History Company, 1890.

Baskerville, Peter, ed. *The Bank of Upper Canada: A Collection of Documents*. Toronto: The Champlain Society in Cooperation with the Ontario Heritage Foundation, 1987.

Bateman, Norman and Paul Selby, eds. *Historical Encyclopedia of Illinois and History of Kendall County*. Chicago: Munsell Publishing Co., 1914.

Beck, Warren A. and Ynes D. Haase. *Historical Atlas of the American West*. Norman: University of Oklahoma Press, 1989.

Berchem, F. R. *The Yonge Street Story 1793–1860*. Toronto: McGraw-Hill Ryerson, 1977.

Bial, Raymond. *The Underground Railroad*. Boston: Houghton Mifflin Company, 1995.

Bigler, David L. *Forgotten Kingdom: The Mormon Theocracy in the American West, 1847–1896*. Logan: Utah State University Press, 1998.

Biographical History of Nodaway and Atchison Counties Missouri. Chicago: Lewis Publishing, 1901.

Biographical History of Page County, Containing Engravings of Prominent Citizens in Page County, with Personal Histories of Many of the Early Settlers and Leading Families; and a Concise History of the County, the Cities and Townships. Chicago: Lewis and Dunbar, 1890.

Bishop, D. M. and Co., comp. *Bishop's Oakland Directory for 1878–79 and 1879–80*. San Francisco: B. C. Vandall, 1878–79.

Bliss, Beatrice L. *Mary Vowell Adams: Reluctant Pioneer*. 2nd ed. Forest Grove, Oregon: Meredith L. Bliss, 1992.

Bowler, Arthur. *The War of 1812*. Toronto and Montreal: Holt, Rinehart and Winston of Canada, 1973.

Breschini, Gary S. "*Mission San Antonio de Padua*." Monterey County Historical Society Local History Website, undated.

Brooks, Juanita. *Mountain Meadows Massacre*. Norman: University of Oklahoma Press, 3rd rev. ed., 1991.

Brown, Dee. *The Westerners*. New York: Holt, Rinehart and Winston, 1974.

Brown, James S. *Life of a Pioneer*. Salt Lake City: Geo. Q. Cannon and Sons Co., 1900. Reprint, New York: AMS Press, 1971.

Buchen, Gustave William. *Historic Sheboygan County*. Resch Publishing Company, 1944.

California Department of Parks and Recreation. *California State Historical Landmarks*. Sacramento: State of California, Resources Agency, Dept. of Parks and Recreation, 1979.

Canfield, Chauncy L., ed. *The Diary of a Forty-Niner*. (Diary of Alfred T. Jackson). New York: Turtle Point Press, 1992.

Carmony, Neil B., ed. *The Civil War in Apacheland, Sergeant George Hand's Diary: California, Arizona, West Texas, New Mexico, 1861–1864*. Silver City, N.Mex.: High Lonesome Books, 1996.

Carson, James H. "Life in California Together with a Description of the Great Tulare Valley." Stockton, Calif.: *San Joachim Republican*, 1852.

Carter, Robert Terence. *Newmarket, The Heart of York Region*. Newmarket, Ontario: Dundurn Press and Elm Tree House Publishers, 1994.

Chandler, Robert J. "In the Van: Spiritualists as Catalysts for the California Women's Suffrage Movement." *California History*, Fall 1995:189–201.

Cheney, Rev. J. W. "The Story of an Emigrant Train" (Ed Akey's story). *Keosauqua* (Iowa) *Republican*, April 22 and 29, 1915.

Chaput, Donald. *Virgil Earp: Western Peace Officer*. Encampment, Wyoming: Affiliated Writers of American, 1994.

Clappe, Dame Shirley [Louise A.K.S. Clappe]. *The Shirley Letters*. Salt Lake City: Peregrine Smith Books, 1983.

Clayton, Lawrence, ed. *William Clayton's Journal*. Salt Lake City: Clayton Family Association and *Deseret News*, 1921.

Cleland, Robert Glass. *The Cattle on a Thousand Hills*. San Marino, Calif.: Huntington Library, 1941.

Cole, S. W. *The American Veterinarian or Diseases of Domestic Animals, Showing the Causes, Symptoms, and Remedies*. Boston: John P. Jewette, 1847.

Cole, Tom. *A Short History of San Francisco*. San Francisco: Lexikos, 1981.

Coleman, Thelma. *Canada Company*. Stratford, Ontario: County of Perth and Cumming Publishers, 1978.

Comstock, David Allan. *1848–1851: 150 Years Ago: A Sketch of Nevada County by Aaron Augustus Sargeant*. Reprinted from an account published in 1856. Grass Valley, Nevada City, Truckee, Calif.: Nevada County Sesquicentennial, 1998.

Conner, Daniel Ellis. *A Confederate in the Colorado Gold Fields*, Donald J. Berthrong and Odess Davenport, eds. and introduction. Norman: University of Oklahoma Press, 1970.

Coon, Delia M. "Klickitat County: Indians of and Settlement by Whites." *Washington Historical Quarterly*, Vol. 15, No. 4 (Oct. 1923):248–61.

Craig, Gerald M. *Upper Canada: The Formative Years, 1784–1841*. Toronto: McClelland and Stewart, 1963.

Cramer, T. Dudley. *The Pecos Ranchers in the Lincoln County War*. Oakland, Calif.: Branding Iron Press, 1996.

Crampton, C. Gregory and Steven K. Madsen. *In Search of the Spanish Trail, Santa Fe to Los Angeles, 1829–1848*. Layton, Utah: Gibbs-Smith, Publisher, 1994.

Cruickshank, F. D., and J. Nason. *History of Weston*. Weston, Ontario: Weston Historical Society, 1983.

Currie, A. W. *The Grand Trunk Railway of Canada*. Toronto: University of Toronto Press, 1957.

Damania, Laura. *Egerton Ryerson*. Don Mills, Ontario: Fitzhenry and Whiteside, 1975.

Davis, Kenneth C. *Don't Know Much about History*. New York: Avon Books, 1991.

Davis, Kenneth S. *Kansas: A Bicentennial History*. New York: W. W. Norton and Company, 1976.

Davis, Richard M. "Where Have All the Wagons Gone?" Part 1, *Overland Journal*, Vol. 15, No. 3 (Autumn 1997):16–39.

———. "Where Have All the Wagons Gone?" Part 2, *Overland Journal*, Vol. 16, No. 2 (Summer 1998):24–42.

Dodge, Bertha S. *The Road West*. Albuquerque: University of New Mexico Press, 1980.

Duffus, R. L. *The Santa Fe Trail*. University of New Mexico Press, 1930. Reprint, New York: David McKay Company, 1975.

Duncan, George W. "Early Houses of Richmond Hill and Vicinity." *The York Pioneer,* 1995, Vol. 90.

Dwelley, Art. *Tenino, The First Hundred Years.* Tenino, Wash.: *Tenino Independent,* 1984.

Eckert, Edward K. and Nicholas J. Amato, eds. *Ten Years in the Saddle: The Memoir of William Woods Averell.* San Raphael, Calif.: Presidio Press, 1978.

Erickson, Paul. *Daily Life in a Covered Wagon.* New York: Puffin Books, 1994.

Faragher, John Mack. *Women and Men on the Overland Trail.* New Haven: Yale University Press, 1979.

Farquhar, Francis P., ed. *Up and Down California in 1860–64, The Journal of William H. Brewer.* Berkeley and Los Angeles: University of California Press, 1966. Reprint, 1974.

Farren, Kathy, ed. *A Bicentennial History of Kendall County, Illinois.* Yorkville, Ill.: Kendall County Bicentennial Commission, 1976.

Fisher, Sidney Thompson. *The Merchant-Millers of the Humber Valley.* Toronto: New Canada Publications, a division of NC Press, 1985.

Folkman, David I., Jr. *The Nicaragua Route.* Salt Lake City: University of Utah Press, 1972.

Foy, Mary E., ed. "By Ox Team from Salt Lake to Los Angeles, 1850, A Memoir by David W. Cheesman." *Historical Society of Southern California,* Vol. 14 (1928):270–317.

Franzwa, Gregory M. *Oregon Trail Revisited.* 4th ed. Tucson, Ariz.: Patrice Press, 1997.

Fraser, John. *Eminent Canadians.* Toronto: McClelland and Stewart, 2000.

Frey, Robert L., ed. *Railroads in the Nineteenth Century; Encyclopedia of American Business History and Biography.* New York: Facts on File, 1988.

Gardner, Mark L. *Wagons for the Santa Fe Trade.* Albuquerque: University of New Mexico Press, 2000.

Giese, Dr. Dale F. *Forts of New Mexico.* Silver City, New Mexico: Dale F. Geise, 1995.

Glendoran, "Pioneer Wright Family." Vol. 16, No. 6 (Nov./Dec. 1998):59–66. Glendora, Calif.: Liberty Publishing.

Goldsmith, Barbara. *Other Powers, The Age of Suffrage, Spiritualism, and the Scandalous Victoria Woodhull.* New York: Alfred A. Knopf, 1998.

Guinn, J. M. *History of California and an Extended History of Its Southern Coast Counties . . . ,* Vol. 2. Los Angeles: Historic Record Company, 1907.

Guthrie, Alfred Bertram, Jr., *The Way West.* Toronto: George J. McLeod Limited, 1949.

Hafen, LeRoy R., ed. *Pike's Peak Gold Rush Guidebooks of 1859 by Luke Tierney, William B. Parsons and Summaries of the Other Fifteen.* Glendale, Calif.: Arthur H. Clark, 1941.

Hafen, LeRoy R. and Ann W. Hafen, eds. *Journals of Forty-Niners: Salt Lake to Los Angeles*. Glendale, Calif.: Arthur H. Clark, 1954.

———. *Old Spanish Trail, Santa Fe to Los Angeles*. Glendale, Calif.: Arthur H. Clark, 1954.

Haines, Aubrey L. *Historic Sites along the Oregon Trail*. St. Louis: Patrice Press, 3rd ed., 1994.

Harwell, William S., ed. *Manuscript History of Brigham Young 1847–1850*. Salt Lake City: Collier's Publishing Company, 1997.

Heath, Kate [Julia Brown]. "A Child's Journey through Arizona and New Mexico." *The Californian*, (Jan.–June 1881)3:14–18.

Henderson, Patrick C. "The Peck Mine: Silver Bonanza in the Bradshaw Mountains." *Arizona and the West*, Vol. 3 (1961) No. 1: 227–36.

Henry, Fern L. *My Checkered Life: Luzena Stanley Wilson in Early California* (with reprint of *Luzena Stanley Wilson: '49er*). Nevada City, Calif.: Carl Mautz Publishing, 2003.

Hicks, Edmund W., Rev. *History of Kendall County, Illinois: From the Earliest Discoveries to the Present Time*. Aurora, Ill.: Knickerbocker and Hadder, 1877.

Hileman, Levida. *In Tar and Paint and Stone: The Inscriptions at Independence Rock and Devil's Gate*. Glendo, Wyo.: High Plains Press, 2001.

Hilton, George W. *Cable Car in America*. Revised ed. San Diego, Calif.: Howell-North Books, 1982.

Hines, Harvey K. *An Illustrated History of the State of Washington: Containing . . . Biographical Mention of . . . its Pioneers and Prominent Citizens*. Chicago: Lewis Publishing, 1893.

Historical Society of Southern California. "In Pursuit of Vanished Days." *Annual Publications of the Historical Society of Southern California*, Vol. 14, Part 1. Los Angeles, Calif.: McBride Printing, 1928.

Hittell, Theodore H. *History of California*, Vols. 1–4. Vols. 1–2, San Francisco: Occidental Publishing Company, 1885, and Vols. 3–4, San Francisco: N.J. Stone and Company, 1898.

Holliday, J. S. *The World Rushed In: The California Gold Rush Experience*. New York: Simon and Schuster, 1981.

Holmes, Kenneth L., ed. and comp. *Covered Wagon Women, Diaries and Letters from the Western Trails, 1840–1849*. Vol. 1. Glendale: Arthur H. Clark Co., 1983. (Reprinted with introduction by Anne M. Butler. Lincoln: University of Nebraska Press, Bison Books Ed., 1995.)

———. *Covered Wagon Women, Diaries and Letters from the Western Trails, 1850*. Vol. 2. Glendale: Arthur H. Clark Co., 1983. (Reprinted with introduction by Lillian Schlissel. Lincoln: University of Nebraska Press, Bison Books Ed., 1996.)

———. *Covered Wagon Women, Diaries and Letters from the Western Trails, 1852: The California Trail.* Vol. 4. Glendale: Arthur H. Clark Co., 1985. (Reprinted with introduction by Glenda Riley. Lincoln: University of Nebraska Press, Bison Books Ed., 1997.)

———. *Covered Wagon Women, Diaries and Letters from the Western Trails, 1854–1860.* Vol. 7. Glendale: Arthur H. Clark Co., 1987. (Reprinted with introduction by Shirley A. Leckie. Lincoln: University of Nebraska Press, Bison Books Ed., 1997.)

Holmes, Philip. *Two Centuries at Mission San Jose, 1797–1997.* Fremont, Calif.: Fremont Museum of Local History, 1997.

Holzer, Harold, ed. and introduction. *The Lincoln–Douglas Debates.* New York: Harper Perennial (Division of HarperCollins), 1994.

Howard, Robert P. *Illinois: A History of the Prairie State.* Grand Rapids, Mich.: William B. Erdman's Publishing, 1972.

Hunt, Rockwell, D., ed. *California and Californians.* Vol. 4. Chicago: Lewis Publishing, 1926.

Hurn, Huston. *The Pioneers.* Series: The Old West. New York: Time-Life Books, 1974.

Jackson, David W., ed. *Direct Your Letters to San Jose: The California Gold Rush Diaries of James and David Lee Campbell, 1849–1852.* Kansas City, Mo.: The Orderly Rat Pack, 2000.

Jackson, Donald Dale. *Gold Dust.* New York: Alfred A. Knopf, 1980.

Jackson, Joseph H. *The Adventures and Experience of Joseph H. Jackson, disclosing the depths of Mormon Villainy! Practiced in Nauvoo.* Warsaw, Ill.: 1846.

Keleher, William A. *Turmoil in New Mexico 1846–1868.* Santa Fe: Rydel Press, 1952.

Kellogg, David. "Across the Plains in 1858." *The Trail* 5:no. 7 (December 1912):6–10.

———. "Across the Plains in 1858." *The Trail* 5:no. 8 (January 1913):5–13.

Kemble, John Haskell. *The Panama Route: 1848–1869.* Berkeley and Los Angeles: University of California Press, 1943.

Kielbasa, John. *Historic Adobes of Los Angeles County.* Pittsburgh: Dorrance Publishing, 1997.

Kimball, Stanley B., ed. *The Latter-Day Saints' Emigrants' Guide by W. Clayton.* (Annotated version of the original published in 1848 in St. Louis.) Tucson, Ariz.: Patrice Press, 1983.

Kimball, Stanley B. and Violet T., and Mary L. Van Camp, eds. *Mormon Trail, Voyage of Discovery: The Story behind the Scenery.* Las Vegas: KC Publications, 1995.

Koenig, George. *Beyond This Place There Be Dragons.* Glendale, Calif.: Arthur H. Clark, 1984.

Koford, Carl B. "Prairie Dogs, Whitefaces and Blue Grama." *Wildlife Monograph No. 3* (Dec. 1958), Wildlife Society Publication.

Landon, Fred. *An Exile from Canada to Van Dieman's Land.* Toronto: Longmans, Green and Co., 1960.

———. *Western Ontario and the American Frontier.* Toronto: Ryerson Press, 1941.

Lane, Lydia Spencer. *I Married a Soldier* or *Old Days in the Old Army.* 1893. Reprint, Albuquerque: Horn and Wallace, 1964.

Langley, Henry G., comp. *The San Francisco Directory.* San Francisco: 1879–1880.

Lauer, Charles D. *Tales of Arizona Territory.* Phoenix: Golden West Publishers, 1990.

Lavender, David. *Bent's Fort.* Lincoln: University of Nebraska Press, 1954.

Leventis, Angie. "Thurston County Honors Trail Blazing Washington Suffragettes." *Tacoma News Tribune,* Apr. 26, 2005.

Levy, JoAnn. *They Saw the Elephant: Women in the California Gold Rush.* Norman: University of Oklahoma Press, 1992.

Lockwood, Frank C. *The Apache Indians.* Lincoln: University of Nebraska Press, 1938.

Loomis, Patricia. "Small Redwood Shack Grows into Gilroy." *San Jose News,* Apr. 26, 1974, 43.

Lyman, Edward Leo. *The Overland Journey from Utah to California.* Reno and Las Vegas: University of Nevada Press, 2004.

Madsen, Brigham D. *Gold Rush Sojourners in Great Salt Lake City, 1849 and 1850.* Salt Lake City: University of Utah Press, 1983.

Mann, Ralph. *After the Gold Rush: Society in Grass Valley and Nevada City, California, 1849–1870.* Stanford, Calif.: Stanford University Press, 1982.

Marks, Paula Mitchell. *In a Barren Land: American Indian Dispossession and Survival.* New York: William Morrow and Company, Quill Edition, 1998.

Matile, Roger, ed. *150 Years along the Fox, The History of Oswego Township, Illinois.* Oswego, Ill.: Oswego Sesquicentennial Days Steering Committee, 1983.

Mattes, Merrill. *The Great Platte River Road.* Lincoln: University of Nebraska Press, 1969.

———. *Platte River Road Narratives, A Descriptive Bibliography of Travel over the Great Central Overland Route to Oregon, California, Utah, Colorado, Montana, and Other Western States and Territories, 1812–1866.* Urbana and Chicago: University of Illinois Press, 1988.

McKinstry, Byron Nathan. *The California Gold Rush Overland Diary of Byron N. McKinstry, 1850–1852.* Glendale, Calif.: Arthur H. Clark, 1975.

Miller, Orlo. *A Century of Western Ontario; The Story of London, "The Free Press," and Western Ontario, 1849–1949.* Reprint, Westport, Conn.: Greenwood Press, 1972.

Morrill, E. N., comp. *History and Statistics of Brown County, Kansas.* Hiawatha, Kansas: Kansas Herald Book, News and Job Office, 1876.

Mossman, Marjorie. "Weston." *Villages of Etobicoke*. Weston, Ontario: Etobicoke Historical Society, 1985.

Mulvaney, C. P. *History of Toronto and County of York, Ontario*. Vol. 1. Toronto: C. B. Robinson, 1885.

Myers, Lee. *Fort Stanton, New Mexico; The Military Years 1855–1896*. Lincoln, N.Mex.: Lincoln County Historical Society Publications, 1988.

Myers, Sandra L., ed. and annotator. *Ho for California*. San Marino, Calif.: Huntington Library and Art Gallery, 1990.

Napton, William B. *On the Santa Fe Trail in 1857*. Reprint, Arrow Rock, Mo.: Friends of Arrow Rock, 1991.

National Historical Company. *The History of Holt and Atchison Counties, Missouri, containing a history of these counties, their cities, towns, etc.* St. Joseph, Mo.: 1882.

Nevada Valley Gold Magazine, "Penn Valley," p. 25. Grass Valley, Calif.: IM, 1998–1999.

Newmark, Harris. *Sixty Years in Southern California, 1853–1913*. New York: Knickerbocker Press, 1916.

Oaks, Dallin H. and Marvin S. Hill. *Carthage Conspiracy: The Trial of the Accused Assassins of Joseph Smith*. Urbana and Chicago: University of Illinois Press, 1975.

O'Flaherty, Joseph S. *An End and a Beginning: The South Coast and Los Angeles, 1857–1887*. Jericho, New York: Exposition Press, 1972.

O'Gorman, Ella Foy. "Foy and Allied Families." *Americana (American Historical Magazine)*, Vol. 25:2 (April 1931):220–301.

Pavlik, Bruce M., Pamela C. Muick, Sharon Johnson, and Marjorie Popper. *Oaks of California*. Los Olivos, California: Cachuma Press and California Oak Foundation, 1991.

Peck, J. L. E., Hon. O. H. Montzheimer, and Hon. William J. Miller. *Past and Present of O'Brien and Osceola Counties, Iowa*. Vol. 2. Indianapolis: B. F. Bowen and Company, 1914.

Peters, Arthur King, comp. *Seven Trails West*. New York: Abbeville Press, 1996.

Peters, De Witt C. *Kit Carson's Life and Adventures, from Facts Narrated by Himself* . . . Hartford, Conn.: Dustin, Gilman and Co., 1874.

Pierce, James H. "The First Prospecting of Colorado." *The Trail* 7:5 (October 1914):5–11.

———. "With the Russell Green Party." *The Trail* 13:12 (May 1921):5–14, and 14:1 (June 1921):5–13.

Pool, Raymond J. *Marching with the Grasses*. Lincoln: University of Nebraska Press, 1948.

Portrait and Biographical Record of Sheboygan County, Wis. (No author noted). Chicago: Excelsior Publishing Co., 1894.

Raible, Chris. *Muddy York Mud: Scandal and Scurrility in Upper Canada*. Creemore, Ontario: Curiosity House, 1992.

Rasmussen, Louis J. *California Wagon Train Lists: Vol. 1, April 5, 1849 to October 20, 1852*. Colma, Calif.: San Francisco Historic Records, 1994.

Rathbun, John C. *History of Thurston Co., Washington*. Shorey Book Store, 1895.

Reaman, George Elmore. *A History of Vaughan Township: Two Centuries of Life in the Township*. Toronto: University of Toronto Press, 1971.

Reid, John Phillip. *Law for the Elephant: Property and Social Behavior on the Overland Trail*. San Marino: Henry E. Huntington Library and Art Gallery, 1980.

Renehan, Edward J. Jr. *The Secret Six*. New York: Crown Publishers, 1995.

Richards, Gil. *Historic Sties of the Mother Lode*. Redwood City, Calif.: Copperline Publishing, 1998.

Roberts, B. H. *A Comprehensive History of the Church of Jesus Christ of Latter–day Saints, Century I*. Vol. 2. Provo: Brigham Young University Press, 1965.

Robinson, Charles M. III, ed. and annotator. *The Diaries of John Gregory Bourke, Vol. 1, Nov. 20, 1872–July 28, 1876*. Denton, Tex.: University of North Texas Press, 2003.

Robinson, W. W. *Land in California, The Story of Mission Lands, Ranchos, Squatters, Mining Claims, Railroad Grants, Land Scrip, Homesteads*. Berkley and Los Angeles: University of California Press, 1948. Reprint, 1979.

Robinson, W. W. and William H. Newbro, Jr. comps. *A Map of the Missions, Presidios, Puebloes and Some of the More Interesting Ranchos of Spanish California . . .* Cartography by Lowell Butler. Published by Westways for the Automobile Club of Southern California, 1954.

Rose, L. J., Jr. *L. J. Rose of Sunny Slope*. San Marino, Calif.: Huntington Library, 1959.

Rose, L. J., Sr. "Cross-Country Reminiscences." *The Californian* 3 (Dec. 1892–May 1893):115–22.

Rothman, Sheila M. *Living in the Shadow of Death: Tuberculosis and the Social Experience of Illness in American History*. Baltimore and London: Johns Hopkins University Press, 1994.

Ryan, John P. *Fort Stanton and Its Community, 1855–1896*. Las Cruces, N.Mex.: Yucca Tree Press, 1998.

Sawdon, Herb H. *The Woodbridge Story*, no date [1961?].

Scadding, Henry. *Toronto of Old/Henry Scadding*, ed. Frederick H. Armstrong. Toronto: Dundurn Press, 1987.

Schlissel, Lillian. *Women's Diaries of the Westward Journey*. New York: Schocken Books, 1982.

Schott, Joseph L. *Rails across Panama, The Story of the Building of the Panama Railroad, 1849–1855*. Indianapolis: Bobbs-Merrill, 1967.

Sheely, Glen and Evelyn. *History of Nemaha County*. Dallas: Taylor Publishing, 1987.

Scheid, Ann. *Pasadena: Crown of the Valley*. Northridge, Calif.: Windsor Publications, 1986.

Sherer, Lorraine M. *Bitterness Road, The Mojave: 1604 to 1860*. Menlo Park, Calif.: Ballena Press, 1994.

Siebert, Wilbur H. *The Underground Railroad: From Slavery to Freedom*. 1898. Reprint, New York: Russell and Russell, Division of Atheneum House, 1967.

Simmons, Marc. *Following the Santa Fe Trail*. Santa Fe: Ancient City Press, 1984.

———. *On the Santa Fe Trail*. Lawrence, Kans.: University Press of Kansas, 1986.

Smith, Jack Beale. *John Udell "The Rest of the Story:" With an Adventure on the Beale Wagon Road*. Flagstaff, Ariz.: Tales of the Beale Road Publishing Company, 1987.

Smith, Herndon, comp. *Centralia, The First Fifty Years, 1845–1900*. Material Written by Students in Her English Classes at Centralia High School, 1942. 3rd ed. Rochester, Wash.: Centralia American Revolution Bicentennial Committee, 1995.

Somerville, Patricia and Catherine Macfarlane, eds. *A History of Vaughan Township Churches*. Maple, Ontario: Vaughan Township Historical Society, 1984.

Spencer, Elma Dill Russell. *Green Russell and Gold*. Austin: University of Texas, 1966.

Stamp, Robert M. *Early Days in Richmond Hill: A History of the Community to 1930*. Richmond Hill, Ontario: Richmond Hill Public Library Board, 1991.

Stanton, Elizabeth Cady, with Susan B. Anthony, Matilda Joslyn Gage, et al. *History of Woman Suffrage*, Vol. 3. Rochester, N.Y., 1887.

Stapel, H. F. *Biographical History, Atchison County Missouri*. Rockport, Mo.: *Rockport Atchison County Mail*, 1905.

Starkey, Marilyn and Juanita Kennedy Browne. *Sketches of Yesterday and Today in Nevada County*. Nevada City, Calif.: Nevada County Historical Society, 1988.

Stegner, Wallace. *The Gathering of Zion: The Story of the Mormon Trail*. New York: McGraw Hill, 1964.

Stewart, George R. *Ordeal by Hunger: The Story of the Donner Party*. 1936. Reprint, Boston and New York: Houghton Mifflin Company, 1988.

Stoddard, Mr. and Mrs. Hugh P. et al., comps. "St. Frederick—A Lost City," *Beauty-Bounty Nemaha County, An Informal History of Nemaha County 1854–1967*, Published for the Nebraska Centennial, 1967.

Tate, Michael L. *Indians and Emigrants: Encounters on the Overland Trails*. Norman: University of Oklahoma Press, 2006.

Taylor, Charles, ed. *Literary Panorama and National Register*. London, England: Simpkin and Marshall, 1819.

Taylor, L. Joseph, ed. *Ontario Directory for 1851: Names of Professional and Business Men and Other Inhabitants in the Cities, Towns, and Villages throughout the Province*. Reprint, London, Ontario: Genealogical Research Library, 1984.

Taylor, Morris F. *First Mail West*. Albuquerque: University of New Mexico Press, 1971.

Theobold, John and Lillian. *Wells Fargo in Arizona Territory*, ed. Bert M. Fireman. Tempe, Ariz.: Arizona Historical Foundation, 1978.

Thompson and West. *Official and Historical Atlas Map of Alameda County, California*. Oakland, Calif.: Thompson and West, 1878.

Thrapp, Dan L. *The Conquest of Apacheria*. Norman: University of Oklahoma Press, 1967.

———. *Victorio and the Mimbres Apaches*. Norman: University of Oklahoma Press, 1974.

Tinkham, George H. *California Men and Events: Time 1769–1890*. Stockton: Record Publishing Company, 1915.

Turner, Glennette Tilley. *The Underground Railroad in Illinois*. Glen Ellyn, Ill.: Newman Educational Publishing, 2001.

Udell, John. *Incidents of Travel to California, across the Great Plains; Together with the Return Trips through Central America* ... Printed for the Author at the *Sentinel Office* in Jefferson, Ohio, 1856. Reprint facsimile. Ann Arbor, Mich.: University Microfilms International, 1980.

———. *Journal of John Udell Kept During a Trip Across the Plains, containing an account of the massacre of a portion of his party by the Mohave Indians, in 1859*. Reprint. New Haven, Conn.: Yale University Library, 1952.

Unruh, John D., Jr. *The Plains Across: The Overland Emigrants and Trans-Mississippi West, 1840–60*. Urbana and Chicago: University of Illinois Press, 1993.

Utley, Robert M. *Frontiersmen in Blue*. Lincoln: University of Nebraska Press, 1967.

———. *A Clash of Cultures, Fort Bowie and the Chiricahua Apaches*. Washington D.C.: National Park Service, 1977.

Walton, George, comp. *The City of Toronto and the Home District Commercial Directory and Register, with Almanac and Calendar for 1837*. Toronto: T. Dalton and W. J. Coates, 1836.

Werner, Emmy E. *Pioneer Children on the Journey West*. Boulder, Colo.: Westview Press, 1995.

West, Elliott. *The Contested Plains*. Lawrence: University Press of Kansas, 1998.

Wexler, Alan and Molly Braun, drawings. *Atlas of Westward Expansion*. New York: Facts on File, 1995.

White, Michael C. and Thomas Savage. *California All the Way Back to 1828, by Michael C. White*. Los Angeles: Glen Dawson, 1956. Testimony given to Thomas Savage for H. H. Bancroft, 1877.

Wilma, David. "Cold weather freezes wharves and rivers in Washington in January 1875," Online Encyclopedia of Washington State History, http://www.historylink.org (search: no. 204).

Wilson, Bruce M. *Crown King and the Southern Bradshaws: A Complete History*. Chandler, Ariz.: Crown King Press, 1990.

Wilson, John P. *Merchants, Guns and Money, The Story of Lincoln County and Its Wars*. Santa Fe: Museum of New Mexico Press, 1987.

Wolcott, Marjorie Tisdale, ed. *Pioneer Notes from the Diaries of Judge Benjamin Hayes*. Los Angeles: self-published, 1929.

Wright, Lyle H. and Josephine M. Bynum, eds. *Butterfield Overland Mail by Waterman L. Ormsby*. San Marino: Huntington Library, 1942, paperback ed., 1991.

Wright, Muriel H. "The Journal of John Lowery Brown of the Cherokee Nation en Route to California in 1850." *Chronicles of Oklahoma* 12:2 (June 1834):177–213.

Wright, Norman E. "Odometers." *Overland Journal* 13 (Fall 1995) no. 3:14–24.

Writers' Program (U.S.) Wisconsin. *Wisconsin; A Guide to the Badger State*. New York: Hastings House, [1954].

Young, John V. *Kokopelli, Casanova of the Cliff Dwellers*. Palmer Lake, Colo.: Filter Press, 1990.

Zillier, Carl, ed. *History of Sheboygan County, Wisconsin, Past and Present*. Vol. 1. Chicago: S. J. Clarke Publishing Company, 1912.

Newspapers

Chehalis (Wash.) Bee Nugget, 1899.

Chehalis (Wash.) Nugget, Washington Territory, 1886–1889.

Kanesville Frontier Guardian, 1850.

Kanesville Frontier Guardian and Iowa Sentinal, 1852.

London (Ont.) Canadian Free Press, Jan. 30, 1849–Dec. 9, 1852; Nov. 8, 1855.

London (Ont.) Free Press and Western Advertiser, (previously *Canadian Free Press*) Jan. 1856–Sept. 30, 1856; Jan. 1, 1857–Sept. 1857.

London (Ont.) Herald, Jan. 15, 1856–Jan. 20, 1857.

Nauvoo (Ill.) Neighbor, 1844–1845.

Nevada City (Calif.) Nevada Journal, 1851–1854.

Olympia (Wash.) Commercial Age, 1869–1870.

Olympia (Wash.) Daily Olympian, 1876.

Olympia Territorial Republican, Washington Territory, 1869.

Olympia Transcript, 1870.

Olympia Washington Standard.

Oregon (Mo.) News, 1857–1858.

Prescott Arizona Democrat.

Prescott Arizona Enterprise.

Prescott Arizona Miner.

Prescott Weekly Arizona Democrat.

Prescott Weekly Arizona Miner.

Salt Lake Deseret News, June 15, 1850–Sept. 21, 1850.

San Francisco Daily Alta California.

San Jose News.

Santa Fe Gazette.

Sarnia (Ont.) Observer.
Sheboygan Press–Telegram, Sheboygan, Wis.
Sheboygan Times, Sheboygan, Wis.
Tacoma News Tribune.
Tarkio Avalanche, 1965.
Tucson Arizona Citizen.
Woodbridge (Ont.) Leader and Recorder, Nov. 9, 1899.
York (Ont.) Christian Guardian, 1832.
York (Ont.) Colonial Advocate, 1831.
Yuma Arizona Sentinel.

Index